'"To love the valleys is to love a mottled sky," writes Ben Wildsmith, beautifully. His memoir is a confrontationally honest and clear-eyed account of a boy damaged, a youth heartbreakingly alone, a man struggling, an addict fighting, an identity forming and reforming, all shot through with the love of music, friendship, Wales and the power of writing. It is deeply moving, piercingly acute on the political and social currents of our times, shockingly human in its self-awareness, and, often, very funny. It is driven by a wonderful feeling of someone coming home to himself the hard way, in whose song many readers will recognise their own.'
Horatio Clare, author of *We Came by Sea* **and** *Running for the Hills*

'This book is everything that a memoir should be: gripping, informative, moving, hilarious, a fascinating doorway into the fun and frozen wastes of being someone else, a glimpse into a life well and vividly lived. Laceratingly intelligent, fearlessly self-analytical, it is, in part, a sequence of joyous, if hard-won, awakenings, into rugby, politics, literature, addiction, adoption, music, Welshness, love of several kinds. All praise.'
Niall Griffiths, author of *Broken Ghost* **and** *Stump*

'I love a memoir and this is, quite possibly, the best one I have ever read – heartstrings suitably pulled and ribs hurting with laughter. What a life and what a writer to document it so skilfully and beautifully for us.'
Rhian Elizabeth, author of *girls etc* **and** *Six Pounds Eight Ounces*

'Ben Wildsmith's life so far – and at a mere fifty-two he's still a bit to go – has been a tormented creative whirlwind. He's one of the best Appalachian pickers I've heard outside the States, a political journalist of curiosity and scepticism and now a memoir essayist of power, entertainment and heart-wrenching recollection. His *Whose Song To Sing?*, which may sound like a disclosure of the life of an adoptee – and it is that – is also, magnificently, a million things more. It rolls from the socialism of Tylorstown to the

renegade leftism of Solihull, from hymns and arias to rock and roll, from the Pendyrus to his grandfather's love of rugby, from dark recollections of adopted fathers to alcoholic breakdowns, wavering recoveries, fiercely difficult work as a carer, then loss and then love. Ben's telling of a life already further packed with incident than most of us could ever cope with is absolutely unputdownable.'
Peter Finch, author of *The Literary Business* and *Walking the Valleys*

'It's a basic need – to belong. Uncertainty as to where you come from, who you belong to and how you fit in can be difficult to wrestle with. This memoir contains the stories that have made Ben Wildsmith. Ben's life is one well-lived, albeit close to various edges. The Rhondda, where Ben now lives and belongs, is fortunate to have such a talented storyteller as an adopted son.'
Leanne Wood

'Ben Wildsmith's charged, generous memoir listens closely to the quiet forces that shape a life: the pressures of secrecy, class and grief, and the strange architectures of power we grow up inside. Written with sharp clarity, disarming humour, and a finely tuned emotional intelligence, *Whose Song to Sing?* reveals how personal and national histories braid together. A humane and brilliant book.'
Ailbhe Darcy, author of *Insistence* and *Imaginary Menagerie*

'With moments of heart-wrenching pain, glorious humour and, ultimately, joy, this is a searingly honest rollercoaster of a memoir that will stay with the reader for a long time.'
Catrin Kean, author of *Salt*

'What truly shines through *Whose Song to Sing?* is the author's empathy and candour. I was deeply moved by his life experiences and reflections on our fundamental human need for love and compassion. This memoir is a triumph!'
Abeel Ameer, author of *Inhale/Exile*

WHOSE SONG TO SING?

A memoir

WHOSE SONG TO SING?

A memoir

Ben Wildsmith

2026

© Ben Wildsmith, 2026

All rights reserved. No part of this book may be reproduced in any material form (including photocopying or storing it in any medium by electronic means and whether or not transiently or incidentally to some other use of this publication) without the written permission of the copyright owner. Applications for the copyright owner's written permission to reproduce any part of this publication should be addressed to Calon, University Registry, King Edward VII Avenue, Cardiff CF10 3NS.

www.uwp.co.uk

British Library Cataloguing-in-Publication Data
A catalogue record for this book is available from the British Library.

ISBN: 978-1-915279-98-9
The right of Ben Wildsmith to be identified as author of this work has been asserted in accordance with sections 77 and 79 of the Copyright, Designs and Patents Act 1988.

For GPSR enquiries please contact: Easy Access System Europe Oü, 16879218. Mustamäe tee 50, 10621, Tallinn, Estonia.
gpsr.requests@easproject.com

Typeset by Agnes Graves
Cover design by Andy Ward
Printed by CPI Group (UK) Ltd, Croydon CR0 4YY

The publisher acknowledges the financial support of the Books Council of Wales.

CONTENTS

Foreword by Jon Gower ix

A journey around Wales xii

Introduction xv

The chosen one 1

Clambering out of the Capri 18

Gwlad! Gwlad! 64

If that ain't country 90

Póg mo thóin 119

Chimpanzee eyes 134

That's a tribe, man 143

Myfanwy 150

Indoor playtime 159

Grit in the sponge 182

Monkey paws 202

Epilogue 230

Acknowledgements 235

For Susie.

FOREWORD

'Adoption is such a fundamental factor in a person's life that its features mimics those of ethnicity,' suggests Ben Wildsmith in this searchingly honest and consistently engaging assemblage of essays. It's an assertion I very much agree with, being myself adopted. I share with Ben memories of an adoptee's perhaps defining moments, such as the day you actually find out you were adopted. Or that other time when you're given a document that is meant to help you better know who you are, only to find out that you once had another name. *Were known by another name.*

I remember that moment well. Having decided to take the first, faltering steps towards finding my birth family, I was in a family centre in St Mellons in Cardiff, where I sat on a little plastic stool to be given a copy of my adoption papers, all arranged by the St Davids Diocesan Moral Welfare Committee.

When I first scanned my way through them, I thought they'd made a mistake and had handed me the wrong documents as they were all about someone else. Then the penny dropped as I realised that the man named on his identity-corroborating and much-travelled passport, David Jonathan Gower, had once been known as Ian Mathias. Perhaps the only person who would have known me by that name was my birth – or real mother – but there it was, in black ink, written by an official hand. It allowed me to try on the new name as if I were donning an unfamiliar mantle to see whether it would fit or not. It felt ungainly, cut from the wrong cloth, an act akin to awkwardly trying on someone else's coat. But at least I knew. I then went on to try to find my mother, but I had left it too late as she had already died. That's another story.

Ben doesn't claim to be writing on behalf of other people who were adopted, although there are many places of such overlap. The emotional impact of adoption is undeniably profound and, in my case, has meant that I have spent my life wanting to be liked or loved, and, mainly, have been fortunate in both regards. As anyone who has read Ben's brilliant political writing knows, that clearly doesn't apply to him so much as he is more than willing to upset those who deserve upsetting, giving voice to the voiceless and railing witheringly against the right. But as the fumes and fuming of political and moral anger clear, this book lets us see that all the while he has been looking for love and the reader's heart surges when he finally finds it.

Personal territory is clearly mapped out in *Whose Song to Sing?*, which charts the author's long and challenging history of alcoholism, with its terrible mornings-after when the pain could only be leavened by whatever dregs of gut-rot cider remained in the bottle. We follow the meanderings of his formal education – both here and in Arizona – and learn of his informal one in important subjects such as working-class politics and the intricacies of rugby. And we follow his musical education, too, from The Pogues through John Prine to the Pendyrus Male Voice Choir, alongside his own journey into guitar-playing and singing.

Intriguingly, there is also the central, pivotal importance of his grandfather, Idwal Morgan of Tylorstown, in his life, which mirrors my own emotional debt to Thomas John Gower of Pwll in that regard. But there is another territory charted here with just as much care and attention to the cartographic detail: namely, Cymru (Wales). It is a country that has long intrigued, nurtured and eventually welcomed the author. In this, he is a beloved member of that extended family, *y Cymry* (the Welsh), a writer who makes our small country a great deal richer for having him here, being one of us.

Jon Gower

A JOURNEY AROUND WALES

I'm on my way to Cardiff with an important load onboard. Already that afternoon I'd made calls at Swansea, Llanelli and Newport. Wales is a small country; environmental brutalities are inflicted upon areas of its size daily. It was yet smaller then, though, and fitted into the ten-by-twelve-feet concrete yard between my grandfather's house and the lawn.

'It's your last call of the day. Drop those spanners off to Dai and tell him we'll be round for the money next Friday.'

With that, Grandad goes indoors to brew a mug of black tea and I trundle the cart he made me towards the corner by the entry gate – Cardiff. It's a hot afternoon; diesel from the bus station opposite the house floats over to mingle with the neat rows of flowers in the back garden. Before I was adopted, Grandad had been working on that bed with a fork when a blonde, blue-eyed boy had smiled at him. He said he recognised me when I arrived a few months later.

I'm determined to make the delivery successfully before he returns. I arrive at Cardiff and knock the entry gate.

'What's this? It's getting late.'

'Delivery of spanners. Urgent, Dai.'

The gate opens and a familiar face underneath a hat examines the cargo.

'Your gaffer has forgotten the adjustable one. We need that for tonight's work. Can you get back to the depot in time?'

That is touch-and-go. Inside, I can hear my mum beginning an argument with Grandma.

'I've told you not to bring that dog round here. It leaves hair on the sofa.'

We'll be leaving soon, that much is certain. The entry door closes and I rush back across Wales to the depot. I'm worried that Grandad's toolshed might be locked. Reaching up, I find the latch loose, so I go inside. Things get made in here: the carved ducks that sit on the sideboard at home and wooden clackers that can be played like spoons, once you've been taught how. In the centre of the workbench is a well-oiled vice that once gripped my mother's pet tortoise so that Grandad could drill a hole in its shell and tie it to a tree to stop it roaming too far. On the back wall hang the tools: saws, chisels, files, a bradawl and the adjustable spanner. Hurriedly I grab it and then rush out, tiptoeing up to close the latch behind me, before putting the spanner in the cart which has 'Ben's Haulage' carved on the side and journeying back to Cardiff.

Time is short. Through the window I glimpse Mum and Grandma leaning towards each other like angry geese.

'He doesn't love you, you silly girl!'

I knock on the gate and Dai opens it immediately, still wearing his cap.

'Thank goodness you are here. That spanner is *vital*. Your gaffer called, by the way. He said to leave the wagon in Swansea. Goodnight.' The gate closes abruptly. I've forgotten something important. I knock the gate again.

'What is it? We've got a job on here!'

'The gaffer says we'll be round for the money next Friday.'

Dai pulls at the peak of his cap and silently shuts the gate. As I pull my cart westwards, the sun begins to dip and the geese inside become louder. I pull a few steps north and take a breather in the Rhondda – Tylorstown to be precise. You can ride a tea tray down the mountainside there.

'Don't pull your airs and graces with me, madam!' Grandma shouts.

I look down at my Start-Rite sandals for a minute before slowly dropping off the cart in the corner of the yard at Swansea, by the lawn.

At the back door, Grandad, minus his cap, is conspiratorial.

'Sorry about the mix-up with the spanner. I've spoken to Dai. Great work today. Here.' He presses a 50p coin into my hand and leans close. 'Don't tell Grandma.'

'Benjamin, we're leaving,' Mum bellows from inside. Grandad and I file in.

Inside, Mum grabs my wrist and pulls me down the hall. Grandma follows, flustered but all smiles. Mum has to release me in her hurry to open the door.

'Have this, but don't tell Grandad,' Grandma whispers as she presses 50p into my hand.

We emerge into the Birmingham twilight and climb inside Mum's Ford Capri.

'Silly old trout!' she hisses, as we roar off towards Solihull.

INTRODUCTION

The adopted experience is often discussed as if it were a process of recovery. There is an initial severance before the child is nurtured back to wholeness by their adoptive parents. Certainly, the circumstances that lead to many adoptions can involve trauma and sadness but, for those of us adopted early, the events leading to our births are never part of our experience as we grow up. Nobody is there to recount them or show us the wounds they left.

In *The Souls of Black Folks* (1903), W. E. B. Du Bois talks about the 'double consciousness' that characterises the Black experience in America: 'One ever feels his twoness – an American, a Negro; two souls, two thoughts, two unreconciled strivings; two warring ideals in one dark body'. I first read that line in an African American literature class at Arizona State University, a year or so before I started to investigate my birth family. It lodged in me like an undetonated depth charge, waiting for my self-awareness to catch up with its pertinence to my own situation.

I know a certain amount about how I came to be, why I was adopted and the motivations behind my adoptive parents' decision to take me on. I won't discuss that in this book, however, because those aren't my stories to tell. *My* story blinked into consciousness after all that was done with. The only pre-history that's relevant to it is that my adoptive parents didn't have a happy marriage – neither before nor after adopting me. That nothing changed in that regard was a disappointment to my mum. She was certainly not the first unhappy wife to try fixing her marriage with a baby, even if her route to having one was more complicated than most.

I learned of my adoption when I was six years old. From here on Du Bois' bifurcation of 'double consciousness' was at play within me as I built the blocks of my personality. A second voice appeared within me which could sometimes seem treasonous. Subjects like family history, resemblance and characteristics seem to crop up *all the time* once you are aware that your own relationship to them is complicated. In my case, discussion of my adoption was discouraged at home and forbidden outside of it. It was a secret. The second voice, though, had questions about that.

If it's fine *that I'm adopted, if I'm no different from other boys, then why* can't *I tell anyone?*

Some of the questions the second voice asked were gut-wrenchingly hurtful.

'So, do I have two mummies, then?'

On my own, I would wonder where I fitted into the scheme of things. *What is it like to look at someone who was related to you? Is anybody like me at all? I'm clumsy; did I inherit that trait? Was my 'other' dad loud like me? Is he alive?*

I am, temperamentally, very different from my adoptive father. He was quiet, precise and practical, whereas I'm loud, messy and imaginative. So, patterning myself after him was difficult. I learned to speak like him and see humour in the dark places where he found it, but mirroring him was inhibiting and awkward. It fed that sense of twoness.

In adolescence, I began to see positive aspects to that. Firstly, I was at an age when it's not uncommon to reject parental templates and I had a bona fide escape clause. *I'm* nothing *like you and thank fuck for that!* Secondly, when it came time to try out different identities for size, I excelled. If you've spent

Introduction

toddlerhood unconsciously aping the physical characteristics of a man with whom you share no genetic information, then becoming a Goth is child's play. I'd learned transferrable skills. Ironically, I've spent my recent adulthood trying to shed my tendency towards dissembling performance in favour of something more authentic, just as the rest of the world seems to have taken it up with abandon. People deliberately confuse their identities with online avatars, filters, personal branding, plastic surgery and AI-enhanced content. This sort of *conscious* creation of identity chills my blood, not because there's anything wrong with it per se, but because I had no choice but to do it. Adopted people are hybrid creations whether we like it or not, and to see people going in for that sort of thing voluntarily feels like, well, cultural appropriation.

I need to stop myself here. I am in no position to speak for all adopted people, not least because the nature of my childhood and adolescence disqualifies me as a suitable control. My experience was an outlier – good for the narrative, but too unusual to have wider implications. I've never talked at length to any other adopted people, either. I have a powerful suspicion that most of them handled the experience better than I did and have therefore emerged with more credit. My fear is that, on publication of this book, Nicky Campbell, James O'Brien, KT Tunstall, Stewart Lee, Steve Jobs, Fatima Whitbread, Jesus Christ, and Michael Gove will release a joint statement condemning it as a whiney and solipsistic insult to the adopted nation.

So, this is solely a personal account. I'm seeking to show how *I* came at life with priorities that were shaped by my adoption. Each chapter is separate because I seem to remember episodically rather than sequentially. Maybe others will chime with some of my story or perhaps they won't. My feeling, though, is that there's something in common for all of us who grew up this way. Adoption is so fundamental a factor in a person's life that its features mimic those of ethnicity. It sits immovably at the beginning of a story, demanding reckoning. It's a big thing to get your head around when you are little and, along with the people-pleasing desire to fit in that comes with childhood, it can produce a flexibility of mind that can then lead a person to interesting places. I hope this book is one of them.

This book is also a love letter to Cymru. I dreamed so hard and constantly about this country as a child that I virtually fetishised it. Whatever was wrong in my life wouldn't be if I could only get there. It was my personal Avalon: constructed from stories, songs and the accent of the one man I knew, without doubt, loved me as his own. There are two versions of Cymru here: one imagined, and one real. I love both. Before I moved here, I had started to worry that the reality of the place would spoil my mythical idyll for me. Day-to-day existence anywhere can be disillusioning, but the reality of Cymru is as inspiring to me as its fictional counterpart used to be. My passion for it endures and, whether I'm staring down at the Rhondda from Penrhys imagining the clatter of colliers, or listening to the heartsongs of the homeless people I work with as they try to repair themselves, I feel the country's nature and the rhythms of its joys and sorrows. Cymru has deepened in my comprehension. If it was an ersatz backdrop to my own concerns when I arrived, then over the decade I have lived here it has come to be a choir of nuanced voices; a wry smile; a warm home in the mist; a long day at work; a happy journey back from the airport to where I belong. Bury my heart on Maerdy Mountain.

Ben Wildsmith, August 2025
Diolch yn fawr.

THE CHOSEN ONE

It's a lovely day in Dudley.* I've been at an American literature lecture and, as I walk down St James's Road under a canopy of sycamores, Thomas Pynchon works on me. 'We await silent Tristero's empire,' I murmur, tossing my empty Coke can into a bin.

Unusually, I have a purpose. I've been carefully avoidant of these during my twenty-three years, preferring consequences to arrive disguised as luck rather than outcomes attributable to me. My life has been a shrug. Today, though, I'm walking to a place to do a thing. I've thought about it, on my own, and I've determined I'm going to do it. I haven't discussed it with anyone, not for a lack of friends or confidence in my judgement, but out of fear that discussion will satisfy my impulse. I've found that if I tell someone of a plan I've made, their affirmation is so sweet that I no longer need to bother going through with the plan. I've already got what it was designed to bring me.

This thing mustn't go that way. Thrillingly, it doesn't seem to be. Where all the books I was going to write, jobs I was going to get and countries I was going to visit became schemes stodged up in nervous prevarication and lazy dreaming, this seems to have my legs pumping. I'm speeding down the hill,

---

* Unreliable narrator alert.

away from the comfort of the university, where life can safely be postponed for three years, towards the concrete council offices in town.

I'm actually doing this.

I thought I might dawdle. I don't have to do this; nobody will know if I don't. Last night, in bed, I was terrified, staring rigidly at the ceiling in the sort of moonlight that reveals all. Now, as the sun dapples the shady pavement that's broken up here and there by shifting roots, I watch my Adidas trainers flashing more and more quickly in front of me. I seem to have certainty. At this moment, I'm the sorcerer's apprentice, moving to some unknown will.

The Adidas trainers are a change. University was one of my many new starts and when my grant money arrived, a week before classes started, I decided I wanted to fit in. My clothes had always been chosen to stand out. I favoured cowboy boots and velvet jackets, bright silk shirts and PVC jeans. This get-up was the perfect uniform for my twin occupations: swanning around with my guitar and convincing the Jobcentre I was unemployable. Starting university, five years late, had been more nerve-wracking than I let on. No pub raconteur wants his intellectual self-assessment to be threatened by agreed-upon academic standards. *What if I'm not as bright as I've convinced everyone I am?* When I arrived for my first day I wanted, for once, to be invisible. Consciously deflating under this doubt, I looked around at what people seemed to be wearing and copied them. If I failed, nobody would notice.

Fuck me, I noticed, though. An introductory hosing-down in post-structuralist criticism undid my identity as profoundly as LSD had ever managed. A month into the course, I began to wonder whether I was legitimately thick. Everybody else's Adidas Sambas seemed to be skipping from lecture to lecture via the union for carefree pints, whilst mine were sinking in quicksand. *What do you mean, 'Who is the author'? It says who wrote it on the front of the book.* As Barthes, Baudrillard, Foucault and Derrida tore apart the assumptions I stood upon, I felt an overwhelming need for firmer ground. And today, St James's Road leads that way, I hope.

Solitude has moods. The Hank Williams, puking-your-desperation-up one has captured the world. Less frequently, you'll hear the monk-on-a-mountaintop smugness of pricks who are compelled to relate the wealth of their human experience. You can experience it as exhilaration, though. I'm in *glorious* solitude walking down St James's Road. Nobody knows where I am nor, particularly, what I'm doing.

I walked out of uni after the lecture but before the scheduled workshop on *The Crying of Lot 49*. Written in 1966, Pynchon's novel warned us we'd be overwhelmed by information. Now, in 1998, the tide is rising as the internet begins to inform, connect and expose us irrevocably. We're being stripped of our mystery by the bleaching light of data.

I don't know where my resolve is coming from today. I'm committing the greatest sin my world warns against and being propelled down this road by pure heresy, accelerating into damnation without a care.

My mum couldn't have been kinder when she explained that I was adopted. I'd like to repeat that. *My mum couldn't have been kinder when she explained that I was adopted.* It was nothing, Mum assured me, just an administrative detail that had been dealt with to bring me here, where I was loved. Not only was I in a real family who loved me just like every family loved their little boys, I was loved a little bit more because I'd been chosen especially and had been so hoped-for.

David, my dad, never mentioned it at all. He may have been persuaded into the whole thing, but his parenting was bracingly unreflective. He did what he did with unflinching authenticity.

It's a radioactive piece of information – your adoption – as elemental as parenthood or grief, but more unexpected and significantly less insulated by common experience. Regardless of how you choose to process it and frame the experience in later life, as a child it's a big, solid thing to know and something that even the grown-ups around you have no experience of.

I was a noisy, wordy child. I liked talking to adults because they had secret caches of words that they would share if you entertained them. I showed off, did impressions, sang and remembered everything adults said. Adults love being remembered more than anything.* This adoption business, though, was a silent thing. Mum had advised caution. 'People might not understand. They could be horrible. It's best to keep it private.' They'd moved house when I arrived. Nobody on our new road knew.

She would discuss it if I asked, but with evident discomfort. Her easy, irreverent humour would dissolve into frowns and peevishness. I learned not to ask. It wasn't pressing for me and it seemed to bother her so much that it wasn't worth it. That's what I told myself. It wasn't a thing I needed to talk about.

It was a thing, though. It *is* a thing, isn't it? I mean, it might be a better idea to go along with it, but there's an air of make-believe about that however you look at it, isn't there?

No, that's wrongthink! A well-adjusted adopted person would never think like that. Only me. To kick-off with, it's ungrateful. *You're in an affluent family that loves you, so shut up.*

Abortion had only been legal for four years when I made my entrance into national life. A little later and there may have been less stigma around it. Contemplating such existential matters in a comfortable suburban bedroom filled with toys

---

* Sometimes writing memoirs to enhance the odds.

felt indulgent. I would tell myself off for it. The snatches of information Mum had about my origins were relayed under duress when my wondering about them became urgent. Each nugget had to be remembered carefully as I knew it wasn't going to be revisited, because these were irrelevant details that I shouldn't be concerned with.

She was eighteen.
Nobody knows who he is.
She might have been Welsh.
She wanted things to turn out exactly as they have.
That is all.

It wasn't a lot to go on. People who are better at being adopted than I am can seemingly create an identity without reference to biology at all. Team Nurture. It must be difficult to sustain, though. When you're looking into the eyes of your firstborn and they are the only pair you've ever seen that reflect your own, it's hard not to notice. Flimsy materials require a craftsman's touch. The possible Welsh connection was improbably convenient. My mum's dad was my favourite person in the world. He had a reassuring certainty in his relationship with me, a grandfatherly authority that derived from wisdom and kindness. I was his only grandchild, and I seemed to matter very much to him. If the only piece of information I had about my origins suggested that I shared his Welshness, then it was taking centre stage. *Cymro ydw i*, I thought, but in English.

I liked doing impressions: Frank Spencer, Frank Carson, Maggie Thatcher, Prince Charles… I could be all these people, flitting from one to the next with nothing more than a change of tone. I was a show-off with a pressing need to be seen. When my Cubs' group's Gang Show came around, I negotiated myself a solo spot and went through my routine. When I was alone, thinking about things I'd been told not to, inauthenticity worried me dreadfully. To belong is everything to a child, and there was an asterisk by my name whichever way I looked at it. On stage, pretending was a virtue, something people admired. It was safe *not* to be yourself there. All you needed to know about how to be Frank Carson was how to say 'It's a cracker!' in a Belfast accent and you were fine. Nobody expected you to convince beyond the superficial. You weren't letting anyone down if you failed, and the stage lights obscured the audience anyway. It was probably good enough.

'Am I a bastard?'

Gleefully looking up rude words in the dictionary had led to this query. *So, that's what William the Conqueror was...*

'That's nothing to be ashamed of, not nowadays,' Mum reassured me in ashen-faced distress. 'Anyway, it's different. You're *adopted* and that changes everything.'

It's in this space that adoptees and their parents must finesse an accommodation. Somewhere between it *changing everything* and being *no different* from any other family lies the tricky terrain that both must exist in. Couples who have been officially scrutinised and vetted have to tell themselves they are the same as couples who, not infrequently, are parents by pure accident. They have been intruded upon, interrogated, judged and their authenticity questioned, whilst a couple who might only have met once are assumed to have been gifted life by the universe. Gratitude stalks this terrain, demanding tribute. Parents must live up to the privilege of bringing up somebody else's child. Adoptees, outsiders often say, are fortunate to be fed and nurtured at all. Everybody is in danger of letting everybody down all the time. If a child is well-behaved the parents lucked out, if not, well... what did you expect?

Subtraction of the biological imperative to go forth and multiply is unthinkable to many. I sometimes hear couples on the radio speaking of their heartbreak because they can't afford another cycle of IVF. Those matching eyes are quite a draw.

Occasionally, people would say that I looked like my dad. It's a kind thing to say to a little boy and also to his dad. It's well meant, a little social lubrication that ordinarily sits alongside complimenting the cut of someone's suit. I liked it when people said that. Someone had told me that we grow to resemble people over time because we mimic their expressions. Maybe that was happening and the stark differences between us were melting away in the warmth of familiarity. Or maybe people just like to bullshit. Because, out of the billions of men on earth, David was the only one who I knew definitively *couldn't* be genetically related to me. The bloke telling us we looked alike had more chance of that – or Eric Morecambe, or one of Bucks Fizz, or Pol Pot, or the milkman. But thank you, it was a friendly thing to say, and you weren't to know any of this, were you?

Family dinners, family values, family pack, hardworking families, family life, 'as a family', 'it's a family matter' – family, family, family. The cultural power of this word sees it harnessed by politicians, supermarkets, religions, television companies and whoever else is tasked with funnelling us through their turnstiles en masse. Its appeal is both broad and exclusionary. 'Family life' is a norm so fundamental that it is protected under human rights legislation. It speaks of pre-civilisation humanity: the instinctual bonds that cohered us before the compromises of society did. To be *without* those instincts, antisocial as they may be, is to lack an element intrinsic to our collective imagination of ourselves. We point approvingly to animals nurturing their young as proof that doing so is the wellspring from which all life thrives. It is the qualifier for Tier One of life as a mammal.

So, ticking 'Don't know' on medical questionnaires that ask if your family has any history of heart disease or mental illness is a miserable experience. Sometimes, the form doesn't even have that option, so you have to put your hand up in class and ask to speak privately to explain that you are biologically unaccompanied in the universe. Your teacher, who has read

Charles Dickens, will look stricken and tell you to put an asterisk and write in your circumstances. Your ears will burn red and amplify perceived sniggers. You were *chosen*, though, so it's alright.

Going for tea at a primary-school friend's house was an early experience of the exotic. The spaced-out mini castles of suburbia didn't allow for much cobble-close communal life; we all had our own worlds, to which admittance was only granted by appointment. Behind front doors, rituals, beliefs and conventions could flourish wildly. A detached house is just that: detached. And ours was as detached as it got. There's no helping yourself to biscuits in these set-ups. They are offered on plates as tokens of hospitality. You might have to take your shoes off or you might not. Sometimes, grace was said, occasionally at elaborate length. I remember a moustachioed father intoning gratitude for the 'fishes on our dishes' as if it were a perfectly unremarkable thing to do. Photographs of devout ancestors looked on in approving resemblance.

One schoolfriend's family had a motto: 'Abbott first and foremost'. I had a conflicted response to that when I heard it. They were kind and welcoming to me – biscuits were on hand – but clearly I was a tourist in their world. If Russia dropped the big one whilst we were polishing off the jam roly-poly, what would be my status in an Abbott-centric response to the news? Would the content of my character earn me a place in their bunker, or would a genetic drawbridge be pulled up, requiring me to seek shelter in the sewage system with other, non-Abbott human detritus? Perhaps I'd make it home, where genetics were a forbidden topic.

'Yes please, another scoop of ice cream would be lovely, Mrs Abbott.'

Across the road, I had a bolthole. Auntie Peggy and Uncle Ern lived opposite us and in a different galaxy. At home, it was quiet. The four-bedroomed new-build only had the three of us to absorb ticking clocks and sighs. 'Prattling', 'verbal diarrhoea' and singing made David wince, so it was best to keep a lid on it and read a book. Visitors were discouraged. Parties weren't held, tongues were. Over the road, the radio was on.

Uncle Ern was a builder. He'd built their house and the two next door. He and Auntie Peg adored each other, so easy together that it made you easy, too. Their son, Ean, was my friend. He was a couple of years older than me but possessed of such a sweet nature that a little kid hanging around was ok by him; the more the merrier.

Auntie Peg's house was a matriarchy in search of waifs to nurture. In contrast to the say-your-grace formality of arranged visits to school friends' homes, I could just show up and fit in. If I was on my own in the school holidays, Uncle Ern would pick me up in his three-wheeler builder's truck and take me to work with him. I'd have a hard hat and lay bricks; he gave me my own trowel. On the way back we'd sing 'Three Wheels on My Wagon' and Auntie Peg would have our tea ready.

I told my Mum how much I loved Auntie Peg's cottage pie.

'It's delicious,' I enthused.

My mum was a fabulous cook; continually learning new dishes from around the world and often spending all day making them. Her own cottage pie – which I'd now sell a limb for a spoonful of – featured a rich, herby gravy and grated cheese in the mash. Aunt Peg's version was mince, Smash and a tin of carrots – as Mum found out when she enquired after the recipe of this longed-for delicacy.

When Auntie Peg, Uncle Ern and Ean went on holiday, I was crestfallen. When I was wishing them a safe journey, that must have showed. Uncle Ern took me aside and asked if I would do him a favour. On his drive, under a tarpaulin, was a pile of building sand.

'Will you check on it for me, make sure the rain doesn't get in? It's an important job.'

Every day, after school, I'd rush over the road to check the tarpaulin was still in place and count off another day until they came back.

'How's the sand?' Uncle Ern asked as he got out of 'Hector', their Volkswagen camper.

'It's fine, Uncle Ern, I've checked every day.'

He went over to look at the sand.

'Well, you've done a great job, young Ben.'

Heading back to Hector, he returned with a large box.

'Something to say thank you.'

Inside was a Burago model racing car – absolutely the stuff of dreams. I'm still not convinced that piles of sand need too much looking after, but it's surprising how comforting a purpose can be when you're missing people.

When the Lebanese family next-door-but-one mentioned that a teenage relative needed somewhere to stay whilst he was studying, it was inevitable he'd end up with Peg and Ern. Another soul at the kitchen table, warming himself in their glow – he became family. Auntie Peg's cottage pie stretched around the world.

David's filing cabinet stood in the spare bedroom – where Sheba our greyhound had her own single bed – and it was a meticulously-maintained archive. Every gas bill, MOT certificate, insurance certificate and school report was in there behind the correct cardboard divider organised by date. It was a monument to order.

It was my school report I was after. My last year at junior school had been strange and upsetting. Mr Darby, our form teacher, was new to the school and had been appointed deputy headmaster. He was different from the other teachers: young, favouring of business suits and extremely strict. The end of his nose was perfectly square; I used to concentrate on it whilst he was bellowing at me.

'*I* say. *You* do!'

I seemed to annoy him. I was always bursting to answer questions and so he would roll his eyes and call me 'the encyclopaedia'. My English compositions – the thing I was best at – came back from him with red pen everywhere and failing grades. I was sent out of class to stand in the cloakroom for a week for giggling when he shouted at another unfavoured pupil. Still, it was my last year there and I'd passed my eleven-plus, so I figured I'd just have to put up with it. At the end of the year, I did well in the exams, coming second in English and fifth in maths. Mum's obsession with education, a teacher's daughter to her core, meant this was a mighty relief.

In the last week, that sunshiny blur when you sign each other's shirts and pinky promise to stay friends even though you are going to different schools, I was heading to the playground at break when Mrs Stevens approached me.

'Ben, can I have a word?'

This seemed odd. Mrs Stevens was a traditional primary school teacher, woolly jumpers and hugs for the little ones when they were upset. She hadn't taught me at all this year.

'Have you had your report yet?'

I hadn't thought about that.

'No, Mrs Stevens, I think we get them today at the end of school.'

Mrs Stevens looked at me kindly and lowered her voice.

'Listen, Ben. It's not very nice. I'm not the only one in the staffroom who thinks it's wrong.'

My guts turned to water. *How bad can it be?*

'The thing is, you need to get your mum to complain. Speak to Mr Curran. Because they'll send it on to your new school and that wouldn't be good.' Then, she put her hand on my shoulder and broke ranks altogether. 'It's nonsense, Ben, and we all know it isn't you. Don't let it affect you.'

Sure enough, when I opened the envelope addressed to my

parents, it contained a harsh assessment of my eleven-year-old character. *Lazy, disrespectful, feckless…*

Worse still, he'd overridden my exam results to grade me bottom of my entire year group for maths and English: D-minus in both. Despite Mrs Stevens's forewarning, I was distraught. I was *good* at school; it was my whole thing. I made my mum proud.

Running tearfully up to the car park, I handed Mum the report and tried to explain what I'd been told. She looked like she'd been shot.

'What the hell have you been doing in there?'

'Nothing, Mum, honestly. Mrs Stevens says you should go and see Mr Curran.'

'Right, wait in the car.'

Sat in the Ford Capri with my bare legs stuck to the vinyl seats in the heat, I had no idea why all this had happened.* My stomach filled with nervous adrenaline, as if I were in real danger. And it felt that way; as if the only thing I had to offer my family, and the world in general, had been snatched away. If I wasn't a *good* boy, a *clever* boy, then what would anybody want me for?

Eventually, Mum came back smiling. Mr Curran had ripped up the report in front of her and promised only to send my exam results on to my new school. We stopped off for ice cream on the way home.

Later, before bed, I watched David at his work desk, carefully sellotaping the report back together. So, a couple of years later, when a perverse desire to read it again gripped me, I knew where it would be.

---

* It wasn't until later that I discovered that some people just don't like know-it-all smart-arses with an answer for everything. Some do, though, so that's ok.

I was not allowed in the filing cabinet. It wasn't locked, though, and I was thirteen. So, when Mum went out shopping, I went in search of Mr Darby's report. In the midst of puberty, with darkness entering my soul like a revelation, it felt good to transgress, especially in search of documentary proof that I was bad to the bone. In the bottom draw, behind the mortgage correspondence, a cardboard divider was labelled 'Benjamin'. Despite legally changing my name to Ben a few years ago, people still call me by the long version when they sense I need taking down a notch or two. It lends itself to a raised eyebrow. Here, in David's cabinet, it had permanence.

Behind the divider, there were dental records, GP letters and… school reports. Swimming certificates and the like were in a separate box that Mum kept. This archive was purely administrative. I found that the sellotaped report that had caused me such anxiety had lost its power. I read through Mr Darby's assessment of my shortcomings with something approaching glee.

Too much for you, was I?

Peering from a teenage summit, I pitied my childish self.

Imagine letting that freak upset you.

Behind the reports, there was an unmarked envelope full of letters. Pulling one out, I saw it it was yellowing and dated 1973. Addressed to my parents, it was regarding the adoption of a child called Gareth Griffin. I stared at it wondering what had happened to prevent this. I mean, I would have quite liked having a brother and, after all, didn't everyone blame my attention-seeking and show-offiness on being an only child? *Where's Gareth?* I wondered.

All the letters in the envelope were about poor old Gareth. He seemed to have come tantalisingly close to a new life as my younger bro. The letters described an evolving process of checks, visits and arrangements. I had around a dozen of them on the carpet around me when the realisation struck. Yes, I was born in 1972, but it was December, so I wouldn't have been delivered to my parents until 1973.

OMFG, I'm Gareth!

I sat very still for a moment, my cheeks burning as I tried to reckon with this. The centre of me seemed to be shifting. I'd always known I was adopted, so part of my confusion was puzzlement at why I was so upset.

'Gareth Griffin,' I said out loud, needing to know what it sounded like.

The name rolled around, a marble on a ship bouncing off the hard surfaces that kept me afloat.

'Gareth Griffin. GARETH Griffin. Gareth GRIFFIN. GARETH GRIFFIN!'

A moment ago, he'd been a conceptual little foundling whose life had nearly intersected with mine. I'd felt sorry for the little sod and wondered if I'd have got on with him. Now he was inside me, mewling and puking up his short story.

I looked again at the letters. Gareth seemed to have turned into Benjamin in March 1973. So, for three months he was somewhere, with unknown people, doing whatever infant Gareths do. Benjamin wasn't a thing until March 1973. The younger kids in my year at school were born in 1973. I associated the year with that hierarchical difference, and so seeing it connected with me seemed all sorts of wrong.

I put the letters back in the envelope, filed it and went downstairs. Mum was out so I mooched about, unable to settle. I wasn't processing this well. It was a retrospective plot twist in my story. A missing three months, let alone a new name, meant I'd been writing it without fundamental information up until now. I hadn't considered either of those possibilities. I'd assumed, I suppose, that I'd been picked up from the maternity hospital by social services and dropped off at my new home before being named – a nice, clean operation for all involved. The revelation that my birth mother had named me rounded out her character in a way that challenged the version of events I had relied on in order to be comfortable with my origins. *What was she thinking giving me a name if she didn't mean to keep me?* It seemed intimate and also an intrusion somehow. What it intruded on was the idea that my adoption had been the natural order of things; something uncomplicated that was for the general good. Mum preferred not to think about it at all, but if I did broach the subject, she characterised my birth mother as a surrogate – someone whose circumstances intersected with ours to produce the happy outcome of our family. 'Gareth Griffin' seemed like someone who had been thought about outside of this contrivance. Perhaps he'd been missed – grieved for, even. Either way, he had spent three months living in a different story altogether, before entering witness protection and having his name changed.

I became angry. I was a *good* adoptee; I never banged on about it or daydreamed about being royalty. I was well adjusted and loyal to my parents. So, why had all this been hidden from me?

By the time Mum came home I was distressed. I stropped about the house until it became impossible for her to ignore, and she casually asked what was wrong.

'Nothing,' I replied, before stropping some more.* Hurling myself down on the sofa, I made my mood as obvious as possible, sighing and shaking my head for further effect, my face like fourpence.

'For God's sake, Benjamin, what's the matter?'

That was more like it: full attention.

But I didn't know what to say. I'm in a similar quandary now, staring at the question on the page. *What's the matter?* I

---

* Absolutely a learned behaviour from her. She was, as I am, laughably dramatic when upset. Score one for Team Nurture.

broke off from writing this yesterday, telling myself I'd come to a natural break. How I was feeling, in that moment, as Mum stood over me, was uncontainable and too much to express. I was angry because something had been kept from me. I was confused because my identity had become even more complicated. I was frightened because it seemed my existence was built on shifting sands. And I was frustrated because nobody I knew had experienced anything like this and, even if I did know someone, I wasn't supposed to talk about it anyway.

'Who's Gareth Griffin?' I demanded, nastily.

That half-brick curved into the air over the still waters of my mum's contentment, and I couldn't snatch it back. For a moment, she looked at me, stricken, and I braced myself for the splash of the impact.

'Fuck off, then. Fuck off and be Gareth Griffin!'

She ran upstairs crying and I just sat there with the mess all strewn around me, some of it hers, some mine, and some belonging to God knows who.

I come to the point as the hill shallows out just before Dudley town centre.

'Mary,' I say, out loud and for no reason I can identify. The tall, concrete building on the left at the end of the road is where I'm due for an appointment. I dawdle outside with a cigarette, then another one. I'm early.

Inside, reception directs me up to the fourth floor and I'm asked to wait on one of those stackable plastic chairs that feature in all things municipal. The cheerful determination that propelled me down the hill from the university to Dudley Metropolitan Council's social services department evaporates as I wait. A woman approaches me carrying a beige cardboard file. Until opened, it contains Schrödinger's origin story. The possibilities within it are limitless but unlikely to be pleasant.

Gareth Griffin's first act can't have been easy, otherwise he'd still be Gareth Griffin, wouldn't he?

Please don't be rape.

'You must be Benjamin. I'm Margaret,' the social worker smiles.

'Ben,' I reply, exerting what control I have.

'Of course. Let's go into the office.'

The file thuds down on the desk. The weight of it isn't mine, though: it's the life choices, biological quirks and happenstances of four other people. My role in it is conceptual; I'm both a problem and an opportunity. I'm known to the authorities even before I receive the first of my assumed identities. I'm in diaries, the subject of meetings and the object of concerns. I'm written about and archived.

This part is not my story, though. And my part in it is not a speaking role. I only emerge from the womb in the second act. The grand acts in the story contained in the file happened around me as adults made big, solemn decisions, like grown-ups do. It's not my business to be poking around in this, really. It's prurient and frivolous of me to rifle through their lives like this. They certainly wouldn't like it.

It's all so 1972. My birth mother is described as 'tallish, pretty'. My other mother's housekeeping skills are noted alongside observations about her home decor choices. There are no villains of the piece, it seems, just young people trying to figure out what's for the best. The shape of my birth mother's name winds its way around me, curling past agreements and language. Outside, with the file under my arm, I say it out loud.

CLAMBERING OUT OF THE CAPRI

I was six in 1979. Mum was about to make the parental sacrifice of trading in her MGBGT* sports coupe for a roomier Ford Capri. For now, I was crammed into the space behind the passenger seat with my knees jammed against the leather, peering out of a small, triangular rear window as we roared down the Warwick Road on our way from Solihull to Acocks Green.† It is about five miles between these two suburban nonentities but somewhere in Olton one crosses a line. The houses become smaller and closer together, cars are parked on the street instead of on block-paved drives and people wait at bus stops – even grown-ups. There was a new difference that day, though. On all the lamp posts there were posters I'd never seen before. In Solihull they were mainly blue, with an occasional orange one

---

* This appeared on our drive as a surprise for Mum's thirty-fifth birthday. What prompted Dad to make this stunning gesture has never been established, but Mum suspected guilt.
† A couple of miles from Acocks Green, J. R. R Tolkien supposedly found inspiration for the 'old forest' in his fictional land of Middle Earth whilst walking around Moseley bog and Sarehole Mill. Had he travelled as far as Fox Hollies Road, he'd have been obliged to pit Bilbo against a tribe of septuagenarian women armed with tartan shopping trolleys. The orcs would have been a warm-up.

in someone's front garden. As we crossed into Acocks Green, though, the posters were almost all red with yellow writing. As these flashed by through my window, I experienced an urgency that defines my character to this day. *Something is going on here and I don't know what it is.* So, under frantic questioning, Mum, hurling the car around bends, explained the rudiments of democracy. *What* is an election? *Why* are they called parties? *Who* will you vote for?

'Maggie. She's a woman. She has common sense and she'll look after our money properly.' Mum might have added that she wouldn't be seen dead in Acocks Green either.

We clambered out of the MG and Mum stuffed her leather Airtex driving gloves into her handbag before pushing her key into Grandma and Grandad's front door.

'We're here, don't get up,' she called through to them.

Mum and I had recently had an unusual conversation. She had been at the school gate as usual but hadn't wanted to go straight home. Instead, we were going to feed the geese in Brueton Park. *Result!* I had happily disgorged the day's scholastic events as we made our way through the immaculate parkland to the artificial lake. She hadn't seemed quite herself, answering me abruptly and avoiding eye contact. I had seen her like this before, though. Dad would become cross with one of us and he would shout at her. She'd be like that for a while after: nothing to worry about.

She kept a very close eye on me, did Mum. I was strong and healthy, but she worried something might happen. 'No skateboard. Don't ask again.' I was top of my class, but I might slip so I should read more… to her… out loud. I had beautiful, expensive clothes but, seemingly, never enough of them, and so she'd risk Dad's anger by buying more. I was her joy, I knew that, but her worry for me was palpable. It was as if she were taking care of something terribly valuable that could break at any moment.

Tossing hunks of Sainsbury's brown bread at the geese, I had burbled on.

'We did timeses today. There isn't a sandbox now we're in second year. David Price says he's going to beat up Max because Max called him a meff...'

Mum had let me exhaust myself of what Dad called my 'verbal diarrhoea' before starting to speak in a deliberate, kind way that was shorn of her usual joyful sarcasm. It turned out that I was 'adopted'. This meant that, unlike other little boys, who were randomly allocated to their parents, I had been *chosen* especially by mine and was therefore *more* loved and *special*. The thing about being adopted, though, was that you must never, ever tell anybody because it is *rude* and would upset everyone. And I didn't want to do that, did I?

I certainly didn't. Mum had always made a point of pointing out badly behaved, *rude* children to me over the years and it was a point of utmost pride that I was the opposite. When we went to Giovanni's restaurant for Sunday lunch, I knew which way to push the soup spoon through the minestrone. Even though it was stupid, it wasn't *rude*, so I did it.

'Will Grandad still be my real Grandad?' I had asked.

'Yes, of course,' Mum replied. There was nothing more to discuss.

Grandma and Grandad's house was a Birmingham Corporation house built just after the war, and they had been the only residents. Their furniture was scrupulously nurtured through long lives, and the china rarely chipped. Grandma's handicrafts sat under the stoic clock in the front room, where we never went unless Grandad felt moved to play me a record from his collection. He taught me to beat time like a real conductor until Beethoven, Mozart and Schubert obeyed my tiny fingers and stern concentration. He told me how an essay he wrote in his schooldays about Mozart's beautiful music rushing out of the window along with the steam from his mother's washing had won him a prize. I plucked books from the shelf under the stairs, knowing that they held the building blocks of this man who loved me so much. Three subjects dominated his book collection: music, rugby and socialism – the Rhondda triumvirate.

So, Mum being a Tory had the potential to be awkward. She'd grown up in that house but always saw herself bound for more glamorous surroundings. Grandad wasn't about to let me go down the same path, so front room music recitals often turned into political education classes, away from Mum and Grandma in the kitchen.

Grandad was born in 1916, so he'd been ten when the 1926 strike turned the Rhondda valleys into battlefields. He was from Tylorstown in Rhondda Fach, just down the road from Maerdy: 'Red Rhondda's Little Moscow'. A little boy needs a storyteller in his life and pre-war Rhondda became a sort of Middle Earth to me: a place where good battled evil unconcerned with the niceties of suburbia that were the be-all and end-all of life back in Solihull.* At my age, Grandad had collected stones to throw at the police who had been given power of entry to miners' houses – houses, mind you, that had to be rented from the mine owners who were imposing starvation wages on their workforce. I wished I had been there too. I recognised what Nye Bevan called a 'deep burning hatred' for the Tory Party from the intensity in Grandad's eyes when he spoke of those times. I learned the thrill of tribal righteousness and had it ringing in my ears along with a Beethoven symphony

---

* This other Rhondda still exists. I keep it hermetically sealed and partitioned away from the actual one that I inhabit in real life. There are similarities between the two, but I wouldn't want inconsistences like the existence of Conservative clubs to infect my version.

as I reluctantly climbed into Mum's MG for the journey back across the Rubicon to where the posters were blue.

There is some debate as to whether the name Solihull derives from the Old English for 'soily hill' and thus means 'shit heap', even if I choose to accept this fact without question or enquiry. What can be asserted as plain fact, however, is that Solihull boasts the lowest sales of books per capita in the UK and the highest uptake of white slip-on Gucci loafers.* Over the course of my childhood there, it went from bad to worse as the traditional population of retired engineering tycoons shuffled off to the celestial golf club, leaving their mock-Tudor palaces to be snapped up by the ascendant young beneficiaries of a deregulated financial services industry. The few pubs that dotted the town became wine bars, and the last vestiges of its rural past were buried under vast estates of executive family homes that increased their value by a grand a week during the property boom. Caravans of voles and field mice could be seen heading down the A41 (now the A4141) towards Knowle in search of asylum.

Every other Thursday, Mum would have her hair done at Raymond's Hair Salon, which occupied the prime spot opposite Beatties department store. This was a two-hour job, and during school holidays, when I was old enough, I would be allowed to roam around the town centre before meeting up with Mum at the coffee lounge in Beatties. The cost of these hair appointments was a matter of some contention between my parents, their necessity not readily apparent from any discernible change in Mum's appearance afterwards. Her mood would be better, though: those two hours of being cared for meant more to her than I understood at the time.

One morning, in 1981, I walked straight past her table in

---

* This is true, but the statistics can only be found on the dark web.

the coffee lounge without recognising her. The soft bob (which had replaced her flamboyant 1960s beehive around the time I came along in 1972) had gone the way of platform boots and collective bargaining. The 1980s had landed on top of Mum's head in the shape of a swept-up perm that sat defiantly rigid and coated in Ellnett hairspray. Shoulder pads completed this new, boardroom look that belied the reality: that Dad forbade her from working. She wasn't going anywhere near an office but looked like she should.

Mum was frantically keen that I get 'somewhere' in life. Her enthusiasm for my schoolwork was born of complex motives, though. Primarily, she wanted the best for me, and this was boosted by a vicarious enjoyment of my achievements that soothed frustration at her enforced role as a housewife. Secondly, she was competitive, and nothing livened up a torpid coffee morning with the girls more than pointing out how much better I had done in my exams than their children.* A regime of flash cards, closely supervised homework and motivational lectures paved the way for boot-camp-like conditions and a siege mentality in my final year at junior school. During the winter term, I was told, I would take two entrance exams and success in either would see me off to an independent school. Failure in both would result in a comprehensive education and the premature death of my mum, whose gravestone would read: 'God forgive me, I tried'.

I was enrolled with a tutor, upon whom the seriousness of the situation had been stressed. Miss Russell was a young, quiet teacher at my junior school who had a specialist practice in the evenings preparing candidates for the exams. On a Thursday evening in October, I was delivered to her home in Shirley for my first two-hour session.

---

* Neatly mirrored by how much better they went on to do at life!

Maths was, and remains, a problem. Miss Russell was a patient and precise soul whose neat handwriting conveyed encouragement rather than condemnation in the space around my imbalanced equations. It was determined that my English was fine, and that the lessons would focus solely on maths. Mum nodded vigorously at this suggestion, to Miss Russell's visible relief and my audible horror. In the Capri on the way home, we discussed the state of play.

'Look, you won't even pass for Solihull School, let alone King Edward's, if you don't sort your maths out. Do you want to end up at *Tudor Grange*?' Tudor Grange was pronounced as if it were a young offenders' institution rather than the best comprehensive in the West Midlands.

'Yes, I do! All my friends are going there and it's only over the road.' Mum didn't dignify this heresy with a response but narrowed her eyes and accelerated recklessly. I knew when to shut up.

During half term it was arranged that all of Miss Russell's students would sit a series of mock exams to see how we were getting along in relation to one another. Five of us[*] assembled

---

[*] It might have been five. Or four. I don't think it was three or six. I can remember where I was sat in the room but absolutely nothing about the other boys who were there. I knew them all as we were in the same room, and if I heard their names I'm sure I could put faces to them, but they are gone from my memory. How much of life goes this way? Presumably, we are editing people out of our memories as we go along; unless they are useful to the narrative we are creating, out they go. If we're not removing people altogether, like ousted comrades in a Politburo photograph, we are merging them into composite characters as used in Hollywood biopics. When the Dalai Lama describes 'this unenlightened guy I met once' in a wry, post-meditational anecdote, he's almost certainly cobbling together a marionette from the living, breathing personalities of countless people he's pretended to tolerate. We do it all the time and, more disturbingly still, are in turn cannibalised to manufacture bit parts in other people's memories.

miserably in her front room where a table was laid out with pens and exam papers. Silent glances were exchanged that told of the shared anguish at having to miss our holidays for this ordeal.

I couldn't seem to get into the swing of it. Whilst all the elements of an examination were in place – silence, serious expressions, a prominent clock – it was still in someone's front room, and so it felt fake. I wanted to do well, but the inauthenticity of the setting underscored the reality that nothing was at stake. I couldn't even think of a decent story for the English paper, so the lost dog in my tale was found prematurely, and I was left with nothing to do for the last fifteen minutes. The others were all still scribbling away, which left me feeling exposed and conspicuous. To show willing, I added an illustration of the canine protagonist, James, being pulled from the river by his relieved owner. I'm not much of an artist, but it filled the blank space on the page and spared me from having to sit unoccupied until Miss Russell signalled time was up. I'd gone the extra mile, I thought.

'Last in maths and second-to-last in English!' Mum was not happy. 'What on earth were you doing drawing a picture? You're not *five*! Well, I'll tell you now, you haven't got a snowball's chance in hell of passing for King Edward's!' Even at the time, her disproportionate fury seemed comic and it was a struggle to appear suitably devastated. 'I don't know why I bother!' she concluded, before marching to the fridge for wine.

The real exams, held on consecutive Saturday mornings, were my first taste of pressure. The Solihull School exam was near to home, and lots of boys from my junior school had entered, so some buffers were in place between me and institutional alienation. King Edward's, however, was ten miles away and it attracted hopefuls from all the suburbs surrounding Birmingham. The Solihull School exam was a warm-up for this: the main event.

A churning terror gripped me as Mum drove down the long driveway to the forbidding red-brick building with arched, oak doors. Even Mum looked cowed by the place. I wasn't alone. Hundreds of fearful ten-year-olds emerged from their mummies' cars, cursing their intelligence. *If I was just a little more thick I'd have my feet up watching* Tiswas *now...*

'Don't worry about it. Just have a go,' Mum said kindly as I clambered out of the Capri.

Some of the other boys had been sent in their junior school uniforms, making them appear even more vulnerable as we entered the towering building and made our way past oil paintings of cane-flexing headmasters from yesteryear. None of us said a word.

'You aren't expected to get all the answers right,' smiled the invigilating master after we had settled in a classroom designated by our surnames. 'In fact, the papers have been designed to render that impossible.' Frantic glances were exchanged around the room. *Not get all the answers right?* Did this man not appreciate the deeply indoctrinated need that boys like us had to *get all the answers right*? 'Just do your best and try to think of the logical solution to the problems.'

The maths paper was a beast with fangs. I looked despairingly at the compound fractions in a list of equations and tried to remember Miss Russell's teaching. Twenty-five little brains heated up the classroom with exertion as we all tried to push self-doubt away and succeed. The exam was designed to make you feel stupid, though, and regular exhalations of frustration drew wry smiles from the invigilator. Then a boy put his hand up. Everybody kept one eye on the master as he walked over and asked what was wrong.

'What's binary?' asked the unfortunate candidate. The master looked at him kindly and suggested he miss out that question. The sense of relief in the room was palpable as every other boy there thought, *I'm not the worst. Thank you, God, I'm not the worst.*

Clambering out of the Capri

September of 1984 found me stood at the bus station in Solihull waiting for the 885 to take me for my first day at King Edward's. The results letter had arrived on a Saturday morning, causing my mum to run upstairs with it and pull me, sleeping, out of bed and onto the floor.

'You've passed for King Edward's! Wake up, you little sod!'

It was a forty-five-minute journey to Edgbaston, and the preponderance of pupils from prosperous Solihull meant there were three double-deckers laid on to take us across the West Midlands to fulfil our parents' dreams and then return us each afternoon. The buses left at ten-minute intervals and each had its own atmosphere and culture. The first was strictly for first years ('sherrings' – a contraction of 'fresh herrings' – in school vernacular) and socially-challenged maths prodigies. The second was where to find the well-adjusted Edwardian: he was relaxed and had done his prep but wanted to arrive at school calmly and discuss matters of interest with his peers before the day's lessons. The third bus would eject its passengers, reeking of tobacco and spiking up their dyed black hair, five minutes before the bell. The morning's lessons were a blurred inconvenience before they could get to the pub at lunchtime.

That morning waiting for the first bus revealed much to me about my nature. I had been so proud of my uniform when I'd tried it on the previous day. Mum and I had gone along with all the other newcomers to the school shop to fork out a small fortune on all the required items. There was an embroidered blazer, a tie, a rugby jersey, rugby socks, rugby shorts, a scarf (optional, but a must for Mum) and PE shorts. When Mum offered the head porter a cheque guarantee card for the payment, he grinned.

'We've got your son.'

Various family members, proud of my achievement, had chipped in and received Polaroid photos of me stood in the back garden wearing my uniform with my hair in a side parting and a smile that spoke of future glories. Aunt Floss and Aunt Renee had insisted on paying for the tie. On Dad's side of the family, they were ten years apart in age, and Floss had brought up Renee as a child. She'd done a good job, too: Renee was a remarkable character who had worked her whole life at the Lucas automotive factory and used to receive a Christmas card from old man Lucas personally, such was her dedication. She was brisk and angular with horn-rimmed glasses, brown brogues, red hair tied up in a bun and a clipped Birmingham accent. She enjoyed talking about engineering and cars in particular. Her own vehicle was a maroon Morris Minor, which she maintained personally and meticulously for thirty years. It looked brand new until her death. Floss's health had failed early and she had never married. Renee provided for her, though. They lived together and were Floss and Renee to everyone who knew them. After a sherry or two, my gran used to like recalling being at their home when something came on the telly about lesbians.

'What's one of those?' Floss had asked.

'Nothing you need worry about, Flossie dear,' Renee replied.

At the bus station, I fingered my tie nervously as Mum's Capri departed the scene. She'd been savvy enough to park away from the waiting passengers and hug me goodbye where my failing confidence wouldn't be so apparent. I remained away from the ebullient crowd with my back to their nervous laughter and cried. *It was so kind of Floss and Renee to buy me this tie,* I thought. *I can't ever live up to this.*

I'm concerned that the contrived *otherness* of the King Edward's experience might not be coming through here. Let's examine it through the microcosm of the lunch break. Since leaving the school I've learned that other 1980s kids were rather restricted in what was available to do during this golden hour of freedom. Our experiences overlapped in that we could also, if we wished, disappear somewhere to smoke fags, slash the tyres on a teacher's car or impregnate a girl from the nearby convent school as well as eat lunch. We also had the option, though, to attend *societies*. I understand that clubs – art, chess etc. – existed at other schools but we didn't have those. There was only one club at our place, the Cartland Club, which is where prefects lazed in leather armchairs smoking and discussing whether or not to go into a career in the City or take over their fathers' engineering concerns. The societies, of which there were over fifty, were lunchtime meetings in classrooms where masters would give up their time to lead discussions about their subject areas of expertise. 'Into geology? Mr Cumberland will be guiding the Geological Society through his collection of slides on Peak District limestone escarpments in room 211 at 13.10 sharp! Get there early to ensure seating.' 'Aspiring poets should note that Mr Trott, who studied under T. S. Eliot in his youth, will be presenting a selection of his early work...' You get the picture.

Each society would produce a report on its activities in the yearly *Chronicle*, which was distributed to all connected with the school. There was even a secret society, the Closed Circle, which published an ambiguous report, and to which one had to be invited. Rumours abounded that it was a far-right think tank. I don't know, nobody ever invited me. Ask Jonathan Coe, he seems to know *all* about it[*].

For the politically committed eleven-year-old, there were two options: the Junior Debating Society and the Parliamentary Society. The JDS was a bear pit with mass appeal. It had two selling points: a reputation for riotous

---

[*] Coe's novels *The Rotters' Club* and *The Closed Circle* depict life at the school shortly before my time.

confrontation and the fact that it was a combined society with the adjoining girls' school. For the newly-hormonal male, this was an attractive proposition. You could rip the piss out of the assigned speakers *in front of pretty girls* who would notice your practiced élan and, doubtless, sleep with you once your balls had dropped. For those at the front, though – the proposers, seconders and refuters of motions – it was an altogether more fraught experience. For one thing, you had to draw lots as to whether you were for or against the motion in play. I found myself compelled to support an equally heartbroken girl in supporting scientific experiments on animals to the derision of our politically disinterested peers, who would no more have bothered writing a speech than checking the ethical bone fides of the ingredients in the Big Macs they had brought along.

The Parliamentary Society, by contrast, had only a few members and sat monthly in a small classroom. Ranging from the fourth form to the sixth, these were boys who had taught themselves the nuances between the economic strategies of Beveridge and Cripps perhaps too early in their young lives and were glad to find companionship for an hour once a month on Tuesdays. I joined in the first year.

'The year's proceedings were enlivened by the contributions of a left-wing member of the Shells,'* was how *The Chronicle* noted my presence that first year. Well, it had been quite a year. Occasionally, we'd go home by bus and then by train through the centre of Birmingham, as a change from the school bus. We could spend some pocket money and see a

---

* The first year at King Edward's was called the 'shells', followed by the removes, upper middles, fourths, fifths, divisions, and sixths. There wasn't a school cormorant into which we rubbed linseed oil but one wouldn't have been out of place.

bit of city life. The life we saw included striking Welsh miners who'd travelled up from the valleys, rattling buckets for small change to help their communities through the action.

Will Grandad still be my grandad?

The strike affected me in a way that was disproportionate to my surroundings. I was living in a four-bedroomed, detached house in Solihull – the Millionaire's Row of the West Midlands. I was attending King Edward's School in Edgbaston, then only challenged by Manchester Grammar for Oxbridge entries and thrashing Eton and Harrow for the same year on year. I had never missed a meal in my life and was, as yet, unaware that I ever would.

Grandad wasn't looking well. His round face had returned to the contours seen in 1930s photographs of him back in the Rhondda. When we went to the rugby on a Saturday, he took along a little silver box with yellow pills inside.

He'd been enthusiastic about Neil Kinnock winning the Labour Party leadership. He'd stressed to me that the intellectual vigour of Michael Foot was all well and good in university debates but that it would never play with working people, especially looking like he did. Kinnock's reforming zeal, I was instructed, made him the man of the future who could remake the Labour movement to take on Thatcher and her criminal friends.

'And it's great that he's Welsh,' I piped up.

'That has nothing to do with it,' Grandad chided, a little unpersuasively.

One Saturday morning, I was in Birmingham city centre to have a look around the record shops, when a boisterous march came down Corporation Street. I edged towards it to see what was going on and a smiling man in his fifties beckoned me.

'Join us, son.'

'What's the march for?' I asked.

'Workers' rights and common decency. Come on!'

I stepped forward and he slapped a sticker on my C&A coat. We marched around Birmingham chanting slogans: 'Maggie, Maggie, Maggie. Out, out, out!'

It was fun and exciting. Everyone was enjoying themselves and it was better than shopping. I peeled off after about twenty minutes with promises to be at the one next month as my back was slapped approvingly by other marchers. As they agitated off around the corner, I looked down at my sticker. Featuring a clenched red fist, it said, 'The Rise of Militant!' I froze in panic for a moment. It seemed I had accidentally joined Militant Tendency. All I knew about them was that they were a *'very* bad thing'. It was rare that all my channels of information were in concert on a topic but *The Guardian*, which I had taken to reading on the school bus; Dad's *Daily Mail*; *The Sun*, in which furtive glances of breasts could be made in a quiet newsagent; Neil Kinnock; Grandad and the Archbishop of Canterbury all agreed that Militant were Soviet-funded thugs intent on destroying Britain forever. I ripped off the sticker, terrified that I had been seen. *Nobody must ever know.*

Grandad went rather quiet when it emerged that Kinnock's reforming instincts ran as far as refusing to back the NUM in the miners' strike. However controversial the decision not to hold a national ballot and notwithstanding concerns about Arthur Scargill's motivations, this was a *strike*. You were on one side or the other, and Kinnock's dissembling refusal to commit was galling, given his coalfield background.

The grim progress of the strike was reflected in Grandad's mood. As his health deteriorated, he was watching the destruction of the way of life that had forged him. His wagon had been hitched to Kinnock, so he couldn't very well complain about that betrayal too much. Instead, old, tribal enmities surfaced. The strike was broken by many miners in the Nottinghamshire coalfield, and Grandad focused his ire on them.

'Nothing has changed!' he would rumble. 'They were scabs in 1926 and they are scabs now!'* He'd explain that the large caverns where Nottinghamshire miners worked made a different type of man than the dangerous six-inch anthracite seams 'back home'. Those soft Midlanders didn't understand the solidarity of men who worked in dangerous conditions and whose mutual trust was a matter of life or death. On one occasion, he rather upset me by declaring that his observation from living nearly fifty years in the Midlands was that the people there were 'born serfs and cap doffers.'

'I was born here, Grandad,' I objected.

'If you were born in a stable it wouldn't make you a horse, would it?'

Well, no, but it might make you wonder if some equine characteristic had brought about that shameful situation. So, when it came to the strike, I was compensatory in my passionate defence of the miners' cause.

The crucible for this early foray into identity politics was the Parliamentary Society at school. You would have thought that the prevailing social turmoil would have attracted radicalised eleven-year-olds, keen to play their part in the national debate, to these meetings in droves, but I was years younger than everyone else there. That meant, though, that

---

* There were parallels, particularly between the 'Spencerite' union of 1926 and the Union of Democratic Mineworkers (UDM) which was set up, with government collusion, to break the 1984–5 strike. In 1992, the Conservative government closed the rump of the UK's mines as Arthur Scargill had insisted they would eight years previously. These included those supposedly profitable pits manned by UDM miners. UDM president, Roy Lynk, honoured with an OBE by Thatcher, staged a hunger strike inside Silverhill colliery with his wife. A sardonic UDM member remarked to television news that Lynk and his wife were down the pit because they were too ashamed to show their faces above ground.

the quality of discussion was pleasingly high. During the first couple of meetings, I thought it wise to keep quiet and assess the lie of the land by listening. 'You have two ears and one mouth,' as Grandad was fond of reminding me.

There was much to learn if I was to contribute credibly, so I took note of what the more impressive sixth formers were saying and looked up what I needed to in the library between meetings. It didn't take long to conclude that monetarism, for instance, was a lot of guff that required urgent challenging, so I decided to put aside my misgivings and wade into the fray.

The results of Thatcher's crude butchery of Friedman's theories had, as it happened, washed up at home, and Dad's firm had gone bust. He'd had to sign on for a while and my school fees were now being paid by a government initiative called the Assisted Places Scheme* whereby paupers could send their promising urchins to independent schools at the taxpayer's expense. I don't think that taxpayers were largely aware of this development, but I'd like to reassure them that I was not incognisant of their maltreatment.

Nothing pricks a young radical like being the unwilling beneficiary of establishment largesse. Alongside the gnawing suspicion that I was inherently a Midlands serf, I found myself in a situation of privilege funded not by my parents but by the system itself. It was as if I had been sat on Maggie's

---

* Before the 1987 election, the Chief Master wrote to our parents instructing them to vote Conservative as a Labour government would cancel this scheme, and the school would be forced to fall back on its investment income to carry on educating poorer pupils. Around this time, the Birmingham Evening Mail reported that one portion of this income derived from rent on a sex shop in Birmingham's Chinatown. 'Forward where the knocks are hardest,' as the school song instructed.

knee and told to give her a kiss because she'd bought me an Airfix model kit for Christmas. I fucking hated Airfix. *See, Mum,* this *is why I wanted to go to Tudor Grange.*

So, when the Parliamentary Society discussion on industrial relations came around, I felt my time had come. The early part of the debate featured a couple of mathematically-inclined boys who were much concerned at the statistical drop in UK productivity by the mid-1970s. This, they unquestioningly explained, was due to the inflated influence of trade unions. We were far enough into the Thatcher regime, by now, that shibboleths like this were beyond reproach. In Solihull, a retired bank manager had trained his daughter's pony to mark out 'collective bargaining' in the stable dust when he shouted, 'What's to blame?'

In the corner of the room, apart from the rest of us, there was an intriguing figure from the fifth form leaning back in his chair. Tall and elegant, he had a quizzical smirk in permanent operation. As the conversation petered into economic technicalities, he engaged obliquely across it.

'The workforce in this country has been a disgrace for decades. They deserve active punishment from the entrepreneurs they have taken for a ride,' he interjected, before leaning back again and extending one leg provocatively. The bean-counters were shocked into silence as, visibly, he relished his effect on the atmosphere. Nature abhors a vacuum – my nature particularly – so I countered cautiously.

'Without the workforce, entrepreneurs couldn't exist.'

'Without employers, they would starve, and many of them would do well to remember that.'

That did it. I launched into a lengthy exposition on the exploitation of labour in the British Isles, complete with a recap of mining conditions in 1920s Rhondda before wheeling back to the present and condemning the short-sightedness of Tory industrial policy, which had condemned so many working men, my own *father* amongst them, to the indignity of the Jobcentre. I explained why, without the crucial intervention of trade union movements, whole swathes of society would be cruelly abused by capital before being slung on the scrap heap when they were of no further use.

When I finished, to curious silence, my opponent smiled languidly.[*]

'It seems to me that if a man has the means to support voluntary employment, then he should do what he likes with his workers. They can always leave.'

At that, the bell rang for the end of lunch.

Later that year, during the summer holidays, I had a taste of the miners' strike that went beyond the theoretical. Dad had found a job, but it paid rather less than what he was used to. He decided to sell his classic car: a pink Ford Anglia.[†] The first response we had was from a chap from Derbyshire. He arranged to come and view it one day while Dad would be at work.

Roy arrived with his wife, Jean, and spent half an hour or so poking around the Anglia, as enthusiasts do, in the morning sunshine. Neither Mum nor I knew the slightest thing about cars so couldn't answer any questions. I innocently volunteered that Dad had given one of the doors 'a lick of paint', which provoked an admonishing glare from Mum. Eventually, Roy thanked us and said he'd have to think about it.

'Well, come in for a cup of tea,' Mum smiled. 'You've had such a long trip.'

---

[*] I can picture this character very clearly. He went on to be a Conservative parliamentary candidate.
[†] Dad named this car 'Pinky'. He could muster wet-eyed sentimentality for anything as long as it didn't speak.

'Oh, we wouldn't want to inconvenience you,' Jean said, Britishly.

'Don't be silly. This way.'

I sat with them as Mum made the tea and they glanced awkwardly around the big through lounge that Dad had built in better times.

'Lovely home you have,' Jean said as Mum returned with the tea.

'Certainly is,' Roy agreed. Mum smiled.

'Thank you.'

'What does your husband do?' Jean asked.

'Well, other than annoy me, he's a civil engineer. What do you do, Roy?'

Roy and Jean exchanged glances before Jean answered.

'Roy's a miner. I hope that's not a problem,' she said quietly.

'We're from mining stock, aren't we, Ben?' Mum replied.

'The Rhondda,' I agreed proudly.

'This must be a difficult time for you,' Mum said.

'It's just that some people make assumptions,' Roy added, 'because of what's on the news, like.'

Mum brushed all this away beautifully and handed out some Marks & Spencer Battenburg. She was a snob – she'd have told you that herself – but only as a hobby. It was a good job she had put them at their ease because I, of course, was straight out of the traps with a barrage of insensitive questions.

Yes, Roy *was* still on strike, but he understood why some of his mates weren't. It was because they still had kids at home and had to provide for them. No, he *didn't* like Arthur Scargill because Scargill wouldn't listen to local branches and had a political agenda that went beyond looking after the miners. There *was* some strike pay from the NUM but it wasn't shared properly and some factions in the union got more than they should.

They were kind people and they treated this strange, obsessive kid with real patience – more than I deserved. Mum eventually brought the conversation round to normal topics like holidays, and we spent a pleasant afternoon before waving them off around teatime.

The next week, Mum received a letter from Jean. Firstly, she wanted to apologise for wasting our time about the car. The truth was that with things as they were, they were not going to be able to buy it. Roy had been so bored stuck at home that she'd encouraged him to drive out for a look when he noticed the advert: it was a trip out to break things up a bit. She also wanted to thank us both for such a lovely afternoon. Truth be told, Roy had underplayed it when he said people made assumptions. Some people this last year had been really horrible when they found out he was a miner. He'd been spat at when they went for a day trip to Derby. So, it had meant more than we knew just to spend an afternoon with nice people away from all the trouble.

I didn't bother with the Parliamentary Society the next term.

The open-top bus struggled to round the corner on to Cross Street in the Old Quarter of Stourbridge. The area is made up of narrow streets of red-brick terraces that were built to house glass makers in the nineteenth century. By 1997, its artisan flourishes were attracting the Black Country's professional class, and today it was receiving us with conspicuous enthusiasm. The bus was bright red, with white roses painted on the side and balloons tied to the chrome rails around the top that accommodated the cheering crowd of primary school children. Downstairs, my mate, Rob – who'd got me into this – and I clutched our acoustic guitars and chatted to the stilt walker, whose stilts were laid lengthways along the floor of the bus. At each stop the routine was the same. We'd exit first and help the stilt walker back up into the air. Then the kids would swarm excitedly into the street, followed by their clipboard-clutching parents. And finally Debra,* the candidate, would touch up her make-up and dance off the bus and down the road as we played something upbeat on our guitars. The press counted Debra among 'Blair's Babes': a large contingent of younger female candidates who were changing the look and style of Labour. Smart, approachable and beautiful, she could wipe Tony Benn from a voter's memory with a single smile. The nearer we got to the Old Quarter, the better she did with the crowds on the street. Young couples broke away from stripping the lino off Victorian tiled floors to reassure her that their votes were in the bag. Old socialists smiled warmly at the excited children and recalled Attlee in 1945.

As we rolled into Cross Street the speakers on the bus Blaired 'Things Can Only Get Better' into the April sunshine, only for things to do just that. Blocking our progress on to Brook Street was a slow-moving flatbed truck from which a solitary, soon-to-be-unemployed man wearing a tweed jacket was bellowing into a megaphone.†

'I believe in law and order! I believe in corporal and capital punishment!'

The children waved their Labour flags and jeered at him as we laughed and hugged each other. From age six until twenty-four, I had known only tyranny. Now the revolution had come, and it tasted of ciabatta dipped in olive oil: middle-class socialism. How could it fail? As went Stourbridge, so did the nation.

To be an educated lefty in a Midlands swing seat was, in

---

* Debra Shipley was the Labour Party candidate for Stourbridge in the 1997 UK general election.
† Warren Hawksley MP, described in his Telegraph obituary as 'a genial follower of Enoch Powell', had held the seat of Halesowen & Stourbridge since 1992.

1997, to inherit the earth. Not only had our side won; we had been cleansed of class guilt by the unifying rhetoric of Tony and his team of Tory-busting messaging experts

Do you remember what you expected from Tony Blair? Despite campaigning for him, I don't think I had the slightest clue what he might actually *do*. It didn't really matter at the time. The final years of Tory rule leading up to the 1997 election had been so alienating that any change would have been welcome. Nowadays, you can't move for people who claim always to have known Tony was a wrong 'un, but they were far less conspicuous at the time. Forcing myself to remember succumbing to his blandishments has the feel of giving evidence: 'Show me on the doll where the man convinced you that an expanded financial services sector was compatible with the restoration of workers' rights…'

Blair had an inevitability about him; something that suggested he knew his destiny before we did. The danger with people like that is that they think every idea they have is governed by a higher purpose. They imagine their misdeeds to be sad duties, undertaken in the service of a fixed narrative.

I came blinking into adulthood through the misty haze of the preceding John Major years. The interregnum period between Thatcher and Blair, purposeless and decadent in character, encouraged an amiable 'will-this-do' attitude that was the antithesis of both Maggie's dogmatic intransigence and the manufactured passion of New Labour. In keeping with the nation's mood, I left school in 1990 during the first year of my A-levels at King Edward's and took the first job I saw advertised in the *Birmingham Evening Mail*. The contrasting attitudes of my parents to this decision conformed to a pattern. Mum was extremely upset upon seeing her dreams for me evaporate into teenage idiocy. Dad was unconcerned: 'Try to make a success of whatever you do.'

By then, both of them were ensconced in new relationships. I lived alone in their former home as they argued over it all the way up to the High Court. I occasionally glimpsed legal documents that mentioned 'the child, Benjamin'. So, fuck them. And fuck school. I didn't tell them I was leaving education until I had. *That'll show them.*

In retrospect, I was temperamentally unsuited for work behind a Halifax Building Society counter, but recruitment processes were less stringent in those days. I was posted to the Small Heath branch which, for a Solihull boy, was a culture shock. Small Heath has had a threatening reputation in Birmingham for as long as anyone can remember. Its long High Street pokes out from Birmingham City football club and runs in a south-easterly direction as an early warning against visiting Coventry. Streets of red terraced houses stretch back from it towards Bordesley Green on one side, whilst the other is separated from Sparkhill by the park and the railway line. It peters out into Hay Mills where the road widens, and Victorian architecture gives way to banal 1960s planning experiments.

The top end, nearest the city, is 'proper' Small Heath. It exists in the Brummie imagination in the same way Hell's Kitchen does for New Yorkers: storied, tough and authentic. If you say you're from there, nobody from, say, Yardley is going to give you any trouble because, even if they prevailed, God knows who you could call on. The area is continually in flux, playing host to successive waves of immigrants, most of whom stay for a while to save up and then move on to somewhere gentler. Amongst them, however, are those who were made for the place and who allow it to fuse with their identity. These families – Irish, Romany, West Indian, Pakistani, Somalian and so on – understand how business in Small Heath works: your word means more than where you came from, and cash is king.

In contrast, I'd spent the previous six years at a school where money was never mentioned and where being a student in the first place was proof that you were special. I was well turned out in a pinstriped suit and I'd fluked an A in my GCSE Maths. It seemed to me that this low-level service job might be fun until I figured out whether to pursue my musical talents or perhaps go into politics.

There were only four of us working in the branch and I was the youngest by ten years. I was also the only male and this could make for an intimidating atmosphere. #MeToo moments included the cackling triumvirate demanding to know whether I was a virgin and changing the door code to 696969.

It also turned out to be a grimly tedious job. For four days a week, I would dole people's money out or take it in at my counter. The only frisson came at the end of the day when I would try to balance the till. One day in the second week, I managed to be over £100,000 out on this calculation, which was at once terrifying and exhilarating as I watched Wendy briefly doubt if my incompetence was a front for criminality.

On Tuesdays, I was given a task that was yet more monotonous but, in retrospect, totemic of the times. A local cleaning company had decided to stop paying its thousands of employees in weekly envelopes full of cash and move them over to monthly bank transfers. My job was to open accounts for all the employees. Armed with a printout of their names, addresses and dates of birth, I was sent to a computer terminal to type it all in. Those thousands of contact details came up a month later when we posted out credit card applications to all of them. The moral implications of this seemed clear to me: people were forced to open a bank account, switched from budgeting weekly to monthly, and then offered credit to cover any shortfall. My grandma had a green, metal box with compartments marked – rent, electricity, gas, insurance, etc. – into which she would decant Grandad's wages minus his beer money. This sort of arrangement was becoming laughable in the tide of electronically-created finance that never touched a human hand. From the stock market's Big Bang to a cleaner's wages in Small Heath, money took life and flew from its box invisibly, like a virus. With each keystroke, I was making people poorer, and they had no idea.

If the Halifax was a chilling glimpse into the future, my next appointment offered a peek at a world that was about to disappear. First Textiles was a large, commercial laundry in Acocks Green that serviced businesses all around Birmingham. It washed tablecloths and work clothes but was particularly known for roller towels. These were long, rolled lengths of stiff cotton that were yanked down out of their holder in public toilets everywhere until electric hand dryers offered a future in which the après-piss experience didn't necessitate handling somebody else's. The new dryers had just been invented, so it was tense times at First Textiles.

It was an intimidating place to start work. There had been no interview, the Jobcentre just fixed it up on the phone, so I had no foretaste of the environment. I came in through a dark, diesel-reeking lorry bay into the processing room. I was the assistant stock controller, so it made sense to ask for the stock controller himself. Dennis was a tall, generously proportioned man with fleshy cheeks, glasses and slicked back grey hair. His stomach flopped easily over his belt, but he wore his girth like a sultan and spoke bold Brummie: slow and loud.

'Right Ben, look at this.' He handed me a stock sheet that had twenty-five codes for different items the laundry washed, with corresponding columns to mark where they were in the process. 'Do you think you can remember all of them today?'

I looked the list up and down with a mounting sense of panic. This was the school entrance exam all over again. *Must not fail, must not fail, must not fail...*

'Erm... Maybe not straight away, but I'm sure—' Dennis silenced me.

'I'll tell you now, Ben, you wouldn't stand a fucking chance. You've got a lot to learn.'

I exhaled.

'Right, let's show you round.'

The processing room was the size of half a football pitch and led directly into the laundry itself. The two entities were, however, strictly demarcated, and fraternisation was not encouraged. The processing room was Dennis's fiefdom that he ruled unselfconsciously, as if he had been born to it. The rest of the staff were female, ranging from school leavers to Elsie, who had been there, at the same table, sorting garments since 1945. She was hard-working, unmarried and inscrutable.

The workplace was honest, if not brazen, in its physical acknowledgement of the forces at play within it. At one end of the factory floor, a staircase led up to a glassed off balcony which housed the white-collar contingent. From here, they could peer down on us as we busied ourselves with the physical labour. Within this enclave, on the right-hand side, was the manager's office. The windows to this had curtains to prevent curiosity and to open randomly for a spot check of the activity below. Its inhabitant was a diminutive chap with a moustache, who walked rapidly and seemed to engender real fear in the women. Sometime between 12.30 p.m. and 1 p.m., he would descend from his lair and march through us to his Jag to go for lunch. Without fail, he would pick one worker to greet as he passed, and I was struck by how paralysed they seemed in his upward gaze. His name was, and I am not making this up, Mr Divine.

After a couple of weeks, I had pretty much got the hang of the job, which consisted of loading up trolleys with cleaned roller towel orders to be put on the lorries in the morning, then unloading and sorting the dirty ones in the afternoon. Dennis was happy enough with my progress to charge me with an extra job on Monday and Friday mornings: I was to shake out the tablecloths and napkins from a new client, the Chung Ying restaurant, and its sister establishment, the Chung Ying Garden.

This twice-weekly, two-hour task lives in my imagination as a foundation myth. Banished to the lorry bay, I would – by hand, mark you – claw the evil-smelling, congealed spillages from hundreds of meals off the peach-coloured fabric until I retched and the whole world seemed to be infused with ginger and soy. *Call me fucking middle class now,* I would think as I hooked my fingernails under yet another welded-on bit of Char Siu pork. And me, a vegetarian.

With musical bookings frustratingly sparse, and having mastered the twenty-five codes, I felt the need for something – anything – else in my life, so I enrolled on a philosophy A-level course at night school. This gives me pause when I see it written down. I had, six months previously, waltzed out of my A-levels at King Edward's, where I had had a straight path to Oxbridge, in favour of a £100-per-week bank clerk job. Now, ensconced on the factory floor of First Textiles on £85 per week, it seemed the most natural thing in the world to re-enter academia at Hall Green College to do a single, utterly pointless A-level, with no goal other than the relief of boredom. Looked at dispassionately, that might seem like self-defeating idiocy, but that would be to ignore the demands of the fictional self I was engaged in constructing: New Ben. New Ben didn't want any residual leg-up from his privileged upbringing and liked the idea of being an authentic member of the toiling masses. He would sit in the canteen at breaktime whilst everyone was chattering, thinking *I am an authentic member of the toiling masses* and feel inwardly thrilled. Granted, it wasn't always an easy fit. On one of the rare occasions a workmate had engaged New Ben in conversation, he had used the word 'abysmal', and therefore been asked if he had 'swallowed a dictionary' but he put that down to teething troubles and adjusted his language accordingly, innit?

Also, education seemed so much more noble than it had six months ago. Rather than some sort of *Tom Brown's School Days* enterprise, I was able to imagine myself as being like a miner in the Institute, educating himself for no reason other than the love of knowledge. There were no expectations of me, and that felt freeing. A little philosophy can go a long way with a seventeen-year-old, especially one who is given to grandiosity and engaged in manual labour.

Dennis's favourite topic was crown green bowls. This game, 'as any fule kno', differs from lawn bowls because of the raised crown that rises in the centre of the green. 'Lawn bowls is played on the flat, so that's the difference right there, Ben. Do you understand? It *rises* in the centre of the green. That's the crown, Ben. Not like in lawn bowls where the green is *flat*. It's completely different, Ben, because of the *crown*, you see. You have to play against the *crown* in the middle of the green which is *raised* with a camber.'

The mornings would pass like this as we loaded the trolleys up with roller towels, ninety-six on each, and wheeled them out to the lorry bay. There is, it turns out, a great deal of horticultural skill involved in maintaining the correct camber on a crown bowling green. A lot of people don't realise that work on the green continues through the winter. Even some of the players who benefit from this in the summer months don't appreciate the efforts of club members who give their time, *whatever the weather*, to ensure that the playing surface is in tip-top condition come the end of March. They are nowhere to be seen in November when the groundsman asks for help with a full surface removal, or in February when the sports sand needs to go down. No, they are sat on their fat arses drinking lager and watching *Coronation Street*. 'But the world's full of people like that, Ben. Lazy bastards the lot of them... Anyway, what did you get up to last night?'

'I was at my college course.'

'Were you now? And what's that in?'

'Philosophy.'

'I'm very philosophical myself. Go on. What did you learn last night?'

'Oh, nothing, just boring stuff.'

Dennis halted the trolley we were wheeling.

'No, I'm interested. What did you learn?' He folded his arms.

'Well, if you're sure…'

He nodded.

'Ok, it was Descartes. He was the one who said, "I think, therefore I am", only it's better translated as, "I'm *thinking*, therefore I am".'

'And what's all that about?' He narrowed his eyes in concentration.

'Well, he's saying that he knows he exists because he's the one wondering if he exists.'

'Well, of course he exists. We all exist. You don't need to go to college for that.'

This piqued me. I'd tried to avoid talking about it, but he'd insisted and now he was dismissing me as some kind of cloud-dwelling college boy. *Well, fuck that.*

'No, actually! He knows that *he* exists, but he can't prove that anybody else does. *He's* thinking about it but that's all he knows for sure.'

The Aristotle of the crown bowling green pursed his lips.

'Well, that's bollocks. Who's he talking to if only he exists?'

'That's exactly what he's considering. For all he knows, he might have imagined everyone else.'

'Don't be daft. He can see everyone same as you and I.' The look of triumph on his face spurred me on. It's surprising how much philosophy you can pick up in an hour at Hall Green College.

'Ah, but *can* he, Dennis? Imagine a slab of beeswax. What

can we tell about it using our senses? To look at, it's white and solid, right? It makes a sound if you hit it, agreed? It smells faintly of honey, we can assume.* To the touch, it is firm. Some people say it tastes like flowers.' Dennis nodded truculently. 'Now, Dennis, imagine we heat the beeswax up! It's suddenly larger and moving like a liquid. It smells different and it makes a bubbling sound and is hot and sticky to the touch. You would burn your tongue if you tasted it, but it might even taste different.† Everything about it is different, Dennis, so how, according to our senses, do we know it is the same piece of wax?'

'What's that got to do with if your mate Descartes exists or not?' Dennis protested.

'He knows he exists because *he's* the one wondering about it. I know I exist because *I'm* thinking about it now. It's you I've got a problem with, Dennis. I can see you and I can hear you.' I squeezed his arm. 'I can touch you and I can smell your aftershave. I won't taste you, if that's alright – we'll take it you taste of something. The trouble is, as we've seen with the wax, that all those things can change, so I can't trust my senses at all. You might be a figment of my imagination. I don't know if *you* exist, Dennis.' As I suppressed a smirk, he picked up a roller towel from the floor plonked it authoritatively down on the trolley. He did not, I observed, have the air of a defeated man.

'Well, Ben, I must exist,' he boomed.

'Why's that?'

---

* Can we? I didn't know then, and still don't now. I have, in fact, never seen, heard, smelled, touched nor tasted a piece of beeswax in my life. I remain steadfast, however, that it exists on a conceptual level.

† I changed this to expand on Descartes' rather scant and ill-thought-through description of molten wax, which said more about his notorious laziness than it did changes of state. Dennis deserved better.

'Because somebody's doing the work around here, and it fucking well isn't you!'

We resumed pushing the trolley to the lorry bay in silence.

At the end of the week, there were three bonuses available to workers who had performed well. I found this out from Brenda, who worked sorting garments on the table by the door to the lorry bay. I was back and forth past her all day, so we ended up chatting now and then. She was in her late forties with red hair and had a gently flirtatious nature. She mentioned someone winning this bonus one Friday and I expressed surprise as I'd never heard of it.

'Well, you wouldn't have. They don't tell anyone about it.'

'What's the point in that?' I asked. 'How are we supposed to compete for it if we don't know it exists?'

Brenda shot me a 'you've-got-a-lot-to-learn' smile and explained.

'See those two over there,' she pointed at two women in their twenties sorting bed linen. 'They're Tom the work manager's daughters. Tom decides who gets the bonus over on the laundry side, and every week bonuses go to Dennis's two daughters who work over there. On our side, Dennis gives out the bonuses and two of them go to that pair every week.'

'What about the other one? Who does Dennis give the other one to?' I asked.

'He's usually riding one or other of us. Goes to her.'

'Have you...?'

'When I was young and stupid.'

I was shocked by this. I looked across the factory floor at Dennis, who was joking around with one of the women, and felt disorientated. I liked Dennis; he was overbearing but seemed to be alright at heart. To learn that he behaved like this was chastening.

'There ought to be a union here,' I said.

Brenda laughed, shaking her head.

'If Mr Divine heard you say that, you'd be fired on the spot!'

'That would be illegal, though!' I protested. Brenda's sigh shepherded me further into a reality I hadn't imagined still existed in 1990.

There was worse to come, though. Mr Divine's two sons were employed as lorry drivers (you'll have noticed the strong family dynamics in the firm). Both were large, boisterous blokes who made their presence felt. One Thursday, I saw the older one grinning at Brenda.

'See you tomorrow,' he said.

Brenda looked a mess, shaking and tearful, so I asked her what was wrong. She wouldn't say at first and seemed scared, angry and embarrassed all at the same time. She was also worried that someone would hear her. Eventually, she disclosed that the two brothers were extorting £20 a week from her wages and that when she'd initially refused, the older one had punched her in the face. As soon as she told me, she started pleading with me not to make a fuss. Nobody would believe her – she needed this job – and it was just one of those things. So, out of my depth, I kept quiet and did nothing.

It's curious how awful things unfold in front of us so calmly. Here I was sampling factory life through a lens of secondhand socialism I'd been given as a souvenir from the 1930s. Suddenly, I was aware of real tyranny happening right there in front of me in 1990. Ok, I was seventeen and pretty much friendless in there, so it's unlikely I could have done anything about it, but the completeness of my acquiescence and willingness to cooperate in that place shames me now.

I'd been there for three months when I put my back out and took a day off sick. The next morning, I was working away next to Dennis and down comes Mr Divine from the office. Jerking his thumb towards me, he asked, 'Where was he yesterday?'

'Off sick, Mr Divine. He said he had a bad back.'

He *said* wasn't lost on me.

'Finish him,' Mr Divine replied, and scuttled off.

'You can finish the day,' Dennis told me. I went to the pub instead.

The place closed for good a couple of years later and sat there rotting for ten years before it got bulldozed. I imagine big, silent Elsie took a Russian novel to her grave.

I was beginning to find out that decent GCSE results and an oversized vocabulary weren't the currency I'd assumed they would be in the job market. My next career move was manning the till at a petrol station. I was fired from this one for accidentally leaving the drive-through car wash on all night at the end of a shift.

'It's lit up like a Christmas tree, how on earth didn't you see it?' demanded the boss.

'I must have been thinking about something.'

What I was thinking about was music. I'd been playing guitar since I was twelve and now, finally, was just about good enough to be paid for it. I was 'a musician'. Being 'a musician' didn't mean making an actual living from it – I've never really managed that – it meant putting music first and being willing to drop anything else I was doing in favour of it. So, if I had a job canvassing for a double glazing company but a show came up that required me to miss work one day, losing that job didn't matter because I'd never been a canvasser in the first place. Being 'a musician' stipulated writing 'musician' as my 'usual employment' on the form for claiming income support.

I was performing blues and country music in pubs with a friend, Jim, from school who had left at the same time as me. We had come to the same decision together during a day we'd bunked off and spent in the Saddlers' Arms in Solihull. We'd get jobs of some sort whilst waiting out the short period between rehearsing our act and achieving professional status. From there, with my gift for songwriting and Jim's guitar prowess, it would only be a matter of time before a recording contract came our way. 'Two more pints of Brew X1 please. We'll tell the school tomorrow and break the news to our parents as a fait accompli.'

As it turned out, this plan was proving frustratingly slow to come to fruition. After twelve months of begging corner pubs for gigs, however, we had arrived at the point where we had between one and three of them every week. Better yet, Jim's dad was happy to drive us anywhere we needed to go. He was less keen on having to pick me up and drop me off in Birmingham before driving the forty-five minutes back to their home in Stourbridge. So, it was decided that, as business was picking up, I'd move to a bedsit over there and sign on the dole so I could 'concentrate on my song writing'. Dole money, plus my rent paid and whatever came in from gigs should add up to enough to live on and Jim's dad could get home at a reasonable hour. That decision would define my next twenty years.

Signing on in 1991 was quite a social activity. You'd pop along to the Jobcentre and inform them of the distressing news that you were between positions. They'd book you in for an interview during which you'd say, 'I am looking for work.' The people working there were sympathetic, unambitious folks who had often taken sabbaticals from the workplace themselves. They'd smile indulgently as you explained your vision for an artistic future and frequently discuss their own musical tastes as boxes were ticked and crisis loans issued. They'd smile and stamp your form, then a jolly green giro cheque would arrive a couple of weeks later in the post. Occasionally, a poorly conceived directive would filter down from John Major's government and lip service would be paid to it in a collaborative fashion.

'Hi, Ben. How's the music going?'

'Exciting times. Thanks for asking, Sam. I've been listening to Townes Van Zandt and I'm trying to incorporate some of those modal structures into my narrative songs.'

'Didn't Nick Drake do a similar thing?'

'Yes! He was working with English folk melodies whereas I favour Appalachian ones, but that's a great comparison. Nice one, Sam. I hadn't thought of that.'

'How about paid gigs, Ben? How are those coming along?'

'Well, you know, I'm calling venues every day. It'll be far easier to get some when I've finished my demo tape.'

'If you do get any, you *will* remember to declare them when you sign on, won't you?'

'Of course, Sam. To forget that would be illegal!'

'Listen, as it's been six months, the government *insists* you do some structured job searching.'

'I've just said, I'm calling—'

'No, Ben, conventional job searching. I'm going to send you to a Back to Basics job club. '

'Oh.'

'Don't worry. It's only three hours in the mornings, for two weeks. It'll keep us off your back.'

'Go on, then,' I conceded. 'I can manage that.'

'Good lad,' Sam smiled, closing my file. 'Check out *Bryter Layter*.'

'Eh?'

'Nick Drake. You'll like it.'

'Cheers, Sam. See you next time.'

And with that, I'd be out on Stourbridge High Street looking for someone to cadge twenty quid off to tide me over until the giro arrived a couple of days later.

I can't stress enough that I didn't feel a moment's guilt about claiming the dole. The final triumph of the *Arbeit macht frei* ethic was some years away and a stint on the rock 'n' roll honing one's skills was a perfectly acceptable career path for the artistically minded dreamer. What was the point in our grandparents winning the war, otherwise? Up and down the country, emaciated doleboys spent our giros on guitar strings, oil paints, notebooks, white cider, weed, charity shop clothes and Para boots from the Army and Navy to clomp around in as we dreamed up something beautiful while everyone else was at work. You will never convince me that we would have been more virtuous citizens had we spent those years studying marketing, phoning people up at random and convincing them they needed a burglar alarm or supersizing your Big Mac meal. Britain was the fourth largest economy on earth, and chucking sixty quid a week at young people who were willing to go without all luxuries so they could stand in front of a blank canvas and feel themselves in kinship with Michelangelo was well within its means.

The Back to Basics job club was held in the room above The Bell Pub on Market Street. At nine on Monday morning, half a dozen of us, all blokes, reluctantly assembled outside, shifting from foot to foot and breathing on our frozen fingers. Nods and grunts served as greetings; this was not the time of day that we jobseekers favoured for much talk.

'Load of bollocks this'll be.'

Except for Barry.

Barry was, and may well still be, a ubiquitous character around Stourbridge. Back then, he was forty-something, red-faced and stocky and he was often to be seen digging around charity shops in his sheepskin coat and woolly hat, beneath which poked straw-coloured hair that was chopped abruptly at his shoulders. He'd talk to anybody in his vicinity and was in possession of a startlingly broad Black Country accent. If an expensively-educated recent arrival from cosmopolitan Birmingham were to describe a stereotypical Yam Yam to his sneering chums back home, it would be Barry.

'Ok, gents, come in out of the cold. There's tea upstairs.'

Enter Geoff to the scene as he opened the doors to the pub. Geoff was the back to basics job club coach who was tasked with turning our cohort into employment-seeking missiles.

'There'd better be God* biscuits,' Barry chimed.

It was going to be a long fortnight.

Tea poured and biscuits dunked, we chose our seats and Geoff began by introducing himself. He was fifty and had just retired from the army. His neat moustache and heavy, elbow-patched sweater bore this out. He could have sat back and relaxed after the army, but no! He still had plenty left to offer and felt that he'd accrued some transferrable skills that would be helpful to people looking for work.

'I doh wanna be a fuckin' sniper,' Barry shouted. Geoff smiled generously.

'Hopefully, it won't come to that.'

First, we went round the room saying what our last job had been. This icebreaker ran aground quickly when Darren, a nineteen-year-old, disclosed that he'd never had a job.

'Never mind,' Geoff enthused. 'By the end of this, you'll have a top-class CV that demonstrates how keen you are to enter the workforce.'

Darren nodded hopefully. Barry sighed.

'So, what about you, Barry? What was your last position?'

Barry sat up in his seat for a moment then leaned right back in it again. 'I was a furnaceman.'

'Well, that's a solid skill base there, Barry. Where were you last working?'

'Round Oak. From when I left school 'til 1982 when it closed

---

* In the Black Country, 'God' is used like 'bloody'. As in: 'Your wench was on one the other night wor she?' 'Tell me about it. 'Er's God yampy.'

down. I suppose you were runnin' round Goose Green with yer Tommy rifle at the time. P'raps you didn't hear about it?'

Time for a fag break. We all trooped downstairs, leaving Geoff to ponder his next motivational gambit.

'I told you it'd be a pile of shit,' Barry railed, as we lit up. 'Straight out the God army and tellin' us how to get a job. It's the only proper job he's had! He'll get no change out of me, just you watch.'

Back upstairs, Geoff's next move was to have us imagine a brighter future.

'Right, gents, I'd like you all to tell me what job you'd have if you had a free choice. Remember, not which job you think you could get, but the one you'd really like to do.'

Darren really stepped up to the mark for this one. 'Retail,' he chimed hopefully.

Geoff was up and running. This gave him full scope to outline a plan of action that would have Darren on a training scheme down at the Merry Hill shopping centre in no time. Merry Hell – as it is still known locally, owing to the exhausting effect of negotiating the crowds there – was the out-of-town shopping centre that had opened five years previously. Depending on where you stood, it was totemic either of the corporate destruction of high street culture or the Black Country's glorious new dawn as the genesis of the service economy.

'Fucking place should be burned down,' Barry hissed.

It had been built on land freed up by the closure of Round Oak Steelworks. How it had been funded and granted planning consent were the subject of lurid rumours.

'Bent as a bottle of crisps, that place is,' Barry continued. 'The week they passed the planning permission, all the councillors bought BMWs! I see'd 'em in the car park.'

The heart of the issue was that Round Oak had provided well paid jobs and was the focal point of the steel industry in an area that prided itself on being the birthplace of the industrial revolution. Merry Hill was touted by Dudley Council and its developers as providing a replacement source of employment that suited the changing economy. The problem here was that it was difficult to imagine Barry, or the thousands like him who worked at Round Oak, successfully retraining as sales assistants for Benetton. The 'thousands of jobs' we kept hearing about were not for the thousands of people who had worked on the site before.

Geoff, though, was all about adapting to his environment and he wasn't ready to give up on Barry yet – even if the rest of the world had.

'The thing is, Barry, the world's changing whether we like it or not. We've got to take what we've learned and apply it to the new circumstances. Take me, for example: you're right, I've been a soldier all my life and I was *crapping myself* when I came out of the army, mate – excuse my French. I mean, what was I going to do at fifty years old? I'd never even used a computer! But I talked to my wife, and she said, "It's not about what you can and can't do, it's about what you *want* to do. Once you know that, you'll find a way." So, I put my thinking cap on, and I realised I wanted to help people. I did a course in computers – turns out they're like engineering really, you'd be better on them than me, Barry, with your experience – and here I am getting paid to help you guys find work. So that's the question, Barry, what do you *want* to be?'

In the moments before Barry answered, I was authentically moved by Geoff's speech. I mean, yes, he was terminally cheerful and overestimated the power of positive thinking, but he'd revealed some vulnerability, and that can't have been easy for a military guy. I got the impression he'd be really delighted if we all ended up doing what we wanted to or at least be able to pretend we wanted to do what we ended up doing – which was doubtless how he kept away from his service revolver at night. Fair play to him. He was a good bloke.

Barry had his arms folded and a malevolent smile on his face.

'Come on, Barry, it's a big old world out there. What's the role you'd like to play in it?'

Barry leant yet further back in his seat.

'Shepherd.'

Geoff and Barry's eyes were locked for an uncomfortably long silence, and I noticed Geoff's knuckles whiten as Barry continued to smile. Geoff could, most likely, have broken the obstreperous fucker's neck with one arm, but where would that have got him? At least he wasn't the one tramping round charity shops, passing off bitterness as humour.

The lesson from all this was that, if the world of industry was to be replaced by something so nebulous as to be indiscernible as a useful activity, then it was marginally better to be the bullshitter than the bullshittee. Geoff and Barry had both washed up on economic shores that were hostile to them. Geoff had negotiated with the natives whilst Barry refused to. I wonder who got screwed hardest in the end.

Stourbridge was an amenable place for the aspirant bohemian. It sits at the southwest tip of the Black Country and has a confused relationship with the area. The Black Country radiates from Dudley, and its boundaries are subject to ongoing saloon bar debates. For instance, Wolverhampton Wanderers F.C. sing of being the 'boys from the Black Country', and a large proportion of their fans absolutely are. Wolverhampton itself, however, is viewed by many not to be in the Black Country at all, as the city doesn't sit on its defining coal seam. Despite this, its council proclaims the city as being part of the region in its ongoing quest to establish a cultural identity. Stourbridge, on the other hand, was, until 1972, part of leafy Worcestershire. Its absorption into Dudley Metropolitan Council is still the cause of rancour amongst those Stourbridge residents who view their town not as the posh end of the Black Country but the beginning of the countryside. This was explained to me over several beers by my friend Brian.

'Look at it this way. London has the most desirable addresses in Britain, doesn't it? Well, the most expensive postcode is W1, because it's closest to the centre of the West End. Now, Stourbridge has the most expensive houses in the Black Country and they are in DY9, because that's as far away from Dudley as you can get. Proximity to Dudley is financially penalised by the market, for reasons that are obvious to anyone who has been there. The underlying reason for this is simple: the Industrial Revolution kicked off in Dudley, with the first blast furnace. After the Enclosure Acts, all the peasants who'd been kicked off the common land pitched up there to work in coal mines and iron furnaces. This was heavy work done with lump hammers and pickaxes. After a while, people started using new technology to make specialist items. So, brighter blokes would move out of Dudley to outlying villages like Cradley, where they made chains, or Lye, which was known for manufacturing nails. The more skilled the trade, the more money you made. At the top of the tree, was glassmaking which was done in Stourbridge. The upshot of this is that Dudley is inhabited by the descendants of metal bashers, who couldn't be trained to make nails. And Stourbridgians, since 1972, have had to pay for those useless bastards when we should be gentlemen of rural leisure, living off the proceeds of our cut crystal decanters in Worcestershire.'

Brian was my conduit into the opaque culture of the Black Country. A decade older than me, he had been a brickie before launching into a series of business ventures, each more unlikely than the last. When we met, he was running a premium-rate phone line that offered horse racing tips. For months, he was evasive about the provenance of his information for those tips, vaguely intimating that he had a contact who worked in the racing stables. Eventually, as our acquaintance flourished into best-matehood, he disclosed that he'd studied the results of the most successful tip services, subscribed to the best one, and cribbed the info off it each morning for his own service. After that, it was all down to advertising, for which he had an enviable knack.

I'd come across him at The Mitre, which was a local music pub I performed at. I was running an open mic night there and he came along with his five-string banjo to see if anyone played bluegrass. A couple of Flatt and Scruggs tunes later, and we had struck up a bromance of Butch and Sundance proportions.

Brian had a robust attitude towards claiming benefits, and ten years' experience to draw on if the Jobcentre became suspicious. Any middle-class guilt that I harboured about earning from gigs whilst signing on was knocked out of me by his evangelical zeal.

'It's a matter of telling them what they want to hear. They know you can't live on it, nobody can, but they've got to justify their existence by going through the rituals with you. Think of your giro as your basic, it allows you the economic freedom to speculate more imaginatively in your business ventures.'

Very much an independent thinker, Brian's political philosophy was an entrepreneurial variant on Marxism: one that recognised class oppression and earmarked state benefits as a source of seed capital for individual ventures, thus disrupting the established hegemony of entrenched interests. When profits accrued, he would buy silver ingots and bury them in the garden behind his council flat.

'Their job is to claw back as much as they've accidentally let you get your hands on, and your job is to stop them.'

It was, of course, exactly the sort of advice that accountants offer to corporations who are juggling government subsidies, profit and tax liability.

'I'm a socialist, Ben, but we've been defeated. If I have to live under free market principles, then fair enough. Just don't expect me to stick to rules that they ignore.'

Under harsh interrogation, it might well be that Brian's outlook could be viewed as somewhat self-serving, but harnessed to his unwavering loyalty and generosity to friends, it struck me as a pretty serviceable way to negotiate the demands of life in 1990s Britain. Brian was reassuring in his belief that the authorities almost never backed up their threats with actual, punitive action.

'Have you ever seen a TV detector van other than on their adverts? Load of bollocks – they don't exist.'

The key to avoiding experiences like the Back to Basics job club, he advised, was to have yourself put on a list of people who didn't get sent to those things.

'What's your worst-paying gig?'

'The Mitre on a Monday night. It's only £25 but it's regular, every week, and a great place to try out new songs, so I don't mind.'

'Right, tell the Jobcentre that you've found a job.'

'They'll sign me off and I won't have enough to pay my rent!'

'Nope, you can earn £15 a week. They'll deduct a tenner from your giro and put you on a list of people with low-paying jobs. They'll occasionally ask if you have been looking for something better but that will be it. No more interrogations and no more job clubs.'

He was right. For about a year I trundled along with my rent paid, most of my dole intact and any money I could earn from gigs and selling tapes of my songs stuffed into my back pocket. I was still in charity shop threads, but I could afford beer, weed and the occasional breakfast in Dee's Cafe. What more could I want?

My life during those years was emblematic of John Major's government in many ways. I was largely well-meaning, lazy, given to pastel-hued imaginings of the past and prone to sudden lurches into absurdity. I usually intuited when real trouble was on the horizon in time, though, and dodged the oncoming train. Not so Mr Major. Whilst the Eurosceptics in his party were sharpening their teeth on the Maastricht Treaty, he was lost in a nostalgic fantasy of warm beer, cricket on the village green and, bizarrely, spinsters cycling to church. By contrast, the Britain portrayed in the press featured crack cocaine, baseball bats in the village post office and spinsters being dragged from their bicycles by pitbull terriers.

Imagined Britain is always a treacherous place to set up camp as its foundations invariably crumble under the lightest historical probing. So, just as Labour's fantasy of a socialist Britain had been undone in the 1970s by the persistently hierarchical nature of its inhabitants, now the Tories' appeal to historical decency had come face-to-face with the observable degradation that our past had led us to. Major believed in his own classless society, he said, yet also yearned for the certainties of the 1950s when class was the guarantor of stability. Meanwhile, every day seemed to bring news of ministers illegally brokering arms deals, 'romping' with teenagers or fatally mishandling oranges. This was, of course, wholly in keeping with behaviour in the 1950s but catastrophically at odds with the make-believe rectitude of the era that Major had evoked.

By 1995, Major had the hot breath of that nice Mr Blair on his neck, and it was time for him to get serious. Suddenly, the unemployed – or cursorily employed – were summoned to a new type of interview at the Jobcentre. Gone were the gentle, amenable hippies who worked there. They were replaced by clear-eyed zealots who knew scum when they saw it. I was never at my best in the mornings and Sam had always been kind enough to schedule our catch-ups for the afternoon. Miss Christine Dee, on the other hand, was clearly no stranger to the sunrise and had me in tears by 9.05 a.m.

'Your so-called business, Mr Smith, has only offset your benefits to the tune of £15 per week for over twelve months. It is clearly not a serious enterprise.'

'It takes time, Miss Dee, I've been working on a new demo tape and—'

'Let me stop you there. You may have had an agreeable time bumping along the bottom of life at everyone else's expense, but it ends here. I suggest you think very carefully about your future, Benjamin.'

Later, in the pub, I was doing just that with a copy of *The Times*. Clearly, my lifestyle was no longer to be tolerated. Blokes like Barry wouldn't mind; he'd just hang in there taking the abuse and daring them to starve him. I couldn't face the humiliation that Miss Dee had dished out but also couldn't face a nine-to-five job. The answer was tucked into an insert detailing clearing vacancies inside the newspaper.

Fuck it – time to go to university.

GWLAD! GWLAD!

Do you remember when we came out of lockdown? The feeling like that of being a newborn foal struggling to its feet was both exhilarating and confusing. Am I allowed to talk to this person directly, or do I have to say hello via a government app? With sanitising stations everywhere, we jittered into public spaces like thirteen-year-olds on first dates and crossed our fingers that it wouldn't all be snatched away again by some novel mutation that specifically threatened whatever it was we wanted to do. That, of course, assumes that you hadn't secretly revelled in the suspension of social and professional responsibilities mandated by the government's response to Covid-19.

Do you remember what the first few weeks of the lockdown were like, after we'd been ordered into our homes? Walking down a deserted Crwys Road to the Tesco Express, I recall seeing a man, potentially infected, coming towards me as if he didn't care whether I lived or died. I had to cross the road and read the menu at the vegan Chinese place that Wales Online rates so highly. It was closed.

I had three irons in the fire when the air got scary. I did nightshifts in homeless shelters for Cardiff Council, sang in pubs and was enrolled on a creative writing PhD at Swansea University. The shelter job paid well, and you can exercise some goodwill in those kinds of positions when your managers are all asleep at 3 a.m. An extra Pot Noodle? Why not? Also, it lent me a temporary heroic air as I strode into work.

I was deployed to a hotel that received sixty-odd homeless people in a matter of days after it was decided that sleeping rough was an arrestable offence. The hotel was in Riverside, shadowed by the Principality Stadium and, over the next few months, we all learned a few things about trauma.

There were standout moments, like the girl who overdosed on Methadone because her boyfriend wouldn't tell her he loved her. I jabbed her with Naloxone and for a moment we shared a novelty, as I pierced someone's skin guided only by the instructions on the box and she was shocked, euphorically, from her stupor. Initially happy and grateful, she tipped quickly into withdrawal, stripping naked and running through the corridors looking for a window to jump from. A security guard from Merthyr wrapped her in his huge arms until the police took her away.

Her boyfriend didn't look up from his book when I told him.

'Pity she didn't die.'

Food for the residents was awful. The council had engaged an outside company to bring in microwavable meals and they were universally despised. A couple of shell-shocked employees from the hotel, who had been retained to look after the property, offered to prepare something more substantial in the hotel's kitchen but were rebuffed. Amongst the homeless community, however, word travels fast and it wasn't long before the hotel was visited by Help for The Homeless, a freelance Christian organisation whose apparent belief is that secular employees act only out of self-interest. On Friday evenings, just after I started my twelve-hour shift, they would arrive in convoy from the valleys and set up makeshift stalls with donated food and clothes. All well and good, you might think, but with gatherings prohibited under Covid-19 restrictions, holding an al fresco souk on Clare Street clearly wasn't on. So, we'd go out front and send them away, to the fury of residents who were helping themselves to the goodies on offer.

'You tell us if they are mistreating you,' the Christians would shout as they packed their stuff away before the police were called. It wasn't meant to be like this…

I also noticed the anguish that my fellow musicians were experiencing at being unable to perform in public. On Facebook, many would announce ambitious online projects that would fade into apathy as they became listless and depressed. For me, though, the enforced break came at the right time. Having invested decades into a musical career that had rarely got beyond pub performances, it took a government order to put my dreams out of their misery. Emotionally, the experience was akin to learning of the death of someone you no longer cared for very much: a muted sadness accompanied by guilt at not feeling more. *He had a good innings…*

The PhD, on the other hand, was a source of continual angst. The MA I'd completed the previous year had been one of my better efforts in life. Having figuratively tumbled down a mountain in mid-Wales, grieving twice-over, I'd finally rolled through the door of an empty council flat in Llanidloes after a period of homelessness in 2015. I had been full of resolve for a fresh start in the countryside. Life had initially been idyllic, full of love and poetry as I started to write seriously and appreciate nature. My relationship with my girlfriend, though, had been volatile. When Mum and then my best friend, Brian, died within weeks of each other, I couldn't support the weight of my grief and collapsed. It was six weeks before I stopped waking up already in tears from dreaming my way through recent traumas.

Step one was to get a job in a call centre in Newtown.

'Good afternoon, you're through to Laura Ashley, my name's Ben, may I take your name…?'

Once the routine had restored my equilibrium, I started

looking for a way out of a life that had gone horribly wrong. Speculatively, I applied to three Welsh universities to do an MA in creative writing. Cardiff offered me a scholarship – they offered one to pretty much everyone, I later found out – so I packed my bag (singular) and headed south.

A year's funded writing and learning in 2019 started to put me back together. I made new friends in Cardiff and, to my astonishment, met and married an extraordinary woman. At the end of the course, though, I felt panicked and cast adrift. I took the homeless hostel job to earn a living, but the sense of belonging to a university had been as important to me as what I had learned there. A university cares for you in a very particular way. It wants you to grow and to think clearly. I was reluctant to lose this nurturing aspect to academia and started a PhD at Swansea because I knew I needed to feel that attachment.

Actually completing the PhD, though, didn't appeal quite so much. I was full of ideas and energised after every meeting with my supervisors, but my impetus dissipated as work and married life took precedence.

So the pandemic, then, was a bit of a Godsend. I did have a demanding job that took up a lot of time and emotional energy, but I could have written if I'd wanted to. Delving about in my past for clues as to who I'd become and what I wanted to write seemed too hard, though. At each online supervision meeting, I'd make my apologies and have a list of bombproof excuses for why my output was so pitiful.

So, when restrictions started to ease, I began to feel a gnawing dread about a reckoning to come. I wonder if that experience wasn't more widespread than we care to admit. There was a gloriously carefree aspect to the reversal of expectations on us whilst lockdown was in force. The requirement not to do things that, in all honesty, we didn't want to do, shone a light on how much of our lives are governed by compulsion, whether external or self-imposed.

So, when a face-to-face meeting was set to discover what the hell I thought I was playing at, my mind adopted its ten-year-old-outside-the-headmaster's-office mode and refused any argument from my adult self that things would be ok. As the moment of truth loomed, I even asked my wife if she'd come with me, and such was my desperation that her eye-rolling response gave way quickly to kind reassurance.

Quite why I descend into these fugue states when confronted by failure is not fully clear to me, although it's likely wrapped up in needing to feel attached to an entity – like a university. If the connection were severed, I'd be adrift and it would be my fault. I'd be rumbled as an interloper and rightfully ejected. Oh God…

So, walking down St Mary's Street in Cardiff, my step slowed as I made my way to the meeting. It wasn't so long ago that I was going nuts in a bare council flat with nobody to talk to and nothing to do. All this opportunity had come my way and, like usual, I'd wasted it. No wonder they were going to throw me out. I'd throw me out in their shoes. Dawdling down Womanby Street, I was gripped with a notion to run. I could go back home, or to Llanidloes, or Birmingham, or wherever Ryanair are flying to this afternoon.

The Principality loomed over me as I approached The City Arms pub, looking vast and forbidding. This stadium that had been the venue of a good ninety per cent of my childhood dreams, the place I had wanted to go more than any other – so much that I'd written to Jimmy Savile begging to be taken there – now stood like a physical expression of my dread.

If this all sounds a bit overwrought about what was essentially an essay crisis, then I agree. Particularly given that the man waiting for me at a table outside The City Arms is universally regarded as one of the kindest, most considerate people in Welsh literature. He already had a drink, so I went inside to buy a pint, my mind racing with apologies and excuses. It was the first day that pubs had reopened and the sense of awkwardness was palpable. Staff and customers alike had lost their easy ways of being. People were speaking too soon or waiting too long to reply. Glasses were fumbled, and whilst being in a pub at all was a great thing, it was evident that we'd all lost something through this collective trauma – something we'd previously not even been aware we had.

Joining my supervisor at the table, I was desperate for anything to delay the conversation we needed to have. Again, the stadium leant into proceedings. It was all of thirty yards away and the perfect conversation piece. Off I went into the woes of the national team, and how can you discuss that without delving into the difficulties of the regional set-up? After all, to assume that ancient local rivalries could be subsumed into support for new commercial entities had been absurd. Sporting support is cultural, not commercial, and here in Wales its beating heart lies at the local level. Yes, it's difficult to translate parochial loyalties into the sort of professional organisation demanded by the global game, but the very identity of Welsh rugby was being threatened… On and on I went, each turn of my monologue making less sense but achieving its aim of forestalling a conversation about the PhD. Eventually, as my train of thought ran up against the buffers, my supervisor turned to the matter in hand. In the space of a couple of minutes, he reassured me everything would be alright and offered a six-month suspension of studies to take the pressure off.

Oh.

Business dispensed with, he fetched us another round and returned to my recent diatribe on the state of Welsh rugby.

'Have you ever considered journalism?'

I laughed at this. 'Nah, I'm just a fan with a big mouth; I don't have any contacts or in-depth knowledge.'

'Well *Nation.Cymru* need someone to add to their rugby offering. How about I get the editor to call you tomorrow and you can set up doing some pieces on the Six Nations? Anyway, I've got to get home,' he said, draining his drink. 'Take it easy.'

I was still functionally speechless when I got back to our rented flat off Newport Road. My wife was naturally concerned about how it had gone, expecting perhaps that I'd be in unmanageable despair. I almost didn't want to vocalise what had happened in case speaking it out loud made it disappear. But when the phone call from *Nation.Cymru* came the next day, it became all very real indeed. A meeting that I'd imagined would signal my ejection from Welsh cultural life had, in fact, turned into an invitation to my own personal nirvana.

The first object I can remember holding was a rugby ball. My grandad brought home a size-three lace-up ball from the school where he taught and set about teaching me the game. From the off, it was clear to me that this was a serious matter. On the narrow strip of lawn at the back of his Birmingham council house, I was taught how to pass off either hand, to sidestep, to tackle and to dummy. But that was only the beginning of what he was showing me. Inside, our conversations were about the history of the game, its ethos and, particularly, how it was played differently 'back home'.

Back home was Tylorstown in Rhondda Fach and its sporting history – and that of south Wales more widely – was given to me as something precious and equally as important as the social history that he'd teach me when I was older.

Five-year-old Ben could tell you all about the 'Tylorstown Terror', Jimmy Wilde: the flyweight champ whom the Americans conceded was the greatest boxer in history and whose slight frame belied his power so much that it earned him a second nickname: 'The Ghost with the Hammer in his Hand'. From the other side of the Penrhys mountain, there had come the heavyweight Tommy Farr, who had kept the whole of Britain awake and glued to their radios in 1937 when, after fifteen rounds against Joe Louis, the American judges had robbed him at Yankee Stadium.

There was pride around Welsh boxers and footballers like John Charles, but figures from the rugby world were introduced to me as a pantheon. Names such as Cliff Morgan and Haydn Tanner were imparted with the reverence Grandad usually reserved for Mozart and Schubert. Beyond sportspeople, these figures were the epitome of a culture and representatives of something distinct and superb that existed only 'back home', and which the wider world could merely look at in envy.

The contemporary rugby scene gave weight to Grandad's assertion that the Welsh game was the gold standard of excellence. I would regularly be required to recite the Wales team for forthcoming games, to prove that I had been reading the coverage in the newspaper during the week. I'd have it learned by rote, and the names – Williams, Davies, Gravell, Fenwick, Williams, Bennett, Edwards, Faulkner, Windsor, Wheel, Martin, Cobner, Squire, Quinnell and their various alternative options – still come easy now.

One Friday afternoon in 1978, I came out of St Alphege Infants School to find that Grandad was standing with my mum to collect me. He'd never come there before, so this was exciting, and he was wearing his Birmingham Welsh RFC tie, so something else was clearly going on.

'I'm taking you to meet someone,' he announced. We walked past the church towards Solihull High Street and into Peters Bookshop. There behind a desk and a pile of books, was a well-built figure with dark hair holding a pen. Grandad marched me over to him and shook his hand.

'Falch i gwrdd â ti Gareth, a gwna ffafr i mi 'nei di a shigla llaw y bachan. Ben ni'n galw fe.'

I like to say that the first person to shake my hand was Gareth Edwards, and who's to say he wasn't?

The days before an international game would be punctuated with phone calls from Grandad as we'd discuss prospects and selection issues. On the Saturday of the game, Mum would deliver me to Acocks Green and we'd settle in to watch with Grandma ordered into silence after she'd served up the egg and chips.

The seriousness with which Grandad watched the games was almost intimidating. Usually jovial and mischievous, his eyes would narrow as he clutched a mug of black tea whilst providing a sparse commentary. A good play from Wales would be acknowledged with a nod, and errors would elicit a quiet 'Clowns.'

I was more effusive; my emotions peaking and troughing with the ebb and flow of the play. This tended to provoke a Kiplingesque rebuke from Grandad, who would remind me that it was only a game and that winning or losing were as nothing to the spirit of the contest.

As the 1970s wore into the 1980s, however, and Welsh victories became less assured, it was noticeable that his murmured discontent during games tended to stretch into silent Sundays, during which *The Observer* would be pored over for further evidence of societal decline in Thatcher's Britain.

When I was old enough, he started to take me to see games at Moseley RFC. At the time they were on a golden run at the very top of English rugby and boasted a fixture list that featured all the top English sides and most of the best Welsh clubs, too (excepting Pontypool, whose brand of play was deemed too vigorous for Brummie sensibilities).

My allegiance on these Saturday afternoons was divided. Mostly, I supported Moseley: they were my home club, and we were members. We even had a card that allowed us into the players' lounge after games, on account of Grandad having taught and coached John White, Moseley's head coach. If the opposition were Welsh, however, I'd support them as a matter of course. It didn't ever occur to me not to. Whether it was Cardiff, Newport, Neath, Swansea, Llanelli, Ebbw Vale or even London Welsh, I became a fan for the afternoon.

We'd either go on the number 1 bus or be picked up by John White's father, Horace, in his distressed 1950s Humber car. Horace was a large, kindly and very loud man a few years Grandad's senior. The car was a powder blue saloon with no seatbelts and a very hard life behind it. Grandad and I would exchange nervous glances as we careered down the Wake Green Road as Horace bellowed out opinions on the game ahead in the sort of Birmingham accent my mother was praying nightly that I wouldn't acquire. Sometimes, when Horace had gone to 'water the horse', Grandad would impress upon me that while Horace was a lovely man, I was to ignore everything he had to say about rugby.

Once through the turnstiles, I'd open the programme straight away to see the teams and whether there were any asterisks by the names. An asterisk meant a player had been capped for his country and a top team like Cardiff would be festooned with them.

Up in the stands, the atmosphere was charged but friendly. Hip flasks would be passed around and supporters of both sides would chat before kick-off. I absorbed all the language, keen to know all the correct terms as well as the gossip and others' opinions about players. Grandad would involve me, ask for my thoughts and correct me if I got something wrong. It was an apprenticeship: learning to be a rugby man and how to talk to other rugby men. More than that, it was a lesson in how to disagree and remain friendly – how to balance different desired outcomes within the greater good – which was that we all loved this game.

The banter was great. Over the Tannoy, a car registration might be read out with a request that the owner move the vehicle.

'It's yours, ref,' someone would shout.

The games would fly by, leaving particular images etched forever in my memory: steam rising off the packs on a cold day as scrums came together with a collective grunt; Ian 'Spikey' Watkins entertaining the crowd during a lengthy injury break by throwing the ball up and catching it behind his back repeatedly and ever higher; Clive Rees streaking down the left wing for London Welsh as if his boots never touched the grass at all.

Afterwards, in the players' lounge, I'd usually be the only kid there, and to be surrounded by full-tilt adulthood on a Saturday night after a game was a rare thrill. Thigh-high to nearly everyone, I'd gaze up, unnoticed, as trays of beer passed over my head, fags were lit and wounds compared. I'd notice the players split off into backs and forwards, that distinction more keenly drawn than between the teams themselves. I'd see the referee in the corner nursing a half before driving himself home, respected but all alone. The committee men would be there, older than God's dog,* blazered, red-faced and slapping the players on the back like indulgent uncles.

I had my autograph book, of course, and would wait until the players had sunk a couple of pints before bothering them, looking first for the asterisks. Handing me a pint to hold whilst he signed, one Welsh international smiled. 'Have a sip then.'

One afternoon, Moseley had beaten Llanelli and afterwards, the Scarlets' skipper, Phil May, was holding court for a post-mortem with his forwards around a table at the far end of the

---

* That, again, is a Black Country-ism. Lars Ulrich, the drummer in Metallica, spent six months in Stourbridge as a teenager following local band Diamond Head around. Thirty years later, on Jonathan Ross, he described himself as 'older than God's dog', clearly thinking it was a UK-wide expression. Hearing it in his LA accent was possibly the funniest thing I've ever enjoyed on television.

lounge. It hadn't been a great afternoon for the eight players there and I could feel a bit of an atmosphere as I approached.

'Could I have an autograph please, Mr May?'

'Course you can. Pull up a chair.'

I hadn't expected that. The Scarlets' stalwart and then the current Wales lock quickly signed my book and passed it on round the table.

'So, do you play?'

'Yes, Mr May.'

'Oh, what position?'

'Number eight,'

'Interesting…' He shot an accusatory look at his back row before turning back to me.

'What are you doing next Saturday?'

When I'd finished collecting signatures and earwigging on snatches of conversation between the players, I'd return to Grandad and his pals who would be a few pints in. Unless the game had been particularly contentious, debate would have moved on to general matters. Tongues would loosen and the little boy, stood quietly below eyelines with his glass of pop, would be forgotten as they unfurled the richly embroidered fabric of their life stories.

'For some reason,' Grandad explained, 'I was pretty good with a rifle; it just came naturally. Some of the new boys from London or Manchester had never seen a rifle, let alone used one. I'm not joking, one of them literally had it the wrong way round and we were supposed to be facing Rommel!

'So, I was asked to take some of these kids off and teach them how to shoot. I took them into the desert with some tin cans and did the best I could with them. Now, while I was away doing that, everybody else had been learning a new drill and the next day we were supposed to perform it in front of the officers. Of course, I haven't got a clue what we're doing, so I went in the middle rank because they inspected from the back as well as the front. My thinking was, whichever way our heads were facing, I'd catch a glimpse of someone and be able to copy whatever he was doing with his rifle. The trouble, of course, was that I was late with every movement.'

I watched Grandad's pals lean in as he left a dramatic pause.

'I thought I was getting away with it but, on the final run-through, before the brass arrived, this Cockney corporal points at me. "Morgan, if you are late one more time, I will not be responsible for my actions with this bayonet!"

'Well! I'm not having that, am I? He was a proper little weasel, anyway. A Cockney weasel. "Just you remember," I shouted back at him, "I've got a bloody bayonet too!" ... And that's how I got my second trip to the Glasshouse.'

With that, he went to the bar for a round. I trailed after him.

'How many have I had, Ben?'

'Five, Grandad.'

'Sure you're counting right?'

'Sorry, Grandad, this'll be your third.'

'That's more like it.'

One evening, after we'd seen Newport play, Grandad was keen to show me something. Fishing a silver box out from his pocket, he opened it to show me his angina pills.

'What colour are these, Ben?' he asked.

'They're yellow.'

'No, they're pink!'

Turning to Horace, he asked him the same question.

'What colour are these, H?'

'Pink.'

'See, told you they were pink.'

'They aren't, Grandad, they're yellow!'

He proceeded to show the pill box to nearly every player in the room, and all of them confirmed that the tiny yellow pills I saw were, in fact, pink.

There must be something wrong with me, I thought. Perhaps my eyes had gone, or I was going mad!

Eventually, Grandad tapped a thickset man on the shoulder.

'Charlie, what colour are these pills?'

This was Charlie Faulkner, formerly of Ponytpool and Wales, who was now coaching Newport. The final arbiter would be a man Grandad had told me was the finest loosehead prop in the world as well as a British Lion and part of of the greatest front row ever to play the game.

But then I rumbled it. Positioned between me and the garlanded scrummager, Grandad was frantically mouthing 'pink' at him.

'They're pink, they are,' he replied.

If Horace wasn't taking us home, we'd walk down to Moseley village to catch the bus in the dark. Punks, goths and skins would be waiting for the number 50 into town, and I was warned never to become like them. Sometimes we'd have a song to fend off the cold: 'I've Been Working on The Railroad' or 'My Brother Sylvest'. Back home, Grandma would have the sausage and mash ready.

'Pretend you're drunk,' Grandad would urge me as we went in.

'How much has he had, Ben?' Grandma would ask.

'Only three, Grandma.'

Those little yellow pills were soon joined by others in Grandad's silver box and the trips to Moseley became less frequent. Sometimes he'd be in hospital, so I couldn't even go round to watch Wales play with him. When this happened, he'd insist that I watch the game particularly closely so that I could report back.

This necessitated my watching at home, which was an altogether more fraught experience than watching with Grandad. On the one hand, I had to contend with my militantly English dad. He had no interest in rugby at all but did enjoy winding me up and, as Welsh performances dipped, he had plenty of opportunities to twist the knife. On the other side of the coin was my mum. She was my predecessor as Grandad's rugby-appreciation protégée but had been dismissed from the position due to her inability to keep a hold of herself during games. She had little grasp of the laws or philosophy of the sport but made up for this with a jingoistic passion that, had we not been in a detached house, would have attracted the attention of West Midlands Police.

Mum particularly relished the outbreaks of on-pitch violence that characterised the game in the 1980s. She'd urge on the combatants and express her contempt at commentator Nigel Starmer-Smith's horrified observations that such thuggery had 'no place in the game'.

'Pansy! What does he think he's watching?'

Mother's commentary also featured ornate descriptions of the players' appearances, rooted in an encyclopaedic command of national stereotypes and particularly, for some reason, those relating to Scotland.

If the game was tight, she'd begin to suffer as it entered the last quarter. Her vociferous support would drop off, to be replaced by a visible terror that Wales might lose. If a penalty were awarded late on, it was too much for her altogether. She'd run from the room, unable to cope with the tension, only creeping back when she heard the cheer from the telly to ask me which way it had gone.

If we lost – and more and more often, we did – Dad would materialise immediately to gloat. As Mum berated the Welsh team and swore never to watch another game, he'd chime in that he'd known we would lose all along and we'd be better off supporting the All Blacks; after all, 'they know how to play the game.'

It was all so different from being round at Grandma and Grandad's, where a knowledgeable ten-year-old could appreciate the game in like-minded company, nodding sagely at the finer points of play and learning to sulk like a gentleman if it all went wrong. But those visits to watch rugby with Grandad became rarer. And Mum knew, better than I, that the little yellow pills weren't going to bring them back for either of us, at least not for long. A Welsh win meant hope for her in a way I didn't pick up on at the time, and her howls at a loss were of mourning to come.

After Grandad had gone, my interest in the game dissipated little by little, like air escaping from a puncture. I still played at school but my bad habits – tentativeness and distraction – grew worse as I drifted away from the standards that had been set for me.

I had nobody to go to Moseley with, so watching rugby was confined to the telly, and it was a grim experience. Wales started to ship cricket scores, players flooded north to play Rugby League and watching the games became an unhealthy ritual for me. As I grew more miserable, the action on the pitch seemed to reflect my descent, as if the two were connected. I persisted, though, and, at senior school I revelled in my outsider status as a Wales supporter. In 1988, when Wales briefly rallied to win the Triple Crown, I wrote the score of the Wales match in big letters on the blackboard to taunt my classmates each Monday. Grandad would have been appalled by that. And so even victory had come to taste bitter: a burnt orange that used to be a peach.

The next year, when we tied for the Wooden Spoon, the singer in the godawful goth band I was in took the piss in much the same way my dad had a few years previously. For good measure he added, 'I don't see why you're so bothered; you're English.'

I smacked him in the mouth, drawing blood.

I'd been drinking.

Whose Song to Sing?

How interested I am in rugby is good indicator of how well I'm coping in life. If things are going well, then I can afford the emotional investment that the game has always demanded from me. If I'm struggling, I shy away from it, unwilling to risk whatever wellbeing I have on last-minute penalties and the whims of referees. The Byzantine complexity of the game demands an intellectual commitment from spectators that is generally reserved for working life, so, if you care, the option of following it casually is off the table. Essentially a riot, rugby is corralled into civilisation by laws that mitigate the risk of serious injury to players. Too stringent an application of them, however, will rob an encounter of its character. Cefneithin mage Carwyn James insisted that it's a 'thinking game', and that extends to supporters, who are expected to understand the yearly revisions of the laws designed to stymie the machinations of players and coaches whose priority is to evade their strictures like steam through a sieve.

If you can prove you 'know your rugby', then admittance is granted to long conversations with touchline strangers whose names you may never know. At work, you'll likely avoid the general chit-chat on Mondays after internationals, wincing silently at the crass nationalism and grotesque misreading of games you have consumed, recognising them as a hybrid of engineering and high art. You'll know who is injured and how long their recovery is predicted to take. You'll have read up on defensive formations that are being developed in France. Increasingly, you'll have an eye on financial investments in the game, mindful as to how their performance might influence your side's fortunes in a couple of years' time. You'll fret, not just about your team but about rugby as a whole: whether it is still attractive to youngsters; if facilities are available for the school game; whether subscription television and high ticket prices are changing the character of the crowds. You'll bristle as other sports set out their stall and tempt people away with the promise of simple rules and trauma-free fandom. You'll take the victories but never get carried away because now, after all these years, you know only too well that heartbreak is round the corner and you'll need to save your energy to cope.

Towards the end of 2003, I was beginning to acknowledge that things had gone very wrong. Academic studies, jobs, relationships and interest in anything other than feeling better right now had been washed away on a sea of booze.

My lifeline was a secondhand bookshop that a supportive girlfriend helped me to set up in which I found if not purpose, then at least something I could tell people I was doing. The shop was in Stourbridge, and I called it Idwal's Books after my grandad. The moment the sign went up, I regretted that decision. It was a constant reminder of how my life had failed to match his hopes for me and, worse, how far away from his values I had drifted. I'd look at the sign, paid for with my girlfriend's money, and be nauseated by how the gesture felt cheap and inauthentic when viewed in the context of my lifestyle.

Memories should be a comfort when you have lost somebody, but shame was in the way of mine. To recall my time with Grandad was to contrast it with what I'd become, and the shock of self-hatred would short-circuit the reminiscence in a flash.

The sign, though, had a peculiar effect. Welsh people who lived locally started to come into the shop to ask about it. One of these was a chap in his seventies whose bearing screamed 'lock forward'. We fell into conversation as he browsed the rugby books and I hid the bottle of red wine I'd opened for elevenses.

Ray Greenway, it turned out, had been capped for Wales Schools and gone on to play in the second row for Pontypool. Appraising his age, I asked, 'You must have known Ray Prosser, then…'

'That's who was next to me in the second row!'

Ray Prosser had been the coach at Pontypool in the 1970s and 1980s, moulding them into the most feared side in British rugby. Their abrasive style of play had seen the more sensitive English clubs – Moseley included – cancel fixtures with them, to the bemusement of their coach.

'There was more dirty play in one match in the 1950s than you get in a whole season now,' he'd remarked to one journalist.

As a kid, I had written to Ray Prosser – as I had every other living figure of note in Welsh rugby – for an autograph care of his club, including a stamped, addressed envelope. I'd done this with other figures I admired. Generally, I'd receive a signed photo with a warm, personal message – Phil Bennett signed six different photos so I could share them out amongst friends. Ray's response was singular: he simply wrote 'Ray Prosser' at the bottom of my letter and sent it back to me. I particularly treasured this one as it was so representative of the man's legend. During a British Lions tour to New Zealand, he remarked to fellow lock David Marques of Cambridge University and England: 'I don't understand you university types. You use long words like corrugated iron and marmalade.'

Over time, it became a habit for the few Welsh rugby fans in the area to drift into my shop on Mondays after international matches so that we could pick apart the Saturday performance. Ray was happy to recount tales from his playing days. He'd played for Pontypool against the All Blacks when he was eighteen ferchrissake! The rugby talk in the shop was sharp and informed, so I started to follow the game more closely again, keen not to sound ignorant.

The new Welsh regions were inaugurated that year and I was able to watch them on telly as S4C and BBC2 Wales now lurked at the far end of the satellite listings even in Stourbridge. On the internet, a forum called Rugby Rebels played host to ferociously partisan debates, and I began to catch up on developments I had missed in the game during my years of laxness.

As my enthusiasm re-emerged, I began to dream again of watching Wales play in Cardiff. In childhood, this ambition had seemed as remote as becoming an astronaut or owning a Raleigh Chopper. As I understood it, all the tickets went to rugby clubs in Wales and were fought over *Charlie and The Chocolate Factory*-style by members who weren't above skulduggery to obtain them. That had to be right because on Grandad's records of Max Boyce live, the crowd erupted in laughter whenever ticket allocation was mentioned. Marooned in Birmingham, our Rhondda family scattered to the winds and not a committee-sitting uncle to my name, I'd dismissed my chances of ever attending an international match. When the stadium that everyone still called Cardiff Arms Park was demolished, it was without my ever having seen it.

In 2004, though, more fixtures and a vast new stadium meant that tickets could be had – for a price – on eBay. Encouraged by my girlfriend – who was relieved by my new, healthier leisure pursuits – I assembled a group of five of us and we paid a king's ransom for tickets to see Wales versus South Africa.

I was acutely aware that my experience of this day was very different to my friends'. On the train to Cardiff, beers were opened at the table, jokes were told, reminiscences were recounted and steam was let off. It was a jolly boys' outing; my friends were English sports fans. We'd go to see the cricket sometimes and today was another pleasant trip to tick a box – see a rugby international in Cardiff.

I joined in best I could, joking along and cracking cans. Inside, I was consumed with nervousness, though. *I'm literally on my way to see Wales play*, I kept thinking as the Gloucestershire countryside sped past and gave way to that of Gwent before, finally, we pulled out of Newport and approached Cardiff. I began to feel queasy, as if an exam or a court appearance was in prospect.

Then, there it was: the Millennium Stadium, visible from the train and looming indifferently over my turmoil as I wrestled with who the hell I thought I was – in my Wales jersey, with my English friends and my heart full of something I had no right to.

Spilling out into the Cardiff streets, my friends, not unreasonably, assumed that I'd have some idea where we were going. Unable to front this out, I was forced to admit that the most fervent Welsh supporter they had ever met had never been to Cardiff and had no idea where anything was. Passing the stalls selling matchday scarves and women who would stencil a red dragon on your face for a pound, I tried to balance the contending forces of shame and wonder that were causing me to dissociate from reality and consume the scene as if it were a film.

Turning on to St Mary's Street, I saw a familiar figure being greeted by passers-by, and without immediately clocking who it was, I shook his hand and accepted his warm wishes for a great day and the right result as we passed. Pressing on, I took it as a good omen that within five minutes of arriving in Camelot, I had met King Arthur, in the shape of First Minister of Wales, Rhodri Morgan. When we got to the bar of the Goat Major, I cheerfully bought the drinks.

'Four pints of SA, please?' I smiled, brandishing a twenty. The barman took the note and poured our drinks without a word.

'Cheers,' I offered, as he handed me my change.

'You've got the wrong accent for that jersey,' he remarked, stinging me right in the soft part.

'If I was born in a stable, it wouldn't make me a horse,' I on the other hand, just about managed.

At least one figure of historical note was born in a stable. I was born in the Sorrento Maternity Hospital on the Wake Green Road in Moseley. I used to go past it on the bus on my way to school in the mornings and on the way back and would always glance at it, every day. Eventually, it became embroiled in a scandal surrounding its infant mortality rate and closed down. Somebody daubed 'Dead Babies' in three-foot letters across its shuttered windows, and it fell into dereliction.

Somewhere in there, an eighteen-year-old girl had followed through on a hard decision and given me my time in the world at an unquantifiable emotional cost to herself. It was also on the bus route Grandad and I took to Moseley RFC, but I didn't glance at it then. I didn't feel the need.

A Birmingham accent, as everyone knows, opens doors the world over. Women want you, and men want to be you. It is, however, difficult to disguise on the rare occasions that it isn't a social asset. It proved not to be advantageous at international matches, which I began to attend regularly after discovering that obtaining a ticket only required standing still for thirty seconds until a tout approached you outside Cardiff Central station.

In the Grand Slam year of 2005, I flew up to Edinburgh with my girlfriend, who had bartered attendance at the Wales versus Scotland game for a weekend's sightseeing. On the bus from the terminal at Birmingham Airport to the plane, we were crammed in with fellow supporters who had clearly had a bibulous trip east from the valleys to catch the 8 a.m. flight. As the bus pulled up next to a rickety-looking propeller plane, one of them asked a flight assistant, 'Jesus, love, is this to take us to the proper plane?' We laughed; she didn't.

In Edinburgh, the atmosphere was charged. According to the press, 40,000 Welsh supporters had made the trip, and the expectations on the team were higher than at any time I could remember. A few weeks earlier, Gavin Henson had kicked Wales to victory over England for the first time since 1999 and seemed poised to become a superstar of world rugby. England had fielded their own wunderkind in Matthew Tait, an eighteen-year-old centre up against Henson. Henson gave him a torrid introduction to international rugby that culminated in the unfortunate Tait being picked up like a roll of carpet, shunted five yards backwards, and dumped on his backside. There were T-shirts on sale around Edinburgh featuring a cartoon of Henson's tackle accompanied by the legend 'Coming for to carry you home'.

The Grassmarket, on the Friday night before the match, was a sea of red. For me, it was a scene I'd wanted to be part of so badly, for so long that I had difficulty absorbing it into my reality. Bursts of song in the streets and accents from around Wales swirled round the eighteenth-century architecture, out of warm pubs and into doorways for a fag in the cold air.

In The Fiddler's Arms, there wasn't a Scotsman to be seen. Trays of beer were being handed back from the bar that was ten-deep with Welshmen. Praise be, the singing started. Not the desultory choruses of 'Hymns and Arias' that had, if I'm honest, disappointed me at the stadium in Cardiff, but full-throated renditions of 'Calon Lân', 'Cwm Rhondda', and half of 'Sosban Fach'. We had got as far as *'Dai bach y sowldiwr'* when three jersey-wearing Scotsmen finally entered the pub. Magnanimous as only those certain of victory can be, the travelling chorale switched immediately to 'Flower of Scotland' in their honour.

'You sarcastic bastards,' one of them responded. He was gifted several pints.

I was deep into the singing and feeling the music in a way that only happens when you are in some kind of choir. It envelops you like a breeze that warms you all and coaxes sweetness from the group. I don't think there's anything lovelier.

Queuing for the loo, I asked a fellow chorister where he was from.

'Gilfach Goch. What about you?'

'Live in England, but my family's from Tylorstown.'

Looking me up and down and then he tweaked my jersey. 'Just like singing then, do you?'

No, I thought as my cheeks burned. *I don't 'just like singing', I learned these fucking songs before I learned to tie my shoelaces.*

'Don't worry about him, butt. He's a prick to everyone when he's had a drink,' the guy behind me said. Bless him.

On the way back to the B&B, I passed a taxi office where a couple of fans were offering the drivers increasing sums to be allowed to stay on the sofas overnight. It was cold – bitterly cold.

The Lakota (also known as the Teton Sioux) describe a time before white invaders arrived when gold was so plentiful around the Black Hills that pieces the size of a baby's head could be found just lying on the ground. If you love words, then your formative years were like that. One morning, you learned the onomatopoeic satisfaction of 'crunch' and in the afternoon, stretched your arm to the languid music of 'elbow', before settling in to 'slumber' because sleep would no longer do. As time rolls on, though, the pickings become slimmer until you're left waist deep in the river scrabbling through your pan of gravel for the tiniest golden speck, not even able to remember the good times.

Here's one for you, though: 'anemoia'*. This is a feeling of nostalgia for times you never experienced. In darker moments, I dream of building a corporation called Anemoia, with the

---

* First coined by John Koenig in *The Dictionary of Obscure Sorrows*, Simon and Schuster, 2022.

sole purpose of purchasing the advertising space on the front of the Wales team jersey.

Because by the time I started writing about rugby in Wales, there was already a queasy feeling that whatever it had once been was disappearing. Whilst the national team kept a seat at the top table of the world game, underneath it, the ground was hollowing out. Attendances at regional matches were plummeting, and the improved fortunes of the Wales football team had caught the national imagination. Rugby had become associated with stuffed-shirt pomposity and royal patronage. Whilst the football fans enjoyed coaches to Cardiff from all over the country, rugby behaved as if the nation stopped at Merthyr. The bucket-hatted rock 'n' roll vibe of football matches contrasted with silver-band quiescence as we played rugby. The songs had fallen away, leaving only 'Cwm Rhondda' and 'Hymns and Arias' to soothe our nerves as we waited for the national side to plummet through the threadbare foundations of the game.

Perhaps it's just a lull. Maybe a star player or two will emerge to entice back the crowds and lift us again into harmonic ecstasy. Or maybe it's gone the way of fags behind the ear and tin-roofed chapels.

I don't report on international matches from the stands very often. My writing has driven me to visit clubs around Wales and watch with the people there. Not only do I hear great comments about the game we are watching, but I get a feel for how people are doing in general through their preoccupations and topics of conversation. The ball, as always, flies around the pitch as a symbol of our wider fortunes. Like an icon in Orthodox Christianity, it is something upon which we can focus to bring forth the truth.

Where I live, in Rhondda Fach, you can't overstate how socially essential the game has been. In an area where governments, both UK and Welsh, have been content for people to experience endemic poverty, the rugby clubs have cohered communities.

In Tylorstown, where the rugby pitch was levelled on the mountain by miners in their spare time, the club has stepped into spaces that have been left abandoned by the authorities. For the elderly, it is a meeting place and a warm hub in the winter. The thriving junior section has girls and boys playing their hearts out but also doing NVQs and courses of all sorts. The women's team mentors young girls and runs assertiveness workshops. If the kids are looking hungry, people *notice*.

The goings-on in the Welsh Rugby Union: its endless scandals and nonsensical decisions have been a source of annoyance for supporters for as long as it has existed. In the warmth of Tylorstown RFC on a cold day, though, you can feel the mighty inspiration of this peculiar and maddening game, and it's the opposite of all that would undo us.

IF THAT AIN'T COUNTRY

I lay a towel out on the hotel bed and get on it to drip dry. I'm so nervous that the nervousness has morphed into numbness. Why do I put myself through this? If Mum had a gravestone, it would say 'Black is so slimming', so I take her advice: new black socks, black shirt, black trousers, black jacket and black boots. I sit on the edge of my bed and open my guitar case. There she is, reclining elegantly on her plush bed: Cheryl, my 1994 Gibson J200 acoustic, with her rare honeyburst finish. Self-esteem in a box.

    I rest her on my knee and rake my plectrum across a plangent E-minor chord. I let it ring and feel the wood come alive in my arms. Pulling Cheryl closer, I ditch the plectrum and switch to E major. With a thumb pick, I dig into the bass strings, which I have muted with the heel of my right hand so they thump like a heart. We, Cheryl and I, fall into an easy swinging rhythm that we both know like breathing. I flick my nails across the high strings, letting them shimmer and then begin to bend notes with my left hand. Cheryl starts talking. My foot's likely tapping; I'm probably rocking back and forth; my eyes must be shut tight because it's working on its own; I do not have to try. Downstairs, the showroom is filling up, but I carry on.

I didn't go to my grandfather's funeral. Initially Mum told me I *couldn't* go as I'd get too upset, provoking an outburst of adolescent defiance effective enough to change her mind.

Then, when the day came, I *was* too upset and stayed with Auntie Peg and Uncle Ern. The details, like Peg's food, were comforting though. The crematorium had been too small to hold the mourners, so they had left the doors open for people outside to hear the service, including the two hymns Mum had let me choose: 'Cwm Rhondda' and 'Alleluia Sing to Jesus'.

He died on 13 December 1985, a few days after my thirteenth birthday, so the first Christmas without him went by in a haze of grief; halls undecked and bells unjingled. A turkey was picked at, but no crackers were pulled. I took a large, metal money box that Grandad had given me and stuffed it full of keepsakes: my cousin's eulogy, a copy of *Eighty Days Around The World* stamped 'Ferndale Grammar School', the Second World War medals he held in socialist contempt, wooden clackers made in his shed to be played like spoons, the last pound coin he gave me and the last birthday card. I wrote his name and the dates of his birth and death out to Sellotape to the lid.

My interests began to change from that moment. When I was playing rugby, I found myself tentative when going into contact and hanging around rucks but not engaging. I lost my captaincy of the school team and then my place in it altogether, but it didn't seem to matter much. Politics started to look like a pantomime that only fools would bother with. Six months earlier, I'd won a public speaking competition by imploring my contemporaries to rise in solidarity and make an enemy of complacency. Well, they could get on with it now. Homework could get fucked, too.

Swearing was one of many issues over which Mum and I began to clash. She was visibly adrift without Grandad, and I resented her for what seemed like weakness. Dad's absences, both physical and emotional, were lengthening and becoming more frequent. He had shown an uncommon tenderness in the days after Grandad's death, but this had atrophied as the weeks went by, and there seemed to be a new urgency to his frustration whenever he was at home. Everything about our home and us irritated him: Mum's food, my voice, whatever was on television. His silences could last for days and there was the sense of an impending explosion around him that created a permanent anxiety in the big, expensive house he had built for the three of us. We rattled around it wordlessly and took the dog for so many walks that it eventually went on strike.

He moved into the guest bedroom and came home late most nights. Mum took to confiding in me about how she felt. He wouldn't talk to her at all most of the time. Eventually, she persuaded him to go on a series of nights out with her so that they could discuss their marriage. I'd pace around the house in mounting panic, waiting for the car to come back. As soon as he went to the loo or to his room, I'd ask her urgently how it had gone.

'Are you getting a divorce, Mum?' These days were redolent of the nights waiting for news of Grandad from the hospital.

She'd shake her head sadly and hug me. 'I don't know.'

During one of these evenings, though, something important happened. A documentary came on the telly about the Everly Brothers. I'd heard of them; Mum had described singing their songs with her school friends. It turned out that these brothers had been estranged for the last ten years but had recently patched things up and started doing concerts together again. The filmmakers had followed them to Kentucky, where they had spent their boyhood summers and learned the close harmony singing that had won them worldwide acclaim in the 1950s. Towards the end of the film, they attended a reunion in a backwoods church hall, along with dozens of family members whom they hadn't seen since making it big. Earlier footage had shown them at their reunion concert at the Royal Albert Hall. They'd been decked out in tuxedos and backed by top musicians as they performed to an ecstatic crowd that included Paul McCartney. Here, they had one guitar and sang in their jeans to a collection of aunts, uncles and cousins. First, they did 'All I Have to Do Is Dream' – their biggest hit. Then the film cut to an interview with the brothers.

'Our dad taught us to sing,' Phil explained. 'He used to sing with his brothers.'

'It got them out of the coal mine,' Don added. 'It seems that it doesn't matter where coal miners are, they sing. Could be Kentucky or could be Wales.' My ears pricked up. Back in the church hall, they took on a new intensity as they sang a song about Kentucky* that their father had taught them as boys.

Over a bluesy, strummed guitar, their voices swooped up into the high notes before gliding back down – sometimes intensifying, at others backing off into breathy reverie but all in lockstep, one voice indistinguishable from the other in timbre, each sensing the other's movement by a familial second sight. It got me in the guts like Grandad's choirs did. By all accounts, Don and Phil had quarrelled with each other for years, but the moment they sang again, they became one being, bound into the music.

The next morning, I was on a mission: I had to get hold of every Everly Brothers record there was. After that, I would need every record they had listened to growing up and every artist mentioned in the liner notes. Their fan club was based in Holland, I discovered, so I sent off my subscription for that.

During half-term, Mum took me along to her regular meet-up with the girls in the coffee lounge of Beatties department

---

* The Everlys didn't grow up in Kentucky. The family moved out of the state six months after Don, the eldest, was born. Growing up in Chicago and rural Iowa, they would still visit Kentucky in their summer holidays. Like Shane MacGowan of The Pogues who grew up in Tunbridge Wells, the Everlys held their culture closely while in exile from it. When the experience of 'home' is dislocated, music seems to define it very powerfully for some of us.

store in Solihull. There were two sections: an open-plan, self-service part where Mother would not be seen dead, and a closed-off restaurant where the waitresses wore black outfits with frilly, white aprons and matching headdresses. Here, the under-occupied wives of Solihull's leafier addresses gathered to gossip and compete. An actress from *Crossroads* habitually took her lunch in there, but not as habitually as we did. Grandad called it the Bats' Cave.

For years, Mum had been meeting up with her best pal – Auntie Susan to me – on Wednesday and Friday mornings for coffee. During the school holidays, I would be brought along and given a series of early masterclasses in smiling sweetly whilst issuing cutting remarks. The waitresses' private lives were of particular fascination; one was rumoured to have performed several moonlight flits, leaving behind credit card debts she couldn't afford. Mum and Auntie Susan would issue sotto voce critiques of the other customers' appearances. 'Oh dear. Madam over there has rather an unfortunate face, doesn't she? Poor woman…'

Around the time Grandad died, a new couple moved in next door. Clive was an up-and-coming bank executive whose wife, Annie, was keen to make friends. She started inviting herself along to the Bats' Cave. The dynamic between Mum and Auntie Susan was a conspiratorial partnership, rich in coded language and entrenched rituals. Anybody would have struggled to breach its defences, but Annie – ten years younger, northern and given to plain speaking – was at a particular disadvantage. She tried to mix in, pointing out the shortcomings of other women and showcasing her own status, but it drew no water with the old firm. Her criticisms were direct and unadorned with mock-sympathy, and her boasts sometimes referenced actual amounts of money. Mum would wince. Auntie Susan's manicured nails drummed the tablecloth.

If that ain't country

By this time, I had to be bribed with black cherry knickerbocker glories to go along to Beatties during the holidays. Mum liked me to go with her so that she had a recipient for pointed observations about Auntie Susan on the way home.* The Wednesday after seeing the Everly Brothers documentary, I was polishing off my ice cream and used a lull in their conversation to make a startling request: 'I want to learn the guitar.'

'Well, you can forget it,' Mum scoffed. 'We already pay for trombone lessons and guitars are common anyway.'

'Common' was a term that followed around my every childhood desire like a restraining order. Clarks shoes were common, and so I was to wear chunky Start-Rite ones. Skateboards were dangerous but, more importantly, common. I wasn't to play with Dean down the road because he was... You get the picture. Common is too subjective and arbitrary a term to argue over, so I had a go at her other objection.

'I intend to teach myself.'

'On what?' Mum countered. 'If you think I'm forking out for a guitar, you have another think coming.'

'I'll save up.'

'Pfft. I'll believe that when I see it.'

I was resigning myself to a drawn-out battle over the issue when Annie piped up.

'I've got a guitar in the loft you can have.' She smiled. 'I never use it so you're welcome to it, love. That's alright, isn't it, Pat?' She looked at Mum who was agape at her temerity.

'That's very kind, Annie,' Mum managed. 'Benjamin, say thank you, you rude boy!'

---

* They were like sisters. Mum was an only child, and this unbreakable friendship meant the world to her. Susan and her family were there for us both whenever things fell apart. I don't know what we'd have done without them.

I suppressed a smile.

'You needn't think you are joining a band,' Mum hissed on the way home.

Annie came round that afternoon with the guitar. It was a half-sized plywood steel-string acoustic in tobacco sunburst, with a white pickguard and a trapeze bridge. The strings hadn't been changed in twenty years. If I was handed it now, my heart would sink but, at that moment, it was the most perfect object on earth. I took it to my bedroom, leant it against the chest of drawers and stared at it. Then I picked it up and went over to the mirror to have a look at my new self. *This hairstyle won't do,* I thought.

Other than singing with Grandad, my musical education had been confined to the tortuous trombone lessons I'd been taking since I was eight. I had wanted to learn the trumpet – in fact, I'd still like to learn the trumpet – but my embouchure had, at a cruelly young age, been deemed insufficiently taut. The trombone is singularly unsatisfying as a solo instrument, and the idea is to become good enough to play in an ensemble as quickly as possible. Each morning before school, I would parp grimly through 'Twinkle, Twinkle, Little Star', or whatever piece I had been set, then present a performance to my teacher once a week. He was a kindly man, possessed of patience only attainable by those whose living relies on retaining students. Five years into it, he continued to reassure me that I would gain admittance to the orchestra soon – very soon.

This borrowed guitar, though – this felt like *mine*. I didn't want a teacher; I wanted to figure it out on my own, thank you very much. I went to the music shop off Mell Square and bought a book called *Instant Guitar*. It was twenty-six pages long and included a floppy 45-rpm record featuring demonstrations of the songs. I started with 'Michael, Row the Boat Ashore'. The guitar had an action like a suspension bridge, and for a month my fingertips burned and bled until they got the message that I was never going to stop and hardened up. Mum took much longer to come to this acceptance. I was practising for two hours before school, and from the moment I got home until I went to bed every single day. Sometimes I would lie in bed in the dark with the guitar across my chest whilst I silently changed chords with my left hand.

'You don't think of anything else,' she would shout at me. I wouldn't even answer; I must have seemed like a member of a cult to her. During lessons at school, I'd lightly grind my teeth to the rhythm of whatever song I was working on and shape my hands to strum imaginary chords under the desk. I drew guitars in my exercise books – Gibson acoustics like the Everlys played. I borrowed books about famous guitar players from the library and ordered obscure imported records from The Diskery record shop in Birmingham.

During this time, Dad was getting stranger. Once upon a time, we could navigate around his temper, but the terrain had changed. Mum knew not to serve fish, that was a given, but now he would come home and claim he could smell that she'd cooked it for me at lunchtime. There had been no hugs since I was tiny, but now he wasn't to be touched at all. 'Don't monkey-paw me!' Mum and I were watching telly one night, when he burst in demanding to know where his wallet was. One of us must have stolen it. Which of us was it? Or were we in it together? He finally found it on top of a kitchen cupboard, where he had put it presumably for safekeeping.

From the starting point of the Everlys, my musical journey could have brought me – via Buddy Holly, The Beatles, The Beach Boys, The Band, Crosby, Stills and Nash, and Elvis Costello – all the way to The Proclaimers, who were huge back then and the obvious aesthetic descendants of Don and Phil. Back then, as far as I was concerned, was shit, though, and I didn't want to be in it any more than necessary. So, instead, I set off backwards, as far as recorded music would let me go.

My studies of liner notes taught me that the lead guitar player on the Everlys' first hits was Chet Atkins, whose thumb-picking style had been heavily influenced by a Kentucky guitarist called Merle Travis, who had been popular in the 1940s. I sent off for Merle's album *Folk Songs from the Hills*, which had recently been reissued. His guitar style was mesmerising: he held down a brisk bass pattern with his thumb whilst simultaneously picking out the melody on the high strings. Occasionally, the thumb would brush over the middle range and create a lush, orchestral effect before locking back into the bass thump that underpinned his vocals. It sounded like three guitars at once. I ran into town to buy a plastic thumb pick after one listen to the album. The songs were mostly about coal mining in Kentucky, and I experienced a powerful sense of synergy as they curled around my grandfather's Rhondda stories, soothing his loss for me like a new friend.

Meanwhile, Dad had started smoking. This was surprising as he was forty-three and Mum said he'd given them up as a teenager. He didn't do it by halves either. He preferred full strength Benson & Hedges Gold with the filter removed, which he would devour at the rate of sixty a day.

His interactions with Mum and me were now limited to unpredictable blasts of anger that punctuated our otherwise silent home. An electricity bill arrived and, after shouting at us for running it up, he went round the house with the kitchen scissors, cutting the plugs off all the electric appliances. We listened in shock as he roared off down the road in the car before screeching to a halt and reversing back and returning to the house. After reattaching the plugs, he told us he wasn't risking us burning the house down by trying to do it ourselves and then left again, this time for the night. We were both caught between terror and hysterical laughter once he was safely down the road.

'He's fucking nuts,' Mum finally conceded.

The last few pages of *Instant Guitar* explained the rudiments of fingerpicking. There was a simple 4/4 arpeggio, its equivalent in waltz time and, finally, a complex pattern called clawhammer. In America, I discovered, this way of playing was called 'Travis Picking', named after Merle Travis himself. And it was the style I was looking for.

To pull it off, you have to keep your thumb and two fingers working continuously in synch for the duration of the song. Each digit is assigned a different role that must be repeated in strict rotation, in time and at speed. There is no shortcut to perfecting this technique. You start by staring at your hand and slowly coaxing thumb and fingers to perform their tasks in order. After weeks of practice, you should be able to do it in time. Some months, or even years, later, you might get up the speed required to perform an actual song, but you have to master doing it all without looking your hands so that you can try to sing at the same time. Nothing I ever learned in formal education was remotely as difficult as this. As things were at home, however, there were good reasons to be locked away in my bedroom with my mind fully occupied by the task. I was relentless in my practice until the pattern sank into my muscle memory and became as much part of me as my speaking voice.

Never underestimate where music can take you. The mathematics behind harmony plays out across the universe. Pythagoras noted that the geometry in the humming of strings correlated with the spacing between the planets. As I dug my way back through the music that had influenced the Everly Brothers, some of the names seemed familiar. I had heard of Hank Williams, Jimmie Rodgers and the Carter Family. They had been present in my life before I'd even heard their music. Why? Dad's record collection was the answer.

When he was home in the evenings, Dad would often shut himself in what was known as the study and listen to his records. I wasn't allowed to touch them, but I had rifled through them unseen when I was little and been mystified by them all – except for one that I recognised. *Parallel Lines* by Blondie. He liked blondes, the old man. The rest were trad jazz, blues and country. When I'd looked through them before, I was into Michael Jackson and Rock Steady Crew like a normal person. Now I'd found out that Don Everly's favourite songwriter was Hank Williams and Dad's collection included *Hank Williams' Greatest Hits,* volumes one and two. I had now read all about Hiram or 'Hank' Williams: an Alabama native, he had grown up with a distant father and an overbearing mother, who had pushed him to achieve from an early age. He'd sung 'Lovesick Blues' on his debut at the Grand Ole Opry and received an unprecedented six encores. He'd been a star for a while before that performance, but Jim Denny, the general manager of the Opry, had been reluctant to book Hank because of his reputation for drinking and abusing prescription drugs. Historians are divided as to why Hank was so self-destructive, but it was accepted that he suffered from terrible pain in his back caused, depending on which biography you read, by a congenital curvature of the spine or a fall from a horse. Either way, his suffering was evidenced in his emotive singing, or half a million people wouldn't have shown up to his funeral in Montgomery after he drank himself to death in the back of a Cadillac on the way to a show in Canton, Ohio at the age of twenty-nine. Oh yes, I'd been reading all about him alright.

It is a fifty-fifty call on whether I knocked on the study door and asked if Dad would play me his Hank Williams records because I saw it as a way of finally making a connection with him or because I just *really* wanted to hear Hank sing. Over the next few weeks, though, it became a habit. I'd knock the door and he'd put on a new record. We would listen to Sidney Bechet, Sweet Emma and Her Preservation Hall

Jazz Band, Stan Getz, Dave Brubeck, Lightnin' Hopkins, Eddie Cochran, Carl Perkins, Emmylou Harris and Waylon Jennings – especially Waylon Jennings. We didn't talk at first; just listened to the music and sat together.

He seemed to be cheering up a bit around this time. The atmosphere loosened and, although he was rarely home, the time he did spend there was calm. I bought him a Carl Perkins double album for his birthday, and we spent a happy hour listening to supercharged rockabilly that seemed to jump out of the speakers as if spoiling for a fight. The songs of dancing, moonshine and knife fights bounced around our silent home like an invitation to another planet.

'How are you getting on with your guitar?' he asked one day. This was highly unusual. If anything characterised our relationship, it was his committed disinterest in anything I did. Rugby, cricket, schoolwork, etc., were topics only suitable for his laconic brand of piss-taking. 'How much did your team lose by today, Benjamin?' Now he showed legitimate interest in something I was doing, and I was thrilled.

'Ok, I think. I'm trying to use the thumb on my left hand instead of barre chords – you know, like Merle Travis does. It means you can leave some strings open when you're picking so they ring better.' He had no idea what I was talking about but nodded kindly.

'There's a woman at work, Jakki, who used to be in a country band,' he announced. 'Her husband is a guitar player. We could go and visit them if you like.'

The following Saturday, Mum and I got in Dad's company car, and he drove us to Leamington Spa to meet Jakki and her husband. I had my guitar with me and Emmylou Harris was on the stereo. My excitement was heightened because I didn't know any proper guitarists. A couple of kids from school messed around with the instrument, but they were hobbyists to my mind and didn't have the single-minded determination to become a real player. This guy had played for *money*. He was the real thing.

Eventually, our car trundled down the rough stone of an unincorporated road in Leamington and stopped outside a row of small, terraced houses. Mum looked a little uneasy clutching her Fendi bag as we rang the bell, but she was happy to be out as a family. It had been a long time since we'd done this. The door opened and we were greeted by a smiling woman in jeans with thick, blonde hair and a very welcoming attitude.

'Come in, come in,' she urged in a rich west-Walian accent. It turned out that Jakki was from Cardigan. Inside, their house was cramped and dark. In the lounge, there was a wall cabinet filled with records, a lot of owl figurines and several ashtrays. Jakki was already smoking and Dad lit up straight away.

'Pat will be down in a minute. Sit down,' Jakki instructed. 'Would everyone like tea?' Mum and I sank into a 1970s velour sofa while Dad remained standing. I scanned the room. Against the far wall stood an original Fender Rhodes Stage 73 electric piano. You'll have seen Ray Charles playing one of these in *The Blues Brothers*. It had chrome legs and was covered in standard black vinyl leatherette. There was an old HH amplifier underneath it. A four-speaker Fender Super Reverb guitar amplifier dominated another wall, and two battered electric guitar cases were leaning against it. Opposite me was an armchair that I hardly dared look at because sat in it, like the guest of honour, was a tobacco-sunburst Gibson J-160E acoustic guitar. It was an old one with gold volume and tone knobs on the top. My own prized instrument seemed silly now. I was ashamed of it and leant it behind the sofa, out of sight.

As Jakki came in with the tea, I heard someone else coming down the stairs. Pat was thin with swept-back grey hair and a matching droopy moustache.

'You must be Ben.' He smiled, greeting me before Mum

or Dad. 'I hear you're a picker.' I must have been beaming like a lighthouse. 'Let's hear you then,' he said, handing me the Gibson J-160E, just like that, and taking its place in the armchair. I pulled out a plectrum from my pocket; a chunky, nylon Dunlop one I'd been using since I started. 'Here,' Pat said, 'try this one.' I took the slim, black Gibson plectrum he'd handed me like a communion wafer and steadied my hands on the guitar. Certain acoustic guitars will haunt you if you are made that way. To a civilian, they are much of a muchness: wood, metal and lacquer, arranged in slightly differing shapes, with a hole in the middle. That, though, is like describing a person without reference to their laugh or the way their eyes show grief. This guitar, for a thirteen-year-old beginner, was too beautiful, too old and too storied for me to comprehend. I'd had my first kiss at a school disco by this time, but now Marlene Dietrich had sat in my lap and was demanding attention. I was sweating. Pressing down an A chord at the second fret, I felt the strings give way with exquisite ease. The action was low and the neck slim, so my adolescent fingers slid into place comfortably over the mother-of-pearl fret marker. I pulled the body of the guitar close and looked at it in my arms. The lacquered dark-brown finish had cracked into faint crazing here and there on the top, and worn away all the way down to the wood at points up the neck that Pat clearly used most often in his playing. Guitars adapt to their owners. If your style favours the bass register, for instance, the wood will start ringing to emphasise that over the years; it's like exercising a muscle. I peered into the sound hole and appreciated the decades of fluff, fag ash and dropped plectrums that had accumulated inside the body. Finally, there was the smell of old lacquer, smoke and sweat that seeped out of it as it warmed against me. I bit my lip and went for the introduction to 'Bye Bye Love' – *Chong kuh chong chong chucka chucka chucka chucka chucka chucka chong*

chong chucka chucka chucka chucka chuck bom bom bom...

Over the next few hours, Pat, in his gentle way, showed me how to barre an A chord at the twelfth fret by stretching my finger across all six strings and playing the chord above it. This changed the opening *chong* to a much more pleasing and authentic *ching* reminiscent of the 1957 Everlys' recording. He opened both battered guitar cases and plugged in two 1960s Fender Telecasters. I'd never played an electric guitar before but, by the time he'd finished with me, I'd mastered the Luther Perkins lead solo on Johnny Cash's 'Folsom Prison Blues'. We all went to see a band in the evening at a country music club, and Pat bought me a pint of shandy.

Life was happier. Dad's mood, always the weather in our house, was sunnier, and Mum had rediscovered her sense of humour. Pat and Jakki became proper friends of the family. We'd go to their house in Leamington and then go out to see a band. They, as professional musicians, would be treated as royalty in the club and Pat took to introducing me as his protégé: thrilling times. I began to realise why they weren't professional musicians anymore and why Jakki had to work in the office at Dad's place. Pat had a glass of something clear at all times. Mostly, it didn't affect him, but, as the night went on, he'd become philosophical; his conversation would turn away from guitars towards Plato. I lapped this up and started devouring Socratic dialogues along with biographies of musicians. After the philosophical phase of the evening, though, Pat would become incoherent and occasionally obscene. Jakki just ignored him when he became like this and Mum didn't seem to mind – he was no threat.

Dad announced that he, too, was going to learn to play the guitar. Not only was he going to learn it, but he would soon outstrip my progress owing to the scientific approach he was going to take. Music, you see, is 'all mathematics', and I would soon learn that my scattergun approach was inferior to the mastery of physics that he would be employing. He had read a book. And he wasn't interested in acoustic guitars, either. No, all the top players used an *electric* guitar. Perhaps I would like to go with him to buy one at the weekend. Until now, Dad's non-participation in making music had been a policy that extended to refusing to join in with 'Happy Birthday' at children's parties. Mum's reaction to this development ran from hilarity to disbelief. 'He's tone deaf, Ben.'

For aficionados, guitar shops are Shangri-La to start with, but when somebody else is paying, they become the playground of the gods. Not that we were shopping for *my* electric guitar, though – this was made abundantly clear on the journey into Birmingham. If I continued to apply myself, I might be granted access to the instrument, but I needed to understand that Dad would be requiring it most of the time as he had planned out a rigorous programme of study. It was to be kept in his bedroom, where neither I nor Mum were allowed.

Somewhere, hidden in the storeroom of every guitar shop in the world, there is an instruction manual entitled *How to Stretch the Budget of a Beginner*. The copy at Jones & Crossland on Smallbrook Queensway must have been well thumbed.

'Looking for anything in particular?' enquired an insouciant employee with Bon Jovi hair. Dad was always very alert in retail environments. He hadn't forged a successful career in highways construction without a keen eye for a deal.

'I'm looking for an entry level electric guitar,' he explained, dressed in his Marks & Spencer suit.

'Cool,' nodded Bon Jovi. 'What kind of axe are you looking for?'

'Nothing too expensive. I can always trade up when I've mastered it.'

'Got ya, my man. Sit down and try this one out.' This was why I was here. Whilst Dad's route to the summit of virtuosity was assured, it had not yet commenced, so actually trying out the guitars was delegated to me.

'You'll be needing a practice amp. We'll plug you into this one.' Bon Jovi pushed a lead into a tiny, black cube as I eyed the vast Marshall stacks at the other end of the shop. 'It's only ten watts but fine to get you going.' He reached up and took down a guitar. It was a Hohner. Now, there is nothing wrong with Hohner guitars; they are reliably made in Germany and have served beginners well for decades as honest, reliable instruments. I sat on the stool and Bon Jovi handed me the guitar. It was a *red* Hohner. I had two things I could play on an electric guitar: 'Johnny B. Goode' and the 'Folsom Prison Blues' solo that Pat had taught me. I wondered why Dad hadn't brought Pat; he'd have been far more useful than me. I cranked out the two tunes as well as I could, conscious of a fake smile above me that wouldn't have disgraced the real Bon Jovi. My playing was disappointing and the guitar – well, it was a Hohner; a red Hohner.

'Hey, cool licks. Mind if I sit in?' The poodle-haired retail worker sat down and plugged a gleaming, *black* Nadine Stratocaster into what I knew – and Dad didn't – was a handmade Peterson amplifier that cost around two grand. As I chugged out the rhythm part to 'Johnny B. Goode' on the Hohner, he ripped out an astonishing salvo of hard rock licks over the top, climaxing with some Eddie Van Halen-style two-handed tapping.

'How much is that guitar?' Dad asked, pointing at the Nadine Stratocaster. The manual had come up trumps for Jones & Crossland, and I sighed in relief as the Hohner was replaced on the rack.

'Of course, an axe that pretty will need a case, dude...'

Logically speaking, music *is* an expression of physics that can be expressed mathematically. Einstein was a violinist. My Dad was a civil engineer. Over the next month, Mum and I developed a keen understanding of the distinction between pure mathematics and mechanics as we huddled in silent hysterics while the latter was applied to the Nadine Strat upstairs. *Why is he doing it?* On reflection, it was the only time I can remember my father attempting something he didn't excel at. The Strat found its rightful owner soon enough.

I started reading a magazine called *Country Music People.* To buy a copy, I had to get the train into the centre of Birmingham, where the large branch of WH Smith stocked all sorts of esoteric goodies. I read the features about star acts like George Strait and the vocal harmony group Alabama. These articles tended towards the sycophantic. I imagine it wasn't easy for a small magazine to secure interviews, so they weren't about to upset the stars with any searching questions. There were advertisements for upcoming shows by touring acts that I would drool over. I wanted to see live music more than I wanted to eat. I'd stare at these little adverts and imagine the venues listed. What was it like in the Mean Fiddler in Harlesden? Why would someone as revered and special as the Texas songwriter Townes Van Zandt be performing at Trysull Village Hall? He described being on the road as something that leaves your skin feeling like iron and your breath like kerosene. If it could take you from Fort Worth to Trysull, then he had a point.

I was not living on the road. I was fourteen and living in the suburbs of Birmingham. No, let's be honest here: I was living in the nicer end of *Solihull,* where the wrong side of the tracks was the raised bed next to your perfectly edged and striped lawn. To go *somewhere* and do *something interesting* is the mission statement of fourteen-year-olds worldwide, and those stuck in mimsy little cul-de-sacs have extra impetus. That yearning was becoming a full-time occupation. My chance came when I saw a full-page advertisement for the Silk Cut International Country Music Festival at Wembley Arena over the Easter weekend. This was a huge annual event that merited televised highlights on the BBC. It was a three-day festival that presented the biggest touring American stars with their bands. Easter Monday was traditionally reserved for the edgier, more progressive acts, and that's where my eyes landed.

I'd heard about David Allan Coe from Pat, who had taped a couple of his albums for me. He was the 'Bad Man' of country music. Liner notes told me that he had been sent to reform school at the age of nine and had then graduated to prison, where he dubiously claimed to have killed another inmate, before leaving aged twenty-nine and becoming a songwriter. During his initial years in Nashville, he had lived in a hearse parked outside the Grand Ole Opry and appeared onstage in a mask billed as 'The Mysterious Rhinestone Cowboy'. He was a former member of the Outlaws motorcycle gang and, as a side project, had released two albums of comic songs that were so filthy, they could only be purchased by mail order from an advert in the back of *Easyriders* magazine. He was third on the bill for Monday behind the Bellamy Brothers and, by the grace of the Lord himself, Emmylou Harris.

I had to word these things carefully. 'Can we go to a music festival in London?' isn't going to work. 'Can we go and see Emmylou Harris?' stands a chance – especially if you've been playing her albums at home for a week and have taken care to leave the sleeves, featuring photographs of luscious, willowy Emmylou, around for your forty-five-year-old father to peruse.

'We can? Why, Dad, you're the best!'

'He's always liked a skinny bird,' Mum sniffed when I told her the good news.

Wembley Arena is a huge echoing shed next door to the football stadium. We arrived around lunchtime and made our way through the car park to the entrance. The UK country music scene was a welcoming milieu for eccentrics and many of the audience had arrived in some variant of cowboy gear.

Cars sported stickers with slogans like 'Keep Yo' Confederate Money, Boys. The South Gonna Rise Again!' One or two people were conversing in fake American accents. For some reason that I didn't understand, Pat wasn't with us, but Jakki was, and she was entertainingly contemptuous of these weekend desperados.

'Once, when we were playing in Germany, one of these guys travelled all the way from Wolverhampton to see us at a US Army base. He had his cowboy outfit on, including two deactivated Colt.45s. Anyway, after he pleaded with security, they agreed to let him into the GI's club, where we were performing on the proviso that he checked the guns at the desk. This was 1975, right, and the soldiers were just back from Vietnam. The only guns they knew about were real ones. This… this *clown* pulls himself up to his full height – in a *cowboy outfit* remember – and says, in a Wolverhampton accent, "I am naked without my guns!" Can you imagine? The Yanks were killing themselves laughing!'

Inside the arena, everyone seemed as excited as I was. The concourse surrounding the showroom was packed with concessions selling Western clothes, boots and records. There were specialist country music dealers who imported the latest recordings from Nashville to sell mail order via adverts in magazines. I sifted through rack upon rack of albums whose names I knew, but which I'd never expected to see. Jakki came over to see what I was looking at.

'Is that the new David Allan Coe?' she asked, cheerfully. Of course it was: shrink-wrapped with an import sticker on it. The man himself stared out from the cover with terrifying prison eyes that promised tales of mayhem in the grooves. It was fifteen quid!

'My treat,' Jakki smiled, snatching it up and handing the dealer a twenty-pound note. 'And here's some spends,' she added, pushing the fiver change into my hand.

'That was kind,' Mum said, as Jakki bustled away towards the *Country Music People* magazine stand. 'Have you seen your father?'

I hadn't. He'd be off in his own world somewhere. Inside the auditorium, the music was about to start. We found Dad at a leather goods stall comparing unsuitable belts and made our way in to our seats. An audience of around ten thousand were anticipating the first act. The stage was brightly lit with a lavish set featuring oversized wagon wheels and hay bales that characterised the British media's condescension towards Country music at that time. The BBC cameras moved into position and on came Sleepy LaBeef: a portly relic of the 1950s rockabilly scene. Sleepy was named for the dark bags under his eyes, but his music rollicked incongruously for four o'clock in the afternoon. He was dressed for a nightclub at midnight: all black with boots and a wide-brimmed hat. Opening acts don't own all that many stage outfits, I figured, whilst trembling to his swamp rhythms and rumbling, baritone voice. *Thank God I'm here...*

Next up was New Grass Revival. They were an experimental bluegrass and jazz group that I'd read about in magazines. I knew Dad wouldn't have heard of them, so I reached across Jakki to offer him the programme so he could read their entry. He narrowed his eyes in a way that said 'leave me alone', so I sat back to enjoy their harmonies and virtuoso playing. He could be in whatever mood he liked today, because this was just the best – the absolute best.

Bluegrass music is structured, using a limited range of instruments to support tight harmonies that are derived from Appalachian gospel music. People often mistake it for old-time mountain music, but actually it's more modern, having been invented in the 1940s. Bands would play melodies in unison in the style of the Scottish and Irish ceilidh music that was brought to Appalachia by immigrants from the eighteenth century.

Musicians like Bill Monroe and Earl Scruggs arranged these melodies to feature intertwining solo passages on banjo, guitar, fiddle and mandolin. They threw in some blues inflections they had picked up from African-American guitarists, added a thumping bass and speeded it all up for maximum excitement. This evolved into a subgenre of country music that attracted virtuoso players who could make the most of the rapid solo passages that defined it and, by the 1980s, there were distinct bluegrass clubs and festivals all over the world.

New Grass Revival was a supergroup of top players, and they specialised in blending the music with jazz and rock to create a modern, sophisticated sound. The crowd thinned out visibly after their first number. I looked over at Dad to see if he was enjoying it. Mum squeezed my hand.

During a break between acts, Jakki and I went over to the *Country Music People* stall so I could spend the money she had given me on some back issues. Mum and Dad stayed in their seats, which suited me as neither seemed very into it. Jakki, though, was as enthusiastic as I was. At the stall, in double-denim and with a heavy cold, was the previous night's headliner, Bobby Bare, whom the magazine had persuaded to come and do a meet-and-greet. He was a bona fide country superstar who has been making hits since the 1960s. His song 'Detroit City' was on the first country compilation album I ever bought. Jakki immediately fell into easy conversation with him.

'Hey, Bobby, are you still working with Shel Silverstein?'

'Well, you know, Shel's a busy guy, but he sends me a song now and then. Just recorded one of 'em.'

'This is Ben. He's started on guitar.'

'Tough road, young man. You take care of yourself.'

I already thought Jakki was pretty cool, but this just sealed it. I forgot to buy any magazines and floated back to my seat to watch David Allan Coe.

Jakki and I took our seats between Mum and Dad with some excitement. Coe had a reputation for unpredictability, and there was a palpable edge to the atmosphere in the arena as the stage was set for him. He came on wearing a large white Stetson hat, a matching ankle-length leather dust coat, boots and Foster Grant shades, and sporting a full-sized American flag as a kerchief. He glowered at the crowd for a moment, then counted the band into 'Longhaired Redneck', a song that addresses anyone who might doubt his outlaw credentials by reminding them of his time in prison.

Then, he slowed the tempo and switched to waltz time as he affected a tearful, faux-sincere delivery that mocked the lachrymose style of days gone by. As the band cooed syrupy harmonies, he crooned mockingly about Texas, sad times and Hank Williams, as if that's all the audience could cope with. As he held the last note, allowing his vibrato to quiver with exaggerated emotion, the band stormed back into 4/4 time and he threatened us all with an 'ass whoopin'' again. As this song drew to a close, feelings in the room were running high. Some were cheering with delight, and others were booing in disgust at the way he was taking the piss out of their beloved music. But nobody could take their eyes off him. Neither could they shout anything either in support or protest because, instead of thanking the audience between songs and telling little stories, Coe just ran one into another with no break at all. The machine-drilled band would switch from a delicate ballad like 'Would You Lay With Me (In a Field of Stone)' before catapulting back into rambunctious, profane country-rock that recalled his sister as a first-rate whore, as well as his mean and drunken father who disowned her. He celebrated his family as white trash whilst daring anyone else to even think that about them.

He finally paused about forty-five minutes in, and a stagehand ran onstage to say something in his ear.

If that ain't country

'She says I need to get off because they can't hear any applause backstage.'

The noise in response was thunderous. Some of the audience seemed unsure by now whether they despised or loved him. He did another couple of tunes and left the stage. By then, the arena had made up its mind. Ten thousand people were on their feet stamping, clapping and chanting for an encore. After ten minutes, there was still no sign of him and the stage was empty, but the ovation continued. Jakki jumped up.

'I'm going to see what's going on.'

She disappeared to the side of the stage where the security people were and I turned to Mum.

'He was amazing, wasn't he?'

She looked a bit overwhelmed. 'He seemed rude, if you ask me.'

Oh, whatever.

Jakki came bounding back with news.

'He's backstage beating up the promoter!' she exclaimed. 'He's annoyed about being told to cut his show short.'

My new hero finally walked back onstage, without his band, to utter delirium from the audience. 'Wembley goes Coe a go-go' was the headline in *New Musical Express* the following week. Still behind his Foster Grants, he said nothing to us but sang a single chorus of his most successful song, 'Take This Job and Shove It'.

'I need some air after that – I'm going for a cigarette,' Jakki said. The rest of us settled in. Mum and I were together, with a gap where Jakki had been, then Dad.

The next act were The Bellamy Brothers. You'll know The Bellamy Brothers' work. They had a couple of monster hits in the seventies with 'Let Your Love Flow' and 'If I Said You Had A Beautiful Body Would You Hold It Against Me?' Whilst I doubt they are anyone's favourite band, it would require some effort to actively dislike them – rather like *Inspector Morse* or Easter.

So, they did their pop-country thing whilst I sat next to Mum with Dad at a bit of a distance. People were chatting during their performance. Coe had been a bit of a rollercoaster that people wanted to discuss and, somehow, it didn't seem like The Bellamy Brothers would mind very much. Mum leant across me to Dad.

'They're good, aren't they?'

Silence. She tried again.

'Really good harmonies, don't you think?'

Dad's eyes narrowed. Mum persisted.

'Remember them in the seventi...?' Dad looked at her with a stare like David Allan Coe must have had behind those Foster Grants.

'You. Can't. Make. Me. Talk. To. You,' he said to her, slow and mean. Then he got up and left.

Emmylou Harris might have been as good as it gets. Her voice undoubtedly cascaded with crystalline accuracy over the backing of her fabled Hot Band. She might have reinterpreted old Louvin Brothers songs so sympathetically that they were, at once, ancient and modern. Her sharp cheekbones must have caught the stage lights so beautifully that any boy's guts would have lurched in rapt desire. I don't know, though, because Mum was crying and she never cried. Wild, angry explosions – yes, she would have those. Several hours of petulant sulking: a speciality. She hardly ever cried though. I do remember that Emmylou wore a black, sparkly dress and did Bruce Springsteen's 'Racing In The Street' at some point.

Jakki and Dad arrived to collect us at the end of Emmylou's show. They'd watched it from the back of the hall. It would have been embarrassing to make their way back to the seats once the house lights went down, apparently. We headed to the car park in the twilight and found Dad's Ford Sierra. Jakki got in the front seat while Mum and I sat in the back. We talked about David Allan Coe on the journey – well Jakki and I did – while Dad glided evenly through the counties up to Warwickshire.

'Just drop me at the end of the road,' Jakki said when we got to Leamington Spa. Getting out of the car, she motioned for me to roll down the window.

'Practise that guitar, Ben.' She smiled and then hurried off down the dark lane. We sat there for a long moment with the engine idling.

'Time for home,' Mum ventured. The engine roared four or five times, as Dad pumped the accelerator, and then we lurched forward. The needle reached fifty through the back streets of Leamington Spa and Warwick before surging to seventy when we reached the countryside.

'No, David,' Mum yelped, only for the engine to intensify. Eighty, ninety, then a hundred miles-per-hour. I clutched Mum's arm and felt my father's rage humming through the car's chassis as we hurtled towards Solihull. In Wroxall, where Mum used to pay for my swimming lessons at a private school every Saturday, a rabbit hopped into the road and perished under the car. Thud. Mum and I clung together in silence, knowing that so much as a squeak would send the needle as far as it would go.

When we reached home Mum rushed out of the car, holding me by the wrist. As she got her key into the front door, I looked back at Dad staring straight ahead out of the windscreen, locked into himself.

'Get up to bed,' Mum implored. 'I'll be up soon.'

Up in my room I looked at my new David Allan Coe record, but he wasn't who I needed to hear right now. Rifling through Hank Williams, Johnny Cash, Waylon Jennings, Willie Nelson, Tammy Wynette and even the Everlys, I willed one of them to speak to me and offer something. At the back of my collection were Grandad's choir records. I picked one up and stared at the cover. The gatefold sleeve featured an aerial view of the Rhondda: close little cottages banked up on the mountain side, each looking down on someone else's chimney. I'd first held this record in Grandad's little council house in Birmingham after he'd gone into town and ordered it for me from Rackhams.

Jumbles of hatred exploded in the kitchen below me and echoed their way to my bedroom at the far end of the house. I couldn't hear what was being screamed and bellowed, so I crept round the landing and down the stairs, holding on to the banister.

Yes, he was in love with Jakki. Yes, it had been going on since before we'd met her. And it didn't fucking matter what Pat thought because that drunk had left for Ireland. In response, I learned that she and I were well rid of him. He was a lunatic and... she'd only had to adopt because he wasn't a real man.

Dad roared incoherently and I heard a glass smash. Mum screamed. My hands seemed glued to the banister, but I knew I had to move. Slowly, and shaking, I padded across the hall to the kitchen doorway. Dad had Mum cornered at the far end with her hair in one hand and a piece of broken glass at her throat. Calmly and slowly, he told her, 'That Easter bunny I ran over tonight
    should
        have
            been
                you.'

'There's nothing you could have done,' Mum tried to reassure me the next morning. 'He's a coward; he wouldn't have done it.'

'I'm sorry,' I mumbled and hugged her.

'Let her have him. It's her lookout now.'

Before he came back to pick up some clothes and toiletries later that day, Mum summoned me and our whippet, James. Lifting the dog's tail, she produced Dad's toothbrush and vigorously brushed his arse with it.

'Do you want a go?' she asked.

I did.

Back up in my room, I took out my guitar and wondered what to practise. Like the night before, none of my heroes seemed to fit the mood, so I tried something new and started to write my own song.

In the lift on my way down to the show I'm grinning like a teenager. Most of the shows I do are in pubs where, if I want to get paid, I sing what the punters want. Thirty years of that can jade you a little. Pressing the button for the ground floor, I recall Bloxwich Memorial Social Club. There, on New Year's Eve 1994, you could see a twelve-piece soul band, a female singer and a comedian – with chicken and chips thrown in – for six quid. It was also where I was hired to entertain the three hundred members in the lounge who refused to pay even that. I rub the precise spot on my head where a 50p coin hit me with the instruction: 'Fuck off home. Here's your bus fare.'

As the lift descends, I recall The Lancaster pub in Castle Vale, Birmingham where, at eighteen, I was sent by an entertainment agent to cover a cancellation and where, after a customer was stabbed to death, people still shouted, 'Do some Irish music,' as his body lay on the carpet.

Before the doors open, I picture the abandoned joy of the residents of a home for people with learning disabilities as they hurled themselves around their dayroom to the Elvis songs they always asked me for. There's a reason he's The King, you know.

Carrying Cheryl across the plush foyer inside her case, I feel none of the nerves that this occasion would seem to demand. At the entrance to the showroom, there is a banner over the door: 'Manchester Welcomes Everly Brothers International'. Martial, the fan club president, whose magazines I anticipated so eagerly as a teenager, greets me warmly in his Dutch accent before introducing me to some fellow fans who have travelled from all over Europe. Finally, he escorts me over to the bar, where a smiling Irishman extends his hand.

'Great to meet you, Ben. Finish that pint and we'll get on stage.' He is Philip Donnelly: lead guitar player for the Everly Brothers, Johnny Cash, Donovan, John Prine, Townes Van Zandt and much more of my record collection. And he is as engaging and gregarious as his legend suggests.

On stage, I can see how excited the fans are to see Philip. I know how they feel. We start to play, and I feel my hands move across the guitar to the familiar chord shapes of the records I've listened to since I was thirteen. When Philip's guitar solos come, they spring from the hands I strained during my teenage ears to fathom as I dropped the needle on the same groove over and over in search of their mysteries. I watch those hands, revealed at last.

'Hey, Ben, do one of yours,' Philip orders. So I do and, in the middle of it, Philip crafts a solo of such intricate beauty that tears spring in my eyes. At the end of the song, Philip asks me – a pub singer, a depressive with no real job – 'Have you recorded that?'

'No.'

'We'd better get you in the studio then.'

Sat on a star somewhere, Mum sighs as the last of her lawyer hopes for me fade away.

PÓG MO THÓIN

I forced myself through a goth phase in the wake of David leaving. It seemed promising, as subcultures go. It was oppositional, I liked the clothes and the girls looked like mythical creatures who could slay you with a single swipe of their Superdrug crimpers.

At fifteen, I glommed on to the scene in a deliberate way. Isolated at home and considered weird at school – 'Hey everyone, who wants to hear about the evolution of the Miners' Federation into the NUM we all know today?' – I needed a friendship group: other marginalised kids with poetic pretensions.

So, I started with the clothes. Relations between my parents were so dire at this point that the situation was ripe for exploitation. When I explained to David that I needed money to fund a wardrobe of all-black clothes with multiple zips and winklepicker boots, he couldn't get his wallet out fast enough.

'What did your mother think of your new clothes?' he asked, gleefully, the next week.

I dyed my own hair, spraying, back-combing and waxing it into points. Accessorising with a fringed Indian scarf and a 'Tune In, Turn on, Burn Out' badge from The Sisters of Mercy tour, I was ready to go and make friends.

Hello, I'm Ben and I am also tortured and sensitive.

There were various 'alternative' venues in Birmingham, but the storied one was The Barrel Organ on Digbeth High

Street. An ugly concrete oblong, it had bands six nights a week and ragamuffin DJs on Thursdays. On Friday and Saturday, it was crammed with sweet suburbanites who just wanted something to happen for once. Dark corners, hormones and pints of snakebite and black ensured the potential of a thrilling fumble or an inspiring heartbreak. Eyeliner, dry ice and fag smoke rounded out the experience for kids with dull lives and ambitions to be interesting.

And it was hard to be interesting. The shiny-new-everything, bubble-perm fascism of 1980s vulgarity seemed to slide its fake-tanned fingers into every crevice of the culture. The television was dominated by ancient light entertainers mugging through summer specials, and aspirational dramas in which blokes in Gucci loafers argued about yachts. On the radio, John Peel and Andy Kershaw acted as a bomb shelter from the relentless artillery fire of Stock, Aitken and Waterman. Youngsters who nowadays enjoy Rick Astley ironically are deeply offensive to me; they are making light of a man who visited unspeakable distress upon a great many people in 1988. Have some respect.

The thudding cheerfulness of all this schlock – and breakfast telly, and *Game for A Laugh* and the Royal Weddings – twisted the concept of happiness for me. It seemed that anyone who smiled was on the make: a grasping, miserable charlatan who was gurning to order.

So, the cultured youth sought out melancholy pleasures, and gothery offered many. This being England, there was a class system in place in the goth world, and it was based on band affiliation. At the top of our society were The Sisters of Mercy. There was no arguing with Andrew Eldritch's savoir-faire. His lyrics had a detached, ironic humour with just the correct seasoning of tortured passion. He looked like we wanted to look: pale, thin and intense. His music had an epic, Wagnerian quality, underpinned by an unsettling but monotonous drum machine. It was also tightly European and never gave in to bluesy flash. Also, their T-shirts were fantastic. You wrote 'Jesus Loves The Sisters' on your RE exercise book.

The Mission, on the other hand, were *not* a band you wanted to be associated with. For a start off, their main guy, Wayne Hussey, had been a guitarist in The Sisters and quit acrimoniously to form his own band. What kind of fool gives up a gig as lead guitarist in The Sisters? He did, however, write very good songs, and the addition of some Led Zep guitar swagger to what could be an austere musical formula could be tempting to the fallible. To turn up at the Barrel Organ in a Mission T-shirt was to mark yourself as insubstantial, though. Some might have played Mission albums at home in private – but I couldn't comment on that.

Occasionally, people would turn up at the Organ thinking it was ok to like The Cult. The real divide in the room, though, was between fans of Fields of the Nephilim and everybody else. The Nephilim subsect were easy to spot as they would dust their wide-brimmed hats with flour to convey the impression of being undead. The rest of us would turn up with our best sombre expressions, but a couple of snakebites would have us laughing, dancing, copping off and behaving like the kids listening to Rick Astley in The Dome – only better. Not so the Nephilites. Their stern expressions were unmovable. They would occupy a large corner of the pub and seemed rarely to interact until their moment would come, about half an hour before chucking out time. The DJ would put on the Neff's 'Celebrate' and they would rise as one, clearing the space in front of the stage. This was a choreographed affair performed in a circle with formal moves and all the seriousness of a ritual. After this spectral barn dance, they'd go back to their corner. Liberal Democrats now, I expect.

For me, though, it was a thin scene musically. The top few bands were great and adjacent acts like The Cure were socially acceptable *and* fun to listen to, but as a genre it felt spindly and passionless after a while. There was no abandon in it. People cried a lot, but not because they were moved by the music. It didn't provoke emotion so much as reflect it back at you, and you've got old age for that kind of caper.

If The Mission became a guilty pleasure – and no proof exists that they were – my enduring love of Country music became a buried memory, resurrected only in snatches of things heard on the radio or television and then promptly dismissed. *You're trying to assemble a life for yourself, Benjamin, with friends and maybe – just maybe – a girlfriend.* Nurturing an obsessive, archival interest in a genre of music that was then the preserve of the over-forties with a penchant for wearing cowboy outfits was not the way to go.

But… there was so much to miss: the storytelling songs; the taut, biting lead guitars; the sweet harmonies that cascaded down from church into barroom regret. Country is a mutant genre of music, a scavenging huckster that sucks up any traditions it can find and bends them through the prism of American commerce into modernity. Its greatest exponents – Hank Williams, Jimmie Rodgers, Loretta Lynn, George Jones – sing over this opportunistic mashup of Irish, Scottish, Welsh, African, Mexican, German and Czech aesthetics with the soothing authority of your mother. Like America itself, the music is as authentic as it is fake. You can pull it apart to see how it works, but as you do, it'll screw right out from under you and break your heart with something new.

On the day that my school pal Vinnie offered me a ticket to see a band in exchange for my scientific calculator, I'd grown away from myself. Six months of living on my own since my mum had left had twisted my course. The nights had become a problem. I didn't want to go upstairs to bed, I'd developed a dread of going up there. Downstairs, the television was always on as I drifted in and out of sleep on the sofa with the lights on. Thinking went to bad places, so I stimulated my mind for every waking moment. There wasn't much enjoyment to be had from telly at one in the morning in 1988, but I took an Open University lecture on mechanics over a compulsive loop of evidence that I was born to be alone.

'You'll love them, trust me. They've got a banjo,' said Vinnie, so I gave him my calculator and got the ticket.

On the train, everybody has band T-shirts on. The older the T-shirt, the higher the status of the wearer. A menacing-looking passenger in a flat cap sports a shirt from 1984, and he's king of the carriage. He's anticipated 'copper interference' and equipped himself with a silver hip flask. Surrounded by younger girls in Doc Martens boots, he produces a tin whistle and starts to play. Everybody seems to know the words to 'Streams of Whiskey', and the carriage erupts in song.

A commuter in his fifties, wearing a pinstripe suit and carrying a briefcase and black umbrella, opens the carriage door. He puts a single, polished shoe on the step to board when the whistle player whirls round to face him.

'Are you a Pogues fan?' the whistle player demands.

'Er, am I a what?' the businessman asks nervously.

'This is a Pogues train! Get off my fucking train! Get off my fucking train!' the lunatic screams.

Outside the venue, touts are scalping tickets. Knockoff T-shirts are on sale, and there's a stall with a petition for the release of the Birmingham Six. Somebody is burning a Union flag, and everyone is older than Vinnie and me.

Inside, the stage is set like a living room at Christmas. There's a huge, tinsel-strewn standard lamp and a Christmas tree; the drum riser is a sofa, and at the side of the stage is a twelve-foot fridge with 'Pogueator' written across it. The music on the PA increases in volume and intensity as crew place instruments on the stage and showtime approaches: Thin Lizzy's 'Whiskey

Whose Song to Sing?

In The Jar', 'Rise' by Public Image Limited, 'Straight to Hell' from The Clash. Finally, the house lights dim, and the crowd starts chanting:

'There's only one Shane MacGowan…'

We've jostled to the front, and it's the most danger I've felt in my life so far. The shove from behind pushes us all so close that we're trapped and can't move our arms in the overpowering heat, sweat and cider fumes. My chest is crushed against someone's arm, and I can feel my heart beating against it. My feet are on the floor but holding no weight as pressure from either side lifts me up like a Subbuteo figure. Suddenly, the mass gives way and about a hundred of us fall like dominoes. *Christ, is this it?* I'm dragged upright by my hair and the Pogueator door opens. Bright white light and dry ice stream out as if to announce our release from hell. Eight figures emerge from the fridge in silhouette, indistinguishable in the light until the last one raises his fist…

'There's only one Shane MacGowan…'

Steadying himself at the microphone stand, Shane surveys the writhing mass in front of him.

'You look like you need a priest,' he observes.

The band jolts into the introduction to 'The Broad Majestic Shannon' and whistle, accordion, cittern, acoustic guitar, banjo, bass and drums sync into an urgent caress. It quickens the heart and calms the nerves simultaneously as centuries of tradition step into 1988 to scorn the tepid mush on the radio. It pounds as it lilts: defiant and nurturing, ancient and young. Shane closes his eyes and sings of Tipperary, of the cross at Finnoe; of old hurly balls, whiskey on Sundays and tears on cheeks.

It's ordeal by joy.

Here it is! Finally, this is the thing!

Teenage love, as we know, has a hysterical quality to it. Most of us look back on our own fondly but with some embarrassment. Maybe we now recognise that it wasn't *really* love, just the adolescent fantasy of it. Well, I fell in love with The Pogues on 12 December 1988, and it was for real and forever.

Full-throated adoration for a *current* musical act was new for me. Always cautious of being fooled, everything the music industry sent my way had me on my guard. I needed my enthusiasms to be rooted in something that wouldn't or change: a bombproof, trustworthy anchor in the past. I wasn't, it turned out, too bothered about *whose* past it was anchored in, either. After cutting off my goth hair and wiping away the eyeshadow, I dived straight into the cultural hinterland that had produced The Pogues.

There were two essential strands. Late-seventies punk was great, but by this time, its original followers had either moved on or become mired in entropic torpor. The punks of Pigeon Park were a feature on the grass outside St Philip's Cathedral in Birmingham, and their good-natured Electric White cider and dog-on-a-string hopelessness looked decrepit and frightening. It was as if they were moored to a single moment in history and their own development. Drunk, dishevelled, and past thirty, they sat like garden gnomes as young executives skirted around them and into new office blocks that cast a shade on their spot.

Serious goths would delve into the Romantics or follow the backroads from The Cure into French existentialism. Both of these are a lot of effort, though, at any age, aren't they? The former were on the GCSE curriculum, and I couldn't be expected to go there in my spare time. And while depressed French goalkeepers interrogating the void at the heart of existence sounds like a lot of fun, I was receiving hands-on experience in that department at home. But, when it came to The Pogues, the obvious thread to pull on was Irish culture.

The barrelling irreverence of Brendan Behan and the kaleidoscopic absurdity of James Joyce were new continents to explore for me. Both were quoted in The Pogues' lyrics that I pored over obsessively. History seemed to explode through the lyrics into the contemporary urban scenes Shane MacGowan described. There were wars behind the eyes of the old street drinkers on benches he sang about: political tides that had brought them to where they were. Everything now came from then; the past was alive in the rhythms and melodies that poked their way through the lies and filth that governed us. From The Pogues, take a left turn at The Dubliners, and you'll find The Wolfe Tones telling you how it is.

I began hanging round in Birmingham's Irish pubs. This was back before these were riverdanced into corporate pastiches. Places like The Mermaid in Sparkhill and The Old Bull's Head in Digbeth catered for an older Irish crowd and offered a sharp cultural contrast to English pubs. They sold Majors cigarettes and Red lemonade; the juke boxes had tunes from Big Tom and Philomena Begley. During the week, you could chat with the old men eking out some companionship with their pensions and content to share a story with you in return for a pint of Harp.

'Before the war, I was in the IRA, young man...'

At the weekends, bands would play, and couples would dance; suits and cocktail dresses were mandatory. If you were respectful, you'd find acceptance. I'd often go on my own, just to be around it all.

My vowels started to soften. I knew it was happening and I knew I was being fraudulent, but I wanted to be in this culture – to participate. God knows what I must have sounded like. I started to daydream about my identity. Mum still had a Year Zero policy regarding my adoption. She'd told me about it but wanted to erase it from history. I was her little boy and that was that. No need to worry about it. 'I said no *need*!'

I'd clung tightly to the Welsh heritage my Grandad had shared with me, applying it liberally over the gaps in my history like Polyfilla. *I'll move to Wales when I grow up*, I frequently reassured myself when things became unhappy at home. I told everyone I was Welsh. I'd started out telling the truth: that I was a *quarter* Welsh. I didn't want to lie, but people would reply that I was, therefore, actually English, as if that was something I'd be happy about. I practised my *un, dau, tri, pedwar, pump, chwech, saith, wyth, naw, deg* until it rattled out like a machine gun. I can still do it. I performatively supported the rugby team, making sure that everybody was aware whose side I was on. I sang the anthem obnoxiously loudly, unless in Welsh company, when I'd mumble, in case I'd got something wrong. So, I was Welsh alright – apart from not speaking the language, having been born there, living there nor having any living relatives there – I was Welsh as *ffyc. Cymru am byth*!

Now, though, with Grandad gone and me living apart from Mum, I'd found this new cultural treasure trove via The Pogues and I began to wonder. *I mean, there must be some reason why I'm drawn to this music, these books and this history. I talk of little else, nowadays.*

My Welshness was a demanding mistress. In nurturing it, I'd purposely set myself apart. In addition to excluding myself from the dominant social group, I had to contend with the knowledge that I'd constructed it with scant regard for reality. In fact, I'll revise that: in defiance of reality. Because I wasn't Welsh, was I? I'd been adopted by a family with one extraordinary Welsh member and wrapped myself in his clothes for warmth. Welsh was learning to sing, a leather rugby ball, pulling up swedes in the garden and learning about the Tonypandy Riots from that loving Rhondda voice. It was well-being. I wasn't Welsh at all.

Unsupervised, I started to think about the things I'd been told not to think about. My other self, the one from God knows where, became insistent for attention. Now that Welshness included a weighty dollop of grief, I told myself that I'd never know where I was from, so it was best to follow my instincts, and hadn't they led me here to the jigs and the reels and the rare talk and the Murphys? Maybe my natural parents were... Irish?

Mercifully, this didn't last long. With a lifetime's experience of pretend-ethnicity to draw on, I soon concluded that the research involved in starting another 'me' from scratch would be prohibitive. The Irish are understandably sensitive about lazy stereotyping and quick to temper, so I put my vowels back in order.

I still enjoyed visiting the pubs, but I gave up on fully participating in the social scene. Instead, I took a familiar position on the sidelines and mainly observed. Sometimes talk would turn to politics, and this could be awkward if you were English. Birmingham's recent history had warped Anglo-Irish relations for many in the city. But it didn't matter, because I was Welsh again. It was easier all round.

Refusing Englishness has been the most consistent component of my identity for as long as I can remember. It's the thing I'm touchiest about; my cheeks burn if people suggest I am English. I don't argue any more because I know it's absurd to. Instead, I lose eye contact and become shifty. It feels like the sand I'm standing on starts to give way at the merest mention of it.

Occasionally, there will be a row in the press about whether a player who has qualified to represent Wales is sufficiently Welsh. This, of course, is a minefield in which self-determination comes into conflict with inclusiveness. If these lines are drawn too broadly, the relationship between culture and nationality is stretched to a meaningless veneer. If they are looped too tightly around supposed indigenous qualifiers, xenophobia and racism are pulled closer towards acceptability. When this is discussed online, I always watch the discussion intently. Comfortingly, many unimpeachably

Welsh contributors speak of Welshness existing in the heart, something that can enter a person by osmosis if they are of the correct disposition. I hope so; I really do.

Others see their nationality as an inherent quality that was set in their formative years, not by cultural training but through immersion in the *political* realities of life in Wales. I was chatting to a writer at the Hay Festival some years ago and suggested that *eisteddfodau* could be a successful cultural export, thinking of how Ireland's artists had flourished at the dozens of *fleadhanna* that are put on around the world. She narrowed her eyes and told me my 'colonial roots' were showing. I died inside a little but took the lesson.

The emotional warmth I associated with Wales as I child has proven to be an enduring lure. I think the best of it, forgive it and defend it reflexively. I'm not *of* it. Although today, with adolescent attachment disorders under some control, I can occupy a space in Wales without agonising about it. *Give it a rest, mun.*

If the pull of Welsh identity can be explained in crushingly obvious Freudian terms, the push away from Englishness is less personal.

Growing up in the English suburbs is a topic that's been explored to saturation point. The nothingness of the experience is so bewildering as to compel artistic expression as a psychiatric imperative for many. You know it from Betjeman, Reggie Perrin, Siouxsie and the Banshees. The striped-lawn tyranny of suburbia is driving a sixteen-year-old to flee to a city *as we speak.*

But it's in places like Solihull that the absence of any meaningful English culture is most apparent. Suburbs exist to bleach away regional identity. Nearly everyone there is from Birmingham but once in possession of a B91 postcode, many choose to eradicate any evidence of that by affecting an off-the-shelf politesse that works as well in Altrincham as it does in Stoke Bishop.

Whose Song to Sing?

The regional identities of England, banished from the dead zone, are as vibrant as anywhere else in the world. If you speak to a Black Countryman *as* a Black Countryman, he'll spellbind you with the self-deprecating whimsy of his offal-focused humour, the sardonic wisdom of his songs about offal and his varied cuisine.

Speak to him as an *Englishman*, though, and he's got nothing to offer except the propaganda of his ruling class. Only Americans think there are English bands. Bands are obviously, and necessarily, bound to the cities that loved them first. Senses of humour vary wildly across England where they are defined by local history, patterns of immigration, economic conditions and dialect. Food is fetishised for its locality. Suburbia is what is left of Englishness when you subtract all those things. The oversized flag that is supposed to cover Jacob Rees-Mogg and Roy 'Chubby' Brown with cultural unity has nothing to defend it from crass nationalism. It offers marching music, waving monarchs, stiff-upper-lip acceptance of injustice and snarling aggression to anything that challenges the established order. It is a top-down insult to the abundant genius that originates from the regions it squats over, subduing, regulating and silencing everything it can. It's the public face of organised crime, and 'Britishness' is its international branch.

So, having grown up in Solihull, was it any wonder that I moved to Birmingham as soon as I could? Imitate my accent all you like. 'Kipper tie with two sugars please.' See, happy to do it for you myself. Tell me how ugly it is and how you can't find your way around the one-way system. Call it a shithole if you like. I'm not the Acocks Green Tourist Board. You can't deny, though, it's *something*: an extant cultural entity with which a person can identify and through which they can defend their corner. Take the piss out of Englishness and the only available response is, and always has been, violence.

Póg mo thóin

Once The Pogues had taken hold of me, I began to see more of life. They were permanently on tour for the next two years and tickets were cheap. Hiding in train toilets to avoid paying is ethical if you are enriching yourself culturally, so distance was no object.

The big one was St Patrick's night in 1989. The band played at Brixton Academy.

Stood outside with Vinnie, as touts offer us £200 each for our green and orange tickets, I feel as if I've finally reached the right place at the right time. Just to *have* a ticket is to be the envy of anyone with a clue. The anticipation as the queue swells behind us up the road towards the market is intoxicating.

The doors open at last, and we rush down the sloped floor to the front. There are Romanesque statues around the circular balcony. A familiar smell building up as the crowd presses in behind us: alcohol fumes, fag smoke and rotting leather rise from the mass of people as we coalesce into one lurching creature.

'There's only one Shane MacGowan...'

It takes about an hour after the support band finish, to set the stage. The road crew usually place the microphone stands in a straight line across the front of the stage because this isn't Freddie and the Dreamers. Shane might be the focus for the press, but the band face the world together with no hierarchy. This time, though, the central microphone stand is placed at the back of the stage.

Orange, white and green lights flash around the stage as the band enter from the back behind the drums. They slow march towards us. The show begins not with the usual hooligan abandon of 'Streams of Whiskey' or 'If I Should Fall from Grace with God', but the sparse, plangent ache of 'And The Band Played Waltzing Matilda'. Shane is wearing a wild beard and dragging his mic stand as the rest of the band create the song's intense dirge in step. Instead of wild nights in pubs or days in fag-stained bookies, we're dragged immediately into the trenches at Gallipoli.

It punctures the wild expectations of the crowd and sets us back on our assumptions. Where there's joy, there's pain, and we're here for both. Before we can figure out how we feel, they are into 'Boys from the County Hell', and the moment is left to ripen over the years in our memories.

Afterwards, Brixton tube station is chaos. We are perched six to a step on the escalator down and nobody's night is over yet. Station staff look panicked as the crowd performs its own encore, using the panels below the moving handrails as a percussion instrument.

'And it's no, nay, never,' THUMP THUMP THUMP-THUMP

'No, nay, never no more… Will I play the wild rover…'

The train is packed with faces crushed up and distorted against the windows as if being transported to a wartime atrocity. At Euston, we have to run. The last train is at midnight, and if we're quick enough… and we are not.

A night at Euston station when you're sixteen is equal parts mythical and terrifying. The shops are all closed, their welcoming, cheerful facades shuttered down as if to say, 'go to bed!' The vast concourse that was full of Londoners when we arrived is empty and echoing. Someone is pushing around a floor cleaning machine to erase the day's sins as best they can. Nobody here wants to be.

We look around the benches to find somewhere safe until 5 a.m., when the first train goes. People are trying to sleep under the harsh, yellow lights. You can be here but only if you're waiting for a train, so every half an hour, a railway employee wakes everyone up and demands to see tickets.

'I'm not actually travelling. I'm meeting my daughter off the first train.' The sleeping bag tells a different story in which family life doesn't feature any more. He is tormented into consciousness and made to recite his lies as if auditioning for a place in humanity.

Two elderly Irishmen are bickering. Their beef has the air of practiced familiarity.

'You fucking Dublin cunt,'

'Dublin? It's *you* who's from Dublin, you gobshite.'

'I know what you fuckers are like: wearing your suit at Mass and sending your daughters over here for abortions. Hypocritical Dublin shithouse, you are.'

They carry on all night, never reaching the pitch of anger nor dipping below belligerence. Like Vladimir and Estragon, they are trapped in eternity.

Inside a railway station without a ticket, time flattens out and spreads over us, forcing enormities into pettiness as we wait for release. The distance between us and them is a few decades and one or two wrong turns. I swig from my can of Special Brew and eye the clock again. For now, I've got a ticket.

CHIMPANZEE EYES

In 2016, I'm back in Solihull, at forty-three, to fashion some kind of role in my mum's death. We do this, don't we: insert ourselves into the expiration of loved ones and try to feel useful? There we are, holding a limp hand, striding about organising logistics or quizzing consultants who – damn it – will find the time because we officially matter in this process. Meanwhile, the soon-to-be-expired counts down the breaths.

My input, I knew, would be limited by the Tiggerish presence of my stepfather, a retired physician whose energy is matched only by his generosity and single-mindedness. He'd called up my mum and asked her out a few weeks after David had left. After a romance conducted on lavish trips around the world, they had married when I was seventeen. These were, undoubtedly, her happiest years, which made the onset of her illness seem all the more unfair.

My stepfather had had this planned for years. Parkinson's Disease allows for that. So, between berating nurses, tying up financial loose ends and advising the consultant, he slotted me in for my goodbyes.

Walking through the hospital, he explains how poorly this might have gone for Mum had he not been there to keep the staff on their toes. I watch my brown brogues move across the blue and speckled corridors. Nurses these days, he explains, aren't trained properly and have no respect. We round a corner, and I glance at an ancient patient who is parked on a bed awaiting staff to move him. He's curled up and foetal, as if anticipating his next womb. Something passes between our eyes, so I nod and try a smile. He knows better.

In his time, Stepfather continues to explain, wards were deep-cleaned every day by matrons who had common sense instead of degrees.

We enter the lift with a tearful woman. Silence in hospital lifts creates a particular space. In the corridors there is purpose, and everything is moving. The lift forces you to focus in on your reasons for being there – your bad toe, if you are lucky. *Ding ding. Swish.* The doors open. Four floors to go. *Goodbye and good luck, love.*

Where we're going is appropriately high up in the hospital. The air is thinner up there, it seems, and the noises are muted. Even my stepfather seems becalmed by it as we emerge onto the top floor. The double doors up ahead hold terrors. In there, abstract anxieties you carry from childhood become real and dance in front of you. In there, nothing gets better. In there, everything is scarce: hope, time, breath. You get orphaned in there. My pace slows as we approach. I take my time applying the alcohol gel to my hands and then take my time noticing its coolness. I look around for more time to take, but it runs out fast up here. I squint and press on in.

My grandmother had a dachshund called Bella many years before I was born. Bella died as Edna entered the menopause, triggering a distress so acute that a stay in All Saints psychiatric hospital was deemed necessary. 'She had a breakdown.' When she had recovered, Edna was adamant that she would never keep another dog; such was her dread at the prospect of loss. Her antipathy to Mum's whippet was surely a defensive tic. I get this entirely. Grief, the presence of absence, towers over the emotional landscape of all it touches; a jagged mountain where once there was blue sky. It menaces even after we learn to live with our backs to it, for we know how suddenly our new view can darken. A good life, long and lived in love, ends hemmed in by Himalayan ranges of loss. I go in to see Mum with only a single mountain behind me, but it's enough to cast a chill on my back.

I saw Grandad for the last time on my thirteenth birthday. The previous, already hormonal months had been fraught as I strained to overhear whispered conversations, noticed new pills in Grandad's silver box and looked up the words 'oesophagus' and 'malignant' in horrified solitude. I wasn't supposed to know that he was for it. He kept up his mischievous humour and endless pride in my achievements throughout the entire ordeal – for both of our sakes, I suppose.

Mum caught the brunt of my frustration: I was being excluded, disrespected and I *needed to know*. Sometimes I'd be taken to the hospital where, invariably, he would have sent out for a book to give me. Sallow and shrinking, he would smile and joke, corralling winces within the dark, Iberian eyes he shared with my mother. You see them all over South Wales – 'chimpanzee eyes', Mum called them. Think of Shirley Bassey or Gareth Edwards. Both Grandad and Mum's eyes were intense and fretted with tiny lines around them when they were brooding. And they both enjoyed the occasional brood. In hospital, I would tell him about school, and we would discuss the world situation. Sometimes rugby.

'Terry Holmes has gone north, Grandad!'
'No amount of money is worth the shame!'
Sometimes other events.
'Ben, those IRA men who bombed the Brighton hotel should be hanged!'
'Why, Grandad?'
'Because they missed the bitch!'
On we would go, smiling at the kind nurses and glowering at bolshy ones until the hour was up. We'd kiss each other

goodbye, and Mum would tear me away from his bedside. The corridors out to the car park seemed endless, like a harshly lit maze. We'd move through one to another and from one lift to another. I'd try to contain the enormity of what was happening by thinking how odd it was to see Grandad barefoot, how crisp his pyjamas looked or how maybe, just maybe, he seemed a bit better this time. Out in the dark and headed towards the car, Mum would be tersely kind.

'He was strict with me, you know. Not like he is with you. I wasn't allowed comics. I had to have *The Children's Newspaper*.'

There were nights that I wasn't allowed to go. I'd be left with a neighbour whilst Mum and Grandma made the trip. These were the nights when there was news. As Auntie Peg or Auntie Susan, or whoever was assigned, kindly made my tea and a fuss of me – 'Cottage pie, love. Your favourite,' – I'd try to seem alright, to behave like Mum liked me to and be grown up. 'Finish your dinner.' The car headlights would flash across the drive around 9 p.m. and my prickling nerves would erupt in jagged spikes through my gut.

'What did they say, Mum? What's happening?'

'For God's sake, let me get my shoes off!'

What had happened was one of two things. Either they were trying something new, in which case I'd jabber with excitement, or something new had failed and Mum and I would stare sadly at each other and I'd go to my room. Once there, I'd put on one of Grandad's choir records and blink through the emptiness of it all while the Treorchy or Pendyrus male voice choirs took me off to my imagined Rhondda.

Eventually, of course, there was nothing new to be tried.

'He's tired, love. Best you don't come until he's feeling better.'

More cottage pie.

As Sunday – my birthday – approached, I began to feel angry.

'He's my grandad. He'll want to see me on my thirteenth birthday,' I told Mum. What would she know anyway? She didn't go to the rugby with him; she couldn't sing 'Sosban Fach', and she'd voted for Maggie. With the limitless persistence of a nearly thirteen-year-old, I prevailed, and we set off to East Birmingham hospital in the December gloom. I took the camera that he had sent for my birthday; he'd be keen to see it for sure.

It feels good to be thirteen, doesn't it? I liked telling people that I was thirteen and the shape of 'teen' in my mouth straightened my back. The plateau of adulthood was at least in view, and it quickened my step. So, I fairly skipped down the hospital corridors with my Canon T50 swinging around my neck. Mum, usually whippet-like, trailed behind. I couldn't wait to see him and for him to see me as a teenager for the first time. I felt sure that there were new levels of wisdom he would open up now that I'd reached this milestone. Maybe the jokes would be saltier too.

The ward was Sunday quiet as I pushed through the double doors and rounded the nurses' desk. Mum was just behind, breathlessly catching me up.

'Ben…' She caught my arm but I brushed her off. I knew where to go. Beaming, I readied my camera and headed for Grandad's bay.

'No!' he rasped, painfully raising his palm at the lens. He was a celebrity and I was the paparazzo intruding. I couldn't comprehend the state of him: face fully thinned out to the photos of his Rhondda youth and arms wisping in the artificial light as he flailed to stop my bloody camera capturing him like this. For thirteen years, I'd known that iron grey hair to be swept back in perfect discipline, even over the single boiled egg and black tea he had for breakfast every day. Now it straggled around his head, somehow infantilising him. His legs lay curled in pyjamas that no longer fitted, and one foot stuck out to the side. Once, that foot had kicked up hobnailed sparks on East Street in Tylorstown, outraging a chapel lady. That outstretched palm had held gravel to throw on the chapel's tin roof during services, outraging yet more of them. It had hurled an empty beer bottle at the wall – to see what sound it would make – catching on the twisted metal top and causing that long, ridged scar along the index finger that conducted choirs and had pointed out everything I needed to know.

I put the camera away and he calmed down. The chimpanzee eyes managed a twinkle, and we spent the time we had buoying each other up, like sailors in a rickety boat.

Idwal Morgan died the following Friday – the thirteenth, as it happened. There was snotty weeping, anger and all you know of grief before I retreated into my bedroom and played his records again. The Dunvant choir are second tier, but they had my back that night. A sentimental song, 'A Valley Called The Rhondda', wrapped me up and offered sweet tea when the hymns were too much.

For thirty years, that was it for me and loss. Relatives passed away, but not unexpectedly, nor with the world-ending implications that losing Grandad had held for me on the cusp of adolescence. It was, as I pushed the doors into Mum's ward that day, the mountain behind me.

My stepfather strides over to the bed with purpose and starts plumping pillows. As always, he's in control; he has to be, or else he would drop like a stone through thin air. I'm more circumspect, edging my way over, unsure of how I'll cope. It's been twelve years since Mum was diagnosed with Parkinson's, and each one of those years has chipped away at her steadily. I've visited less as the communication staggered and then halted, and hardly at all since I moved to Wales. I don't want to see this and I move towards it as if wounded. A senior nurse bustles over. And he's off.

'Sister, it should not be up to me to make my wife comfortable. Standards in this hospital are a disgrace!'

'Mr—'

'*Doctor*!'

'I can assure you, Dr Hunnisett, that my staff have done everything possible—'

'In my days working in this hospital, you would have been disciplined.'

I quietly move round the side of the bed and face Mum at last. She is shaking violently.

'It is quite possible, Dr Hunnisett, that your wife can hear this and is distressed by it.'

Mum's eyes are closed tightly but I can see them moving about under the lids.

'I'm sure my wife would be as disgusted by her level of care as I am.'

I take her hand and stroke it a little to see if I can calm her convulsions. They accelerate.

'Dr Hunnisett, I understand your distress, but I am not willing to permit this abuse towards me or my staff.'

Mum lets out a couple of little gasps. I try to intervene.

'Let it go. This is upsetting her.'

'What's upsetting her is being left to slip down the bed for God knows how long. Keep out of this. You don't know what you are talking about.'

He's right, as well. I don't know what's going on here. *Can she hear us? Is she in pain? She looks like she's in pain. They wouldn't let her be in pain, would they?* I stroke her hair. It is flat and limp against her head. In her pomp, she paid a fortune each week to have it permed and primped up into the intimidating bouffant that challenged every woman in town. Even in the care home, she had it done until last year.

I can still hear my stepfather. I lose my patience.

'Look, can you leave me alone here for a bit, please?'

The medical professionals huff off together, my stepfather still arguing the toss.

It's quiet and I sit holding Mum's hand. She's still shaking but seems less agitated. There is defiance in her lips which are set against her environment – her fate – and… well, I should have visited her more. That defiance has seen me through some times. When I was six, I broke the news that Annette Bishop was on the reading book ahead of mine at school. Mum was hosting a dinner party that night for puce-faced construction allies of Dad's with their wives.

'Go to bed, I'll see you later,' she told me at 6.30 p.m. At around 10.30 p.m., she woke me up and brought me downstairs. I could hear the dinner party laughing away over her brandy snaps as she brought me into the little room off the kitchen, sat me down with a glass of milk and produced the next three reading books on the curriculum. For an hour, she had me read them out loud to her until I had them word perfect.

'That sees off Annette Bishop,' she said, hugging me and tucking me back into bed before returning to her party.

I have to tell her how much I love her.

I stroke her face.

'Mum,' her eyes tighten faster shut. 'Mum, I—'

Across the ward an elderly woman lurches out of her bed. 'You're a fucking bitch!' she spits at the senior nurse.

I persist. 'Mum, I love you so much.'

No visible response.

'Get back into bed,' the senior nurse orders.

'Mum, I'm sorry. I know I haven't…'

The elderly woman's daughter weighs in. 'Don't you talk to my mum like that, you bitch!'

I hold my mum's face in both hands.

'Mum, it's Ben. Can you hear me?' Her lips are rhythmically mashing against each other as she shakes. My hands tighten around her face.

'If you don't behave, I'll call security,' the senior nurse tells mother and daughter. The mother lumbers back into bed and the daughter shuts up.

I can't shut up.

'Mum, please.' Still she is closed to me and looks like she is raging against all of existence in defence of her own corner of it. I relax my grip, fall back on my training and sing.

'Mae bys Meri-Ann wedi brifo,
A Dafydd y gwas ddim yn iach.
Mae'r baban yn y crud yn crio,
A'r gath wedi sgramo Joni bach.
Sosban fach yn berwi ar y tân
Sosban fawr yn berwi ar y llawr,
A'r gath wedi sgramo Joni bach.
Dai bach y sowldiwr, Dai bach y sowldiwr,
Dai bach y sowldiwr, a cwt ei grys e mas.'

The one verse I can remember of her daddy's song.

'Mum, I love you,' I tell her half an inch from her face. For an instant her eyes open and the dark brown glitter emerges.

'Ugh,' she says.

I don't know – maybe that's Welsh for 'I forgive you.'

THAT'S A TRIBE, MAN

Towards the end of the second year at Wolverhampton University, I had to choose where I would go in the United States on my exchange programme. The options were New Hampshire (not far enough away); Akron, Ohio (too rusty and industrial); Flagstaff, Arizona (a contender) and Arizona State University in Tempe, Arizona. A bit of research revealed that ASU housed William S. Burroughs's literary papers and had just won *Playboy* magazine's 'Party College of the Year' title, so August 1997 found me at Gatwick airport bound for Tempe. David had, surprisingly, offered to drive me to Gatwick,* but once in the departure lounge, I was on my own with an overwhelming sense of anticipation. Nervously checking my passport every couple of minutes, my head was swirling in Jack Kerouac; Hank Williams; Muddy Waters; Lee Harvey Oswald; Lee Van Cleef; Townes Van Zandt; Thomas Paine; Rita Hayworth; Tempest Storm; Operation Desert Storm; Manifest Destiny; the right to keep and bear arms; the right to remain silent; Copland's 'Fanfare for the Common Man'; and Wendy's 'All Beef. No Bull.' cheeseburgers. I mean something good had to be at the end of this flight, right?

My first taste of America was at George Bush International Airport in Houston, Texas. After going through immigration,

---

* Refused to pick me up on the way back, mind.

I had to collect my luggage and catch another flight to Phoenix, Arizona. Around the luggage carousels, the scene seemed unsettlingly stuck in an era I had assumed had passed. Texas businessmen were hurrying around wearing the grey business suit and cowboy boots combo beloved of J. R. Ewing in *Dallas*. So far, so quaint. Around them, however, guys in baggy, white T-shirts and red baseball caps vied for business. Stooping low, they would approach the J. R.s and ask, 'Help with luggage, Sir? Help with luggage?' whilst pulling down on the peaks of their caps in deference. The ease with which the J. R.s negotiated the exaggerated servility of this entirely African-American workforce was jarring. Crocodile skin briefcases were put in one hand, dollar bills in the other, and not a word was spoken. I pressed on through the enormous airport, conscious that my next flight was leaving soon.

The pace and agility of American commerce was on display when I arrived at the gate just as it was closing and presented my ticket.

'Oh, you're here. No problem.'

A flight attendant hurried down the boarding bridge onto the plane and removed the unlucky passenger who had bought my seat in the hope that I was a no show. He was brought off, scowling, and I was on my way to Arizona.

Late afternoon in the Valley of the Sun is a unique experience. If you arrive by plane, you'll be struck by the perfect square of the Phoenix Metropolitan Area – 14,500 square miles and counting – mostly low rise because there is no shortage of space. It's ringed by desert mountains and decorated with real, imported lawns that require constant sprinkling with real, imported water that sinks into the desert, never to return. On the ground, you'll stroll through the air-conditioned swishness of Sky Harbor International Airport and into a taxi. The driver will already know you're heading for Tempe because that's where ASU is, and you look like the type. He'll gesture at the mountains turning peach in the late afternoon sun and then cruise down Rio Salado Parkway onto Mill Avenue, which, next week, he assures you, will be shoulder-to-shoulder with 'primo quality pussy'.

'Really?' I asked, as I took in the adobe bars, the GMC pickup trucks and the palm trees.

'Believe it,' he affirmed. 'When term starts and they hear that accent, they'll tear you apart. They're as dumb as you want 'em to be, too.'

I checked into the Mission Palms Hotel and tipped the porter five dollars for carrying my guitar because I was getting the hang of the place now. I had a shower and laid on the super-king-size bed watching televangelists before pulling on my boots, my new white Levis, my best silk shirt and my round-collared velvet jacket. Then, as the sun set and the mountains began to glow a deep ochre, I stuffed a hundred bucks in my pocket and headed out into an Arizona night – ready for anything.

'Fuckin' faggot!'

Silk shirts and velvet jackets, it turned out, were controversial apparel in these parts. The guys in the back of the pickup truck didn't look authentically angry, though, so I blew them a kiss as they sped by.

I was hungry and came across a bar on Mill that did burgers. It was called Islands and had a Hawaiian theme. I ordered a Maui burger with fries and a longneck Bud and settled in to enjoy the scene. Further down the bar, a guy who'd put on a Hawaiian shirt for his visit was entertaining two women by loudly explaining how he was the top guy at his workplace, which was unsurprising as he'd also been the top guy in sports when he'd been in college. He was standing up and they were sat on stools.

My burger and fries arrived and I beamed. So far, America had lived up to all my stereotypical hopes and fears for it, and this mighty slab of food was another box ticked. I ate a bit of my burger before I was politely interrupted by a calm voice.

'Hey, is that Maui burger any good? I'm thinking of getting one.'

The voice belonged to a tall, powerfully built guy with black hair to his waist and a large turquoise pendant around his neck.

'I'm liking it,' I replied.

'Hey, buddy, send me over a Maui burger – no fries, I don't have his appetite. Mind if I join you?'

'Carry on.'

He asked where I was from and what I was doing there.

'ASU? Cool, I'm a professor there.'

'Really, what do you teach?'

'Native American literature. I'm Chiricahua.' He fixed me with an intense gaze and clarified, 'That's a tribe, man.'

After a discussion about native writing and his time at Oxford, he wished me good luck. I pushed on into the night infused with the belief that I was living in a mythical dream in which everyone I met here would be extraordinary. As the bars closed for the night, I explained this to a woman finishing her drink. She was kind enough to prove me right, and America smiled hello.

ASU is home to 50,000 students and occupies a mile square campus in Tempe. Its walkways are lined with lime trees that exude a powerful fragrance just before rare bursts of desert rain. Its buildings are peach-coloured to reflect the sky at sunset, and at one corner of the campus stands the Gammage Auditorium: a circular concert venue designed by Frank Lloyd Wright. My thoughts occasionally turned to the ASU student who had swapped their expensive semester here for the dreaming spires of Wolves Uni's Dudley campus. Each to their own.

On my first day, I found that I'd been enrolled in four literature survey classes that concentrated on the established

American canon. A bit of swift negotiation allowed me to dodge the prospect of ploughing through *Moby Dick* in favour of a full slate of classes focussing on hyphenated America: African American literature, Chicano literature, ethnic literature and Native American folklore.

These sorts of ethnically defined courses didn't exist in the UK but often sat as part of wider degrees that American universities offered in African American or Transborder studies. University here seemed to be a place where identity was as important as theory, and these classes were chiefly attended by students looking to explore their own cultures. During one African American literature class, the discussion turned to personal experiences of racism. I sat in silence as the young woman next to me related how her family had moved to a white area of New Mexico when she was a child. She had come home from school during their first week there to find a thirty-foot burning cross in their garden. The press had already started to report on the rise of 'political correctness' in classes such as these but, when confronted with lived experiences such as that one, the necessity of forging a mode of language through which they could be discussed openly seemed clear to me.

The British, I have noticed, are equipped with a large armoury of painfully respectful language, but it is never related to anything we've experienced ourselves. So, we can perform streams of Kipling-and-Owen-influenced rhetoric in tribute to historical events but sometimes have absolutely no words for our bereaved friends at funerals. Mostly, we shuffle along wordlessly, hoping that our awkwardness will serve as evidence that we empathise. Put us in front of the telly when *The World at War* is on, and you can't shut us up. It is as if all our finer feelings must be reserved for anniversaries long after the things they commemorate.

The ease with which many Americans seem to discuss their feelings provoked envy in me, something I safely disguised as sarcastic contempt. Amongst ourselves, the British contingent scoffed at the earnest way they took emotions so seriously and related such personal stories to each other. It seemed gauche and unsophisticated when, in truth, they were processing what we could not.

All of this came into sharp focus one night in late August. The Wolverhampton students who had opted to go to Flagstaff came down to visit us at ASU for the weekend. We all went out to an Egyptian restaurant, expecting to carry on around the bars and clubs afterwards. We were a voluble lot and I suppose our accents must have been noticeable because, towards the end of the meal, the lady who owned the restaurant approached us in a nervous fashion.

'Excuse me, are you British?' she asked in a Middle Eastern accent. We confirmed that we were, and she stood to attention.

'I am very sorry to inform you that Her Royal Highness The Princess of Wales has passed away.'

'What the fuck?' we all gasped, and she went on to explain about the crash in Paris. We asked to pay the bill so that we could go over to a bar and see what was unfolding on television. As we were paying, her husband joined her and, equally formally, announced, 'I would like to say that, although we are Egyptian, we despise the Fayed family.' His wife nodded in agreement.

At the bar over the road, we busily fed quarters into payphones so that we could wake up our mothers with the news. The television sets had commentary over a picture of Diana with 'RIP' and her birth date and today's date – so it must be true. We fell back on our culture and drank heavily as a mark of respect.

The next few weeks were quite surreal. Every single American who spoke to me about it was unwavering in their belief that Charles had bumped her off. That was a given. Tower Records opened at midnight so that people could queue to buy a copy of Elton John's ghastly tribute record. It was a big story. But America processed it and then moved on.

Back home, meanwhile, people seemed to be struggling. My mate Brian rang me daily to describe what was going on.

'Everyone's gone round the twist, Ben. I went into Stourbridge today and there were about twenty people just standing at the war memorial for no reason at all. There's a book of remembrance in Tesco – fucking Tesco!'

The Wolves contingent watched the funeral together on television. Not only were we eight hours behind and watching the future, but it was a Britain we struggled to recognise. People were filmed losing the run of themselves altogether – wailing and so on.

At one point, in the preceding week, anger had seemed to be mounting over the queen's phlegmatic response to events, and my Marxist heart thrilled briefly at the notion that the flag-waving shriekers might piece together the symbiotic relationship between the fate of poor, bulimic Diana and their own collective abuse at the hands of the Establishment. Her Maj, however, pulled off a last-minute show of performative empathy and the revolution was postponed yet again.

Looking at it from the blazing sunshine of Arizona, I was struck by how childish it all seemed and how fragile the emotional state of the nation was. A monarchy demands that its subjects live vicariously through it and invest their hopes and fears in it. If they don't, how could it sustain itself? Every 'mustn't-make-a-fuss' suppression of personal grief that we'd all been encouraged to make when it came to our own losses found expression in this poorly scripted end to a fairy tale.

On a liquor store across town in Phoenix, there was a sign marking a hard week for everyone: 'RIP Princess Diana and Mother Teresa. Cold Beer To Go.'

MYFANWY

I'm forty-four and stuck up a Powys mountain at the dog-end of love. Our four years have been the filmic, irrational symphony for which I've always believed myself destined. Now that the timpani has died away, a resigned calm has set in as we start to ready ourselves for the necessary trauma of severance.

Eve is painting away happily, so I broach the subject.

'The Pendyrus Choir are singing at the chapel in town tonight. Fancy it?' She carries on putting the gleam into a pine marten's pupil.

'That one from [insert name of Powys town that isn't Newtown] was absolute shit,' she says. 'You said it was as if Vic Reeves had been cloned forty times and locked in Treowen Community Centre with Linda McCartney on piano.'

'No, this is the *Pendyrus*, from Tylorstown in the Rhondda – where we visited. They are *the only musical ensemble in the world to have performed at both the White House and the Kremlin*,' I quote directly and solemnly from Wikipedia.

'Kay,' she breezes, holding an empty coffee cup back towards me. Reasonable mood.

Driving down from Tylwch to the chapel in Llanidloes is a tense affair. Eve is incongruously glamorous in the passenger seat of my knackered Polo but consciously so: satin dress, red tresses, green eyes. Beautiful people can seem cruel. They have to be; how else would they ever get rid of us?

Myfanwy

We park outside the China Street Chapel, right where they put the black traffic cones for the funerals that the town is so enthusiastically fond of. The chapel towers at you from the pavement: fierce columns, solemn ironwork and inscriptions on tablets with fervent dates. There are around a dozen chapels in and around little Llani, and I often wonder what they were like during the revivals of the nineteenth century. These chapels must have been bear pits of tumult, raging against the Establishment and each other in competition for the souls of Wales. Their stone, oblong faces are set like resolute jaws, daring passers-by to defy them, dwarfing pubs and taunting the Church.

An old boy in a choir blazer is sat on the wall catching a breather and having a fag.

'I'm looking forward to the concert,' I say, rolling one myself.

'Last time we were here was 1956,' he replies. 'I was a kid myself.' His accent feels like a childhood blanket. The melodious precision of Rhondda vowels is unique and as far from the Powys accent as Scouse or Mancunian.

I do the mental arithmetic. Grandad left in the 1930s so he wouldn't have known him. Still... 'My family's from Tylorstown,' I announce. 'My uncle, Trevor Morgan was headmaster of the school there... perhaps...' On I go. I can't help myself – like one of those Americans who, on discovering you are British, asks if you have met their niece who is studying at the University of Huddersfield.

The old chorister negotiates me kindly.

'The name sounds familiar,' he offers, unconvincingly.

'You can hear the musicality in his speaking voice, can't you?' I whisper urgently to Eve as we go through the chapel gate.

'Whatever,' she replies.

The quality of the Rhondda accent was instilled into me as immutable fact and the reason that the Pendyrus and

Treorchy choirs were the best in the world – in that order. Whilst it's true that male voice choral music was not centred in the 1982 zeitgeist for many nine-year-olds, I'm sure that it would have been, had they known about it. The first cassette my grandfather gave me was a compilation of choirs from across Wales. Along with ersatz favourites like 'We'll Keep A Welcome In The Hillside', I was introduced to the mighty minor key hymns 'Tydi a Roddaist' and 'Laudamus'. Both of these feature dramatic shifts of dynamic where the choristers start by menacing in the bass register, before building to full throated crescendos that the tenors cut through like clashing pipe organ chords or buglers in battle. It is fierce music that points accusatory fingers at hypocrites, mine owners, landlords, police, Maggie bloody Thatcher and anyone else threatening the culture from which it sprang. It's physically demanding to sing and emotionally exacting to engage with. It is the Death Metal of its time.

We pick up a programme in the foyer of the chapel and hurry in to find seats. It's otherworldly in there. The chapel has rows of polished oak pews in a main bank facing towards the lectern, with five rows at each side facing inwards opposite each other. No incense. No candlewax. A balcony sweeps out above us and the pews up there await the choir, who will face each other across the room.

The pews are already full of everyone I don't know in town. My familiar faces are gin blossomed, bearded, braided and down the pub. These here are the scrubbed initiates of deep Llani: shop owners whose sisters have keys to the community centre and Rotarians who know where the bodies are buried. A practised hum floats across the sold-out audience and I shoot Eve a sour look.

'Where are we going to sit?'

She is pretending to ignore the snatched glances of respectable men who clearly appreciate the time she took getting dressed. Focussing, she scans the room sharply, like the red kites she paints. Goneril.

'Over there!'

It's true. There are two seats left on the right-hand side under the balcony facing inwards. We make our way there in silence as I note that I won't even *see* one half of the choir who will be singing from the pews directly above my head. You can have enough of this shit, I can tell you, being late to everything all the time and fending off simpering blokes who would run a mile if they knew what actually being with her took. Fair play though, she would have told you that herself.

I look at the programme and find that the first half is what I'm here for: a couple of ambitious classical pieces and an old African American spiritual are to be followed by a suite of Welsh songs. Feeling a bit guilty about my frostiness, I nudge Eve and point it out. Her tastes run more to the psychedelic, but she remembers the dramatic heft of 'Tydi A Roddaist' from my YouTube-assisted lessons on Welsh culture and nods approvingly.

The second half of the programme looks boring. Here is another example of Wales failing to live up to its doppelgänger that lives in my imagination. Despite ongoing efforts to reach them, my Welsh-born contemporaries seem no more enthusiastic about choral concerts than their English counterparts. The chapel, though, is heady with Estée Lauder's Youth Dew and excited by the promise of an extended medley of 'Songs From The Shows' after a nice cup of tea and a macaroon during the interval. I envision them whipped up in Methodist fervour and pouring out into the streets to vent centuries of rage in a reprise of the Chartist riots, but it isn't going to be that kind of night. Pity.

However, the choir itself, from what I can see of them, contains a handful of members who are my age and younger. As the audience settles down, I watch the young tenors in their blazers, surrounded by older men. One has long hair tied in a ponytail. He is smiling and joking with the septuagenarian next to him and I feel a pang of something – envy, probably. A senior chorister rises to introduce the choir and describe its history.

'To the people of Rhondda Fach,' he explains, 'male voice choir singing comes as naturally as tax evasion'. Pausing to allow laughter to scatter nervously around the pews, his eyes narrow and his chest expands as he sweeps an arm around the choir: 'This… is Pendyrus!'

They rise in concert and breathe into their first note. I watch the perfectly synchronised lips of the tenors opposite on the balcony, their eyes fixed on the choirmaster who conducts, cajoles and restrains his charges with the graceful animation of a lion tamer. Directly above me, the baritones and basses rumble with melancholic menace, and I feel my hamstrings tighten.

The first two songs are the classical pieces: serious music to demonstrate the choir's technique. After a break of decades, Pendyrus has recently returned to the competition scene, immediately trouncing all comers at the semi-National Eisteddfod. In the 1920s, choir competitions proliferated and were followed with the same parochial zeal as rugby in the Valleys. Pontypridd was the grudge match and usually settled long after the judging when the respective choristers would discuss their merits, frankly, outside the pub.

The choir are drilled to perfection. The posture, the breath control, the unswerving focus and cohesion of the choir speaks of hard rehearsal time in Rhondda Fach Sports Centre on Mondays and Wednesdays.

Presently, a lone microphone on a stand is produced and a white-haired, round man steps forward. His fellow tenors pat him on the back as he moves through the ranks. Every inch a self-effacing star, he quietly positions himself about a yard behind the microphone. His eyes dart around the microphone before his first line. The next song is a spiritual: 'Lily of the Valley'. Welsh choirs have long favoured these pieces for concert performance. When Grandad conducted the choir at the school he taught at in Birmingham on television – *television,* mind – he chose another African-American song: 'Steal Away'. The cultural fraternity between the Valleys and Black America is personified by Paul Robeson who stood with the miners during the 1926 strike and later observed, 'Wales, you know, is a part of England[*] where I first understood the struggle of white and Negro together. When I went down into the coal mines, into the Rhondda Valley – went down to the mines with these workers and lived among them – later did a picture, as you know, called "Proud Valley" – and I became so close that, in Wales today, as I feel here now, they feel me a part of that land.'

'Lily of the Valley' is a call and response song, similar in structure to work songs in which a solo singer puts out a line and the choir respond to it. The choir strike up with the refrain:

'He's the lily of the valley, oh my Lord!'

It is sung quietly, by eighty men with mighty voices in harness. The soloist, I notice, sings along as if vibing himself up. He is a conspicuously diffident man and obviously uncomfortable with the spotlight that has been shone upon his talent. Every written version of the lyric concludes with an exclamation mark, and he delivers it perfectly but with aching restraint.

'King Jesus in his chariot rides!'

Still the choir hold themselves back. The conductor makes frantic, suppressing motions with his hands and threatens them with his eyes. To do this, he has to pivot on his platform

---

[*] Ferchrissakes, Paul! Alright, carry on. You're forgiven, just this once.

and exhort tenors one side, then basses and baritones the other. It is the look your mother flashes you when you are five and about to tell an approaching aunt that she is fat. They comply.

'Oh my Lord...!'

The chapel is strung out on tension. It is as if we are being tuned up across a Stradivarius. The soloist leans into his microphone again.

'With four white horses side by side!'

This time, the conductor just smiles, he has them where he wants them. The choir drops almost to a whisper.

'Oh my Lord.'

It feels like all my constituent parts have been assembled into a performance and made to dance in front of me: a ballet of music, socialism and Ancestry.com. Who knows what all the pensioners in the audience are thinking about. Macaroons? Brexit? Maybe some of the choristers are distracted by gas bills or intrusive sexual fantasies. Perhaps the chapel itself is considering a sudden collapse at the shock at this recreation of former glories. God knows it is empty the rest of the year. Still, never mind. For me, it is something else.

The pay-off is glorious. All that restraint bursts out of the responding lines with abandon before ratcheting back down into grace.

Soloist: 'What kind of shoes are those you wear?'
Choir: 'Oh my Lord.'
Soloist: 'That you can ride up in the air.'
Choir: 'Oh my Lord.'
Soloist: 'These shoes I wear are Gospel shoes.'
Choir: 'OH MY LORD!'
Soloist: 'And You can wear them if you choose.'
Choir: 'Oh my Lord.'

The piece finishes, the soloist retreats back to his place and the microphone is discreetly removed. I issue Paddington Bear's hardest stare at Eve to alert her that the main event is on. 'Tydi a Roddaist' is next in the programme and, if she loves me, and she said she did as recently as two months ago, then this must be important to her, too. This is not a time to be wondering if colloidal silver is the key to eternal life or if dinosaurs left us clues to solve climate change. No, this moment now is about me and the elaborately sacred identity I have constructed for myself. *You owe me this, Eve, and you know it.* She smiles weakly.

I'm in Wales – actual Wales – in a *chapel*, and the Pendyrus are about to sing the hymn I've nailed myself to since the age of eight. I live in a cottage on a mountain with an artist girlfriend who stops the hearts of bats with her eyes so she can paint them. Her mother bought me a floppy fedora hat with a feather in it last Christmas. Take it away, boys, take it away.

It's a mug's game trying to describe music once it really hits you. If your legs are gone, you can't be expected to memorise much of it technically.

It's loud.

It's doomy.

The basses above me grind like cogs in an abattoir.

The tenors opposite caw and keen like corpse-eating birds over our mountain.

The conductor snarls when he wants something.

It intensifies like mob violence.

God is definitely present, cackling along.

There is an uncomfortable silence when it stops: people cough when they don't need to. The tenors smirk: they know what they have done. We can take no more. Then one piano chord rings, and they pull themselves back out of demonic possession to stroke our hearts, velvet-like with 'Myfanwy'.

Paham mae dicter, O Myfanwy,
Yn llenwi'th lygaid duon di?

(Why is it anger, O Myfanwy,
That fills your eyes so dark and clear?)

The harmony is close, with the baritones at the top of their range. I imagine them above me staring at the tenors, who are about to close their eyes and soar into a white oblivion where nothing is certain. The last few notes of this song are for the precarious summit of the broken, male voice.

*A rho dy law, Myfanwy dirion
I ddim ond dweud y gair 'Ffarwel'.*

(Give me your hand, my sweet Myfanwy,
But one last time, to say 'Farewell'.)

I can feel Eve next to me: her breath, her warmth, her fugitive soul stilled for a moment.

On YouTube, there is a video of this song taken by somebody on the balcony using their phone. On the right-hand side, at the front, you can make out a couple holding hands for the last time.

INDOOR PLAYTIME

I'm thirty-seven and stood on the bridge over Lye railway station, waiting for a hug.

My on-off girlfriend, Dawn, pulls up and jumps out of the car. 'You'll be alright; it'll be fine.'

'You'll look after the shop while I'm away?'

'When I can.'

She's put up with a lot.

'I'd best get the train, then.'

I'm on my way to Hull, and I'm very, very frightened. After the last of five detoxes, administered by friends who cared more for me than I did myself, I'm trying something drastic to try to end the cycle of addiction. I've got a CD that I've burned with my most significant songs: the Pendyrus doing 'Cwm Rhondda', the Everlys, The Pogues, John Prine…

I figure that if I lose myself altogether in this treatment, these might bring me back, like those celebrities who record messages for comatose fans. It's a lonely thought to take on to the train. This is a lonely business.

Tabernanthe iboga is a tree bark from Africa that is used in Bwiti spiritual ceremonies by tribal peoples in Gabon and Cameroon. If ingested in large quantities, it provokes a near-death experience and, according to medical authorities in countries where it is prohibited, an actual-death experience for around one in three hundred users. It's also supposed to reverse addictive thought patterns and 'reset' the brain. All aboard!

It's a four-hour journey, and I've got much to ponder on. I'm thirty-seven and seem to be out of options. Each bright new start has brought diminishing returns, as jobs, bedsits, relationships, health and fatherhood have become subordinate to drinking. My girlfriend pities me, on a good day, whilst propping up our bookshop with money from her difficult job. I wear rags. I wear rags because they suit me. I don't shave. When I perform music, it's sloppy and disrespectful. I've had 'six months' to live for years according to doctors and, mostly, it seems like six months too many. I wear rags.

On a Sunday, when I was little, I'd sit at the dining table, holding the correct knife, and Mum would pour me a glass of watered-down wine.

'The French do it like this. They are so much more sensible about alcohol.'

I agreed with her. I was a *grown-up* little boy. I behaved myself and was a credit to her. If drinking this odd stuff meant I was adding a layer of sophistication, then why not? It was alright.

Until it wasn't.

I received my first lesson about the awesome power of alcohol at a neighbourhood wedding reception in a Chinese restaurant. A Lebanese family lived next door but one to Mum, Dad and I, and were by far the most interesting feature of life there. They had homes in Beirut and Sierra Leone, where Hamad worked as a lawyer for the President. Their hospitality was ostentatious and jarring in the buttoned-down, encroach-a-millimetre-onto-my-lawn-and-I'll-sue environs of West Midlands suburbia. At least three times a week, A'Ishatu, a servant from Guinea who worked for them, would knock the door with Tupperware boxes of hummus and shawarma for us.

'From the mistress...' she would say, smiling.

Twice a year, they would invite the whole road for a meal in the Shirley Temple Chinese restaurant. Hamad, who had been expensively educated in London, would wave away the menus, give £50 to the waiter and say, 'Tell the chef to bring the best.' Fifty or so people, some of whom he barely knew, would soon be smeared in lobster and belching Moet bubbles.

His daughter Amira's wedding reception was the same, with extra-lavish, no-expense-spared bacchanalia assured. Eleven at the time, I was seated on a table with the other kids. As the evening went on, the adults got blasted. Hamad, whose devotion to Islam was fierce but selective, gave a speech that was so derogatory to his new son-in-law that it had to be cut out of the official video. Nobody was taking much notice of us kids.

The waiters seemed happy to bring anybody whatever they wanted.

'Can I have a sherry, please?'

The waiter returned with a bottle and left it, as he did with the whisky, brandy and gin I asked for later.

I had to be taken home. The couple next door were leaving early to relieve their babysitter, so they looked after me while I puked and cried myself dry. The party carried on.

I'd forgotten that night by the time I was fifteen, though. With David and Mum absent, the long nights in an empty house undid me.

After David left to be with Jakki, Mum had spent a few weeks in near-breakdown, hysterical one moment and euphoric the next. To put the top hat on it, her ill-natured whippet, James, had chosen that time in her life to succumb to a heart attack whilst stealing a tissue out of a handbag. He'd reared up on his hind legs and careered over to Mum so that he could die on her lap, the little sod.

One afternoon, she had taken to her bed when the phone rang. Our kindly GP wanted to take her for dinner. I was sat on the bed when she took this call and can still see her look of astonishment. Within a couple of weeks, he had taken her to

New York, and then India, China, Malaysia… She began to spend nights away at his flat and, before long, she was living there. Food would be dropped off for me, and they'd take me out to restaurants regularly. The big, four-bedroomed house that had been constructed for Mum and David and me was mine whilst they argued over it in court. I rattled around it in adolescent confusion whilst everyone moved on.

In the cabinet were two bottles of Chivas Regal whisky, and I found that a nip or two of that stopped the swirling in my head. A nip before school also made it easier to face my disappointed teachers. A nip was a friend.

So, when we all started hitting the pubs, as fifteen-year-olds do, I had some tolerance built up already. Teenagers roam in packs, and I was a straggler, rarely invited but not unwelcome. Drinking helped my social situation no end. I was good at it, conspicuously good.

Of all the places, people and things I've clung onto in a bid to project an identity of my own, alcohol held me the tightest. It offered freedom from awkwardness, a sense of doomed-youth romance, faux-masculinity when required and oblivion when life became too much. It was something to recognise me by – a party-piece point of difference that was more socially acceptable than the empty, restless ache of mourning and abandonment that drove me to turn to it. I was a hard-drinking, guitar playing rake and not a terrified, lonely child whose family had either died or gone away.

I'm skipping the reminiscences of wild times. They were routine for decades, as boring in the telling as they were in the living. Living in a sensory straitjacket, you can feel very little and judge even less. It is a discount version of life. A girlfriend once observed that having sex when you're drunk is like doing it in black and white. Joys don't fully imprint on you, miseries are filed under the wrong headings and ascribed to innocent parties. *I* felt myself to be unaccountable for the hurt *I* caused other people because – well, look at me – I'm a shambles, so nothing I do matters.

After a particularly long night when I was sixteen, we all assembled at the Old Wharf pub in Digbeth for no reason other than we were cohered and had no reason to separate. I felt all kinds of dreadful, my stomach and head trying to parent me the best they could. Everyone was groaning in the good-natured camaraderie of self-inflicted misery that accompanies snatches of memory and little bottles of Britvic orange juice to wash down the paracetamol. I managed to smile and take the plaudits for once again winning the drinking.

Something had changed for me, though. Along with the hangover, I could feel dread. I looked at my hands, and their usual slight tremor had intensified so that I couldn't still them with will alone. I ordered a pint. I had to hold it with two hands to keep it in the glass, but once it went down, all that floated away. It was fine.

In that gulp, I sold my wellbeing to the licensing trade. The first yelps of physical addiction had sounded, and I'd begun the cycle of ill–drunk–ill that bites away a larger piece of Hemingway's marlin with every revolution.

I was still living by myself at seventeen when Mum remarried. On a Friday, I gave her away at the ceremony and delivered a speech at the reception wearing a grey, double-breasted suit that I'd been issued for the occasion.

After she'd left with her husband for their honeymoon, I was sat around drinking leftover champagne at the venue with twenty quid in my pocket for a taxi home. Then I was offered a lift. Rob and Jane were there as guests of Mum's new husband, but I knew them as the aunt and uncle of Liz, a sometime girlfriend from the school next door to ours. Hard-drinking and outrageous, Rob was a sentimental old-school bloke who, despite the drinking problem, remained a producer at the BBC in Birmingham. Jane was arachnoid with a mass of untamed black hair and expressive, emaciated limbs. She had a snorting laugh and six black cats. They were childless and liked the company of younger folks. They would pour you a stiff drink and crash the fags if Liz took you round.

'How are you getting home, old boy?' Rob enquired. He wouldn't hear of my getting a taxi so we crammed into their little car and Rob weaved erratically through Solihull until we reached the house at around one in the morning.

'Good God. You don't live in here by yourself, do you?'

'Yep,' I shrugged, as they gawped at the huge, four-bedroomed suburban echo chamber. They invited themselves in, which was a bit awkward. The place was a tip. I had a foot-diameter terracotta plant pot serving as an ashtray. It was overflowing on to the Axminster where there were enough empty beer cans to manufacture an Austin Metro. Rob and Jane sat down on the leather sofa in disbelief.

'You mean to say they've just left you here?' Rob demanded, surveying the detritus. 'How long have you been on your own?'

'About eighteen months.'

Glances were being exchanged and I began to feel uneasy.

'I'm sorry, we can't have this,' Rob announced, looking at Jane. 'Can we?'

'Certainly not!' Jane confirmed. 'You're coming back with us.'

'I'm fine. Don't worry about me. I like it here.'

Rob stood up and grabbed my arm.

'No. You're coming with us.'

I was escorted, or bundled, back into the Renault 4 and taken back to their Bohemian pad near the BBC in Stirchley. There, Rob insisted that the arrangement would be permanent.

'You can live with us. I'm not having you rattling round that place on your own at your age. It's a disgrace!'

The next couple of days were a kaleidoscope of brandy and insanity. Grand plans would be hatched, Rob and Jane would occasionally ignite into drunken fury with each other, and sleep would be snatched sitting up before it was time for another snifter. Periodically, I'd be dispatched to the corner shop for more cigarettes. We didn't eat anything at all, but the cats were fed royally. The crescendo arrived on Sunday night when Rob fetched his Royal Marines beret and donned it whilst Rod Stewart's 'Sailing' blasted from the stereo. Standing upright, he saluted with tears running down his cheeks as he recalled 'that fucking great ship, the Ark Royal.' He passed out immediately after Rod finished singing. I followed suit.

By Monday morning, a hungover sense of reality had seeped into proceedings. They were still *extremely* unhappy about my living arrangements, but, having thought things through, perhaps it was *impractical* for me to live with them on a permanent basis. I was delivered home in the Renault 4 and never saw them again.

If you had asked me at the time what I thought of the way I was living, I'd have told you I had it made. I had freedom, a bit of pocket money and nobody to tell me what to do. The callousness of David's role in recent events had settled as a narrative within me. I was comfortable with blaming him for any emotional difficulties I was facing. He hadn't left me all on my own, though; that had been Mum. The story didn't allow for that to be something bad. I was fine. Fine.

It took eleven years of committed drinking to reach the next port on the voyage. By the time I was twenty, I could do anything I needed drunk. I didn't do any of it very well but could turn in passable facsimiles of work and love in combination – enough to keep me in shelter and nurture.

At twenty-seven, I was working at Waterstones bookshop in the now-enormous Merry Hill shopping centre near Dudley. The promise of the Back to Basics job club had finally become manifest. The delivery drivers would arrive throughout the day in the loading bay underneath the shops and call me in the goods-in room. I'd assemble as many roll cages as they estimated I'd need and go down in the lift to fetch the boxes of books. The morning before one of the *Harry Potter* volumes went on sale, I shifted three hundred boxes.

The routine was good for me, though. I'd ditched my only strand of stability by breaking up with Dawn in favour of a riotous nineteen-year-old Londoner I'd met while playing music in a pub. Jenny was *fun*: argumentative, playful and reckless. She wasn't worried about me, didn't bug me to rein it in and always thought it was a good idea to open a bottle or spark-up another one. I'd go to work at seven, after a couple of hours to sleep off the wine and dope we'd get through every night. Carting those boxes around sweated it all out, and she'd still be in bed when I got home.

'I hope you've brought some wine back!'

I was taking up some empty roll cages one morning when the goods lift stopped abruptly. It bounced slightly before coming to rest between floors and something happened to me. My centre of gravity seemed to remain suspended at the height where the lift had jolted; the rest of me was a couple of inches lower, where it had settled. Recovering myself, I pressed the alarm and heard it echoing up the shaft.

Being trapped in a lift on your own is a monastic experience. I put my hands against the dimpled aluminium walls of the square box that would be home for as long as it took, and wondered how anybody could bear my company. The white, artificial light in there wasn't entering into any negotiations, so fears that I had gathered in the dark had their moment under my own, private sun. Stuck between the floors of a concrete temple to retail* and lit up in my fragility, a vulnerability settled

---

* Without a book, ironically.

on me. My adult life had been an evasion: show to show, girl to girl, drink to drink. I had kept moving, outrunning the suspicion that I was stood on quicksand and apt to disappear if I took a breath.

When, finally, the maintenance crew winched the lift up to the first floor and let me out, I stepped on to solid ground and noticed something peculiar. I couldn't feel the floor beneath me and still seemed to be suspended above it. I was walking around as usual but had no sense of my weight.

'Christ, you need a drink!' Jenny correctly prescribed when I arrived home with the tale.

The next morning was a trial from the off. Walking to the bus stop, I was aware of the hangover to come. If you drink enough, it saves itself until you are ready to appreciate its majesty.

I still couldn't feel my feet beneath me. It was as if my perception was still in the lift, suspended. The feeling carried on all morning. I floated around collecting the smaller deliveries and inputting them into the system as my stomach started to roil. When the articulated lorry arrived with the main load, I was sweating before I even lifted a box. The delivery would mean two trips up in the lift with five cages each time. I didn't mind the lift; it had done its worst. I wasn't right at all, though.

Up in the stock room, fight-or-flight chemicals were bubbling away in my solar plexus to the point that I was rubbing my tummy to try to relieve the discomfort. As I unpacked the boxes, I found my thoughts racing ahead of what I needed to do. I had to input books twice to rectify mistakes. It seemed hot in my windowless room. The artificial light wasn't white in there, as it had been in the lift, but yellow like school on a rainy day. *You can't go out to play, so draw a picture.*

The green lettering on my ancient computer flickered as I tried to type the order numbers from invoices. It was so stuffy in there. I found it hard to breathe.

No wonder this place has a chaplain.

The boxes were stacked up around me, higher than my head. Radio 5 was playing in the background: something about fiscal responsibility.

Fiscal, fiscal, fiscal.

My stomach was on fire. An entire crisis seemed to be happening down there.

I steadied my hands and tried to type in an invoice number. C5076401. C5074601. *No, ferchrissakes…* C50747601. *At last. Maintain fiscal discipline, Benjamin.*

I couldn't drink my tea. Couldn't have held it down. *Why's it so fucking hot? Ok, try another one.* C5287234…

The flames in my stomach started to lick further up towards my chest so I forced them down, away from my heart. *What the fuck's happening?* I could hear my pulse banging through my ears and started pressing my fingers into my neck to slow it down. My left arm went numb and the flames broke through. I cried out as pain engulfed my chest and took over from my thoughts. Running on to the shop floor, I gasped, 'Heart attack,' to the gentle assistant manager, Andrew, and fell on the floor of the philosophy section.

It was good the lift had been repaired, as the paramedics were saved from carting me down the steps where I threw all my fag ends. Hooked up to all the bleepy stuff in the ambulance, the end was clearly nigh. The grand, romantic arc of this tragic youth would close before he could create his masterpiece. A foundling strung tautly at birth across the vicissitudes of providence, his potential would live in the hearts of those he touched—

'You'll be alright, son. It's a panic attack, trust me. I've been doing this forty years. So, let's get you to the hospital and have you checked over. You're going to be fine.'

'Oh.'

'Do you want us to call someone for you?'

'Yes, please.'
'Who is it?'
'Dawn.'

After a few hours of shaking and crying in a cubicle, a nurse arrived with a big, black pill. Heminevrin is a blunt, old-style sedative that's used to treat alcohol withdrawal. People call it alcohol in a pill. Despite all the evidence, I hadn't made the connection between my drinking and what was happening to me, so I was shocked.

'I just like a drink,' I protested.

It kicked in after about twenty minutes and I felt fantastic. The relief of fear is euphoric and common to all addictions. No consequence, however dire, can be imagined so vividly that it competes with the rush of mortality leaving your system as the poison kicks in. Being in withdrawal is to be locked in a cage with a lion. You've got a key, but they are telling you to stay in there until Simba goes to sleep. Well, fuck that, thank you very much.

Dawn dropped me home, kind and without judgement, before returning to work.

'Fuckin' hell darling, what's happened to you?' Jenny enquired.

I recounted the day's events, half spaced-out and half full of importance. 'It was a very serious incident…'

'You're not giving up, are you?'

I saw genuine fear in her when she said that. She shouldn't have worried.

I'd had, I decided, 'a funny turn'. Yes, I'd been overdoing it with the drink, so this was my warning to cut down a bit. I liked to have lots of drinks, so rather than cutting down the frequency, I diluted them. I'd have shandy, then alternate shandy with a proper pint, then…

Within a couple of weeks, I was back to where I started, except something had permanently altered in my body's response. The sweating, headache and nausea that we all recognise after too much alcohol was joined by the ghost of the panic attack I'd had at work. It seemed always to be there, awaiting its next chance to overwhelm me. A burning terror at the top of my stomach would have me clawing at it, pushing the flesh around to try to dissipate its effect. It was fear in search of a reason and, as it intensified, I started to fabricate reasons according to my circumstances. *I've got an ulcer that's about to burst…*

Once my mind was fully engaged with the issue, the rest of me would follow suit. As I carted boxes around at work, my heart rate would accelerate, informing me that it was in trouble. Accordingly, I'd produce stress chemicals to wash around my ragged, booze-lacerated stomach, and I'd scratch at it more urgently, sometimes punching it in the hope of replacing the sensation temporarily with a more bearable type of pain.

Eventually, one day, I broke. I was on my way up the fag-strewn steps from the loading bay and each step seemed to send my heart faster and faster. Jabbing my fingers into my neck, my pulse seemed to be vibrating rather than beating and I froze. Blood rushed to my extremities, leaving a hollow – a weakness where my sense of self usually was. If I took one more step upwards, my heart would explode; I was certain of it. After five minutes stranded, placing and withdrawing my foot on the next step, I surrendered. Abandoning hope, I decided to run at the lion and let it put me out of my misery. I could see the door to the back of the shop at the top of the stairs and launched towards it, crashing through and straight into the manager's office where Andrew, who was inputting data, swivelled round in alarm.

'I've got to go. I'm not well,' I managed.

'It's peak time, Ben. And there must be 300 boxes to do in your room.'

Indoor playtime

I was *done*, I couldn't manage an explanation and burst into tears. 'I *can't*.'

Andrew softened out of managerial mode and looked empathetically at me. 'Of course. Yes, go home, Ben.'

I rushed into the goods-in room and used the phone.

'Dawn, I need you. Please pick me up. No, not the shop. Meet me in the Robin. Thank you. Sorry.'

The Robin Hood was up on the main road, so I half-ran through the shopping centre's endless car parks and past the disused monorail that had once heralded the region's emergence into a post-industrial future. In happier days, I'd played music in the Robin, supporting Eric Bibb as well as the Strawbs – pitifully, it still says this on my musical publicity material. I'd even headlined a couple of times. It was a place of excitement. Now, I was in the bar at midday, and it was a functional space, somewhere that people who need alcohol at midday go. I ordered a pint and a scotch, draining them whilst stood at the bar before asking for the same again. As I returned to myself and the lion slunk away, I took stock. *This can't go on.* With a mountain of evidence casting a shadow at my back, I consulted the only counsel I ever truly listened to. The beer and the whisky didn't hesitate to answer.

You should chuck in this job. It's making you ill.

The obvious plan, of course, was to get more gigs and make a proper living from music. I'd been paid for playing music as soon as I started. At fifteen, on a pub crawl around Birmingham, I'd got talking to the landlord in a corner bar called The Gothic. I saw the posters up on the wall for singers and told him I could do a night of country music for him. He was amused, being well aware of my age, and asked me what my stage name was.

'The Lone Star' I improvised.

'Oh, right!' says he. 'And what financial remuneration does a 'lone star' command nowadays?'

'Thirty quid.'

He smiled.

'And my drinks.'

'Done! I'll see you a week on Saturday. Make sure to put on a good show. They'll let you know if you don't,' he warned, gesturing to the characters at the bar who were several pints in at teatime. I stuck my head in later in the week, and there was a poster on the wall advertising my show. 'The Lone Star – Country & Western, Rock 'n' Roll, Irish! The Gothic welcomes the debut of a future showbusiness legend!'

From the moment I saw that poster, I was a 'professional musician'. Every time I got paid, I became surer that this was all I needed to do. If I could just get four gigs a week, it would be the same as a working wage. It was obvious! This sort of thinking, as any mother will tell you – especially mine – is calamitous. No matter what job I was doing – bank clerk, estate agent, laundry worker, part-time lecturer – if you asked me, I was a 'professional musician'. Even when I had my own bookshop, named after Grandad and beloved by many, I still couldn't fully inhabit the role. All my efforts were half-arsed, in other words, because my guitar made up most of my personality.

Set up in the corner of The Gothic, I had my first Saturday night crowd to negotiate. People have a right to be demanding at the weekends. They've put in the work over the week and are left with two nights to wipe away the sweat and dress up. If you're out of time or playing stuff they don't like, you're stealing pleasure from them – the little pleasure they have.

After bashing out every song I knew over two forty-five-minute sets, I'd gone over well enough to win an encore.

'Do "Blanket On The Shelf",' a woman shouted.

'Sorry, I haven't heard of it.'

'Course you have. The one about being married and the moonlight…' She started to sing, swaying as she held on to her big, kindly looking fella.

I obliged with 'Blanket On The Ground' before accepting my sixth pint of Guinness.

My hangover the next day was intense. I had to borrow a Distalgesic to kill it, but I had money in my pocket and a family-sized dose of validation. The line from there to quitting school was direct and short.

The trouble with my plan was that I wasn't quite good enough to make a full-time living. There was always enough work to keep me in fags and tins of beans but never enough to sustain independent living. I didn't see it that way, though. More often than not, shows would end with cheering and offers of drinks that ensured that my faith never wavered. I could live with next to nothing as long as I was *told* I was good enough.

By the time I eventually left Waterstones, nearly fifteen years on, I'd begun to entertain the idea that I was deluding myself. It was the most private of thoughts and off limits to absolutely everyone. I still wrote 'professional musician' on my dole application and lorded it over open mic nights as if I were an enviable member of a musical Brahmin caste. My hangovers transmogrified into spiritual trials as I approached thirty. Then, either by fear, despondency or encroaching age, I suddenly couldn't ignore it. *I'm not good enough at this to live by it.* Audiences, in the moment, on a sweaty Saturday night, have goodwill to spare if you've given them what they want to hear. They might have danced to 'Blue Suede Shoes' or cried to 'My Elusive Dreams'. They might tell you that you're the best they've seen in that pub; that you should have a recording contract. They might buy you a drink or even take you home for the night. On Sunday morning, though, it's a different world, and the shaky vocals on the tape they bought from you don't have that elusive quality that can turn anything into Saturday night. I've seen quite a few of mine in charity shops over the years, and I always buy them because the kid on the front wasn't all bad.

Without a day job, I discovered the terrible power of addiction for real. Other people had been calling me an alcoholic for years, but I knew better. I was an adventurer. The egg cups of sherry they winced at would never have been enough to float my dreams and they needed a name for me to compensate for their envy. *Of course* I drank a lot. If they'd have been paying attention, they'd have noticed I wrote a lot of songs too, and took whatever drugs I could get hold of, and tarted around as much as my middling looks would allow. I wasn't some shuffling drunk – I was… bacchanalian!

Increasingly, though, the drinking portion of my lifestyle was gaining supremacy. Hair of the dog in the morning became more frequent and less unpleasant. Activities that didn't allow for a civilised drink – particularly day jobs – seemed irritating, then difficult, then unachievable. Poverty and shame settled in for the long haul as my ability to counter them atrophied.

I wake up under a duvet and a donkey jacket, fully clothed, wearing two pairs of socks. It isn't giro day until Thursday, and today is Monday.

Reaching down the side of the bed, I find a two-litre bottle of Broadoak cider. It's still one third full, and I've remembered to screw on the cap before going to sleep, so it shouldn't be flat. I pick up the brown bottle and open it. A sulphurous, agricultural smell hisses out limply and I down it. I used to gag when I did this, but nowadays my tongue knows the breakfast routine. It already tasted of cider; now it tastes of wet cider. Get over it. I put the radio on and pull apart the nub of a Lambert & Butler cigarette to cannibalise for a roll-up. If I'd had a proper one left, I'd have smoked it before having a drink. It's hard to roll them before you've settled your nerves. *Woman's Hour* mingles with the smoke, so it must be mid-morning. That's good: waking up in the afternoon is bad for my state of mind. Not enough light. I swing my legs out of

Indoor playtime

bed and crunch over the cans and fag packets to the bathroom. My piss comes out strong and silver, like vodka.

The milk's still ok, even though I hadn't bothered to put it in the fridge. I stare sadly at the kettle before downing the milk. Immediately, it won't settle in my stomach; it's gurgling around urgently, so I run back to the bathroom and throw it up. To purge the taste of its regurgitation from my mouth, I drink water straight from the tap. It hits my stomach and freezes it for as second before it lurches again. I throw up the water, but my stomach is still spasming. My vomit slows to a green trickle of bile as I retch again and again, pulling muscles that haven't yet recovered from the same ordeal yesterday morning. The effort makes me so dizzy that when I pull myself up off my knees, I'm disorientated, grasping little shards of information from which to assemble reality. The black, speckled tiles on the bathroom floor fill my eyes and conspire with the women on the radio talking about a change in the pension age to distract me from my squalor.

When I enter the lounge, I put the light on. The curtains are permanently closed. I'm going to need more cider. Pushing my hand through the foam base of the sofa, I feel around between the springs for coins. There are lots down there; they fall out of my pockets when I'm sleeping, and I deliberately leave them there for when I'm skint. I need £2.79 for a bottle of Broadoak, and I've already fished out a pound coin and a 50p piece. The rest comes in 20ps, 10ps, 5ps, 2ps, 1ps…

I can't do supermarkets anymore. Their bright, family-orientated commercialism is so at odds with my condition that I feel like a shoplifter even though I'm paying. So, I go to the corner shop. It's more expensive but dark and quiet. Barinder judges nobody, even when it's 6.30 a.m. and they're buying two litres of cider. He always has a smile.

Back in the flat, I drink the second bottle slowly. I'm going to have to make it last until later this afternoon when I can borrow some money. It's enough to stave off panic but not to bring about any sort of warm glow. The radio doesn't help.

'The government has announced a crackdown on long-term benefit claimants...'

I secure a tenner off my mate who got his giro today and head back to see Barinder. Carting four bottles of Broadoak back to the flat, I watch the parents picking up their kids from school. I haven't seen my son for a year. Can't think about it. Just can't.

Back in the flat, I chug down a bottle as quickly as I can. *Crackdown on that, you cunts.*

I lie on the sofa, counting the empty Broadoak bottles on the laminate floor. Forty-three, plus a bin liner full from tidying up a couple of weeks ago when Dawn had come round to see me. Bless her.

I wake up after a couple of hours and I'm crying because of a dream I've just had. I'd been holding a tiny hand and singing softly. The third bottle seems to make it worse. The flat has hardly any furniture and my snotty sobs echo around it. I have a picture in my mind of being a cork bobbing in the middle of a vast ocean, unconnected to anyone or anything. I put on a comedy DVD, not to cheer myself up, but to force myself to follow linear thought patterns – to be anchored.

It's the middle of the night when I wake up next. The DVD is showing the menu page, so I start it again immediately. I don't want any of my own thoughts, not now in the dark. I'm ravenous and find a tin of peas. I tip them into a bowl and mix them with some mayonnaise. It's better than it sounds. I think so, anyway. Opening the fourth bottle, I listen to Stewart Lee make sense of the world on the television, clinging on to his reasoning in place of my own. I hope there's more riches at the bottom of the sofa for tomorrow because it mustn't get worse than this. It just mustn't.

By the time of my fifth home detox, things had become a touch frosty with Gavin the alcohol nurse, and he was a dedicated and empathetic professional, non-judgmental and positive in circumstances that would try anyone. I'd proven a tough nut to crack, however, relapsing time and again. The detoxes became progressively more gruelling as my physical dependence spiralled. The doses of Librium would go up in order to counter seizures, and it would take longer for me to give a clear breathalyser reading as my liver began to falter. The skin across that poor organ was hot to the touch; things were getting serious.

'You need to understand you *are* going to die if this carries on, Ben.'

'Yeah, I know. I'll do better this time. I understand.'

'You don't though, do you? What about if you *don't* die straight away? Do you get what that would be like?'

'What do you mean?'

'You could get wet brain?'

'Eh?'

'Wet brain is when you sustain permanent neural damage from excess alcohol. You would need lifelong nursing care.'

'I like nurses.'

'Not when they're wiping your arse for you, you won't. Wise up, Ben!'

Eventually, Aquarius, the private company contracted to do this work by the NHS, refused to fund any further treatment. I was officially a lost cause, and it came as a relief. At last – finally – I had no potential to fulfil, nobody left to disappoint.

'Ben, it's Paul. How you doing, brother?'

Paul is the sort of friend I wish everybody had. Funny, creative, haphazard and troubled, he doesn't even hope that you'll be light, easy company. Having been through the mill himself, he sees a good day as being as interesting as a bad day and is happy to share either with people he likes. I don't remember how we met but, within minutes, we had established that we were both adopted and could talk to each other about it. He'd get me round for lunch and introduce me to interesting people, and we'd go down rabbit holes of conversation, safe in each other's company.

'Well, you know, Paul, pushing a boulder up a hill.'

'I *do* know, brother. Something tells me you haven't left the flat in a while, have you?'

'Well, you know, working on some songs.'

'Yeah, I know, Ben. Still, nothing better for that than an injection of nature, is there?'

Oh, God. Nature. Paul loves nature and wants me to love it, too. He's convinced that light and fresh air can improve any situation. I'm frightened of both.

'Come on, Ben, just come for a *walk*. What's the worst that could happen? I'll pick you up in fifteen minutes.'

I glance around the flat at all the cans, upturned ashtrays and discarded ready meals. The curtains have been shut for a month. I don't want to go, but it's hard to argue with him.

Outside is an awful place if you're not in the mood for it. It's bright, noisy and full of hostile-looking primates, often with their offspring. Paul's never steered me wrong, though, and whilst languishing in a *Leaving Las Vegas** fantasy has its comforts, it wouldn't hurt to see if anything feels different out there from how it does in here.

'Alright, see you outside.'

I get downstairs and Paul is outside in the car. He's tall, blonde and fifteen years older than me. His life has been a kaleidoscope of creative success and emotional hardship. He's smiling like he always does.

---

* The sequel, set between Colley Gate and Stambermill.

'Just a little walk, comrade – catch up on how you're doing.'

We end up walking around an overgrown graveyard. Paul has always been fond of blunt symbolism, and it's not lost on me.

'So, what are you actually *doing*, Ben?'

I have nothing to say. It's easy to relinquish everything if you're on your own. Under the glare of another human being, it starts to feel like a betrayal of the collective. This is why I keep the curtains closed.

I look down at a nineteenth-century tomb. It has an anchor on it, meaning that whoever is in there must have died at sea. It's elaborate, with marble walls extending around the earth where Able Seaman Enoch Jenkins's remains lie. The earth is overgrown with weeds and has shifted in the time since anybody tended to it, so much that the marble has cracked into a haphazard attempt at a rectangle. The earth on top of it is also swelling with the regenerative gifts of decay so, being the showbiz chancer I am, I lie down on it and stare up at Paul. I doubt that poor sailor beneath me had the luxury of kind eyes when he needed them. Circling kites, more likely.

I'm done, though. When Paul drops me home, it's Broadoak time. The authorities have given up on me and I've served notice to my friends. From here on in, nobody will be remotely interested in what I have to think or say. I'll be overgrown soon.

'I need to speak to you, urgently.' It's my friend, Brian: the crassest and best person I've ever met. One Christmas Eve, we had to be held on opposite sides of the street by the police because we'd belted each other in the pub. We grinned at each other across the road as they held us back. It was funny.

We are always falling out, so I haven't heard from him for a while.

'What about?'

'Look, it's important. Come to Rimski's at four. I'll explain.'

If it was important, then it was *important*. He and I would fall out regularly – hit on each other's girlfriends and badmouth each other to strangers. There was an understanding, though, some kind of tacit acknowledgment that, when it mattered, we'd be there. I don't know it now, but I will be holding his hand when he dies, the glorious cunt.

Rimski's, though? That's a coffee shop in Stourbridge inhabited by students and wankers only. Have I got enough for the bus, or do I have to walk?

I'm there first, sweating from the walk and prickled with otherness. Coffee shops have no dark corners; you're on display, and I'm not in a condition for that. I've had this T-shirt on for two weeks. It's late afternoon and a bit chilly, but I take my lemonade to a table outside. Fucking lemonade. I can't drink coffee or tea; they make me panicky, so sweet fizz will have to do. Inside the shop, the optimism is overwhelming. People have art portfolios and whole lives in front of them. This is exactly what I hide from with my curtains closed. Other people's bright futures are deeply offensive to the hopeless community. *What am I doing here?*

'It's Ben!'

I look up to see Paul and Brian approaching with big grins and tangible warmth.

'See, Brian, he's absolutely fucked!'

'State of you!' Brian observes cheerily.

They are both wearing badges cut out of cardboard with 'Team Ben' written on them.

'Right, shut up and listen,' Brian instructs.

I don't know how interventions work in Hollywood, but the Black Country/Cockney approach was no-nonsense, kind and *funny*. Having arrived at a point where I fully accepted my life was coming to an end, there was no point trying to shock me anymore. I *could*, it turned out, be motivated by absurdity.

If there was nothing to lose, then why not go down laughing? I'd had enough of the other thing.

Paul and Brian had been collecting spare Valiums from our circle of dysfunctional friends. They had enough to get me through a three-day detox, and the spare room had been set up at Paul's flat.

'Come on, let's go…'

That was my last detox so far. There was an experiment done once where rats were isolated in empty cages with a bottle of plain water and another that contained cocaine. The rats quickly became hopelessly addicted, sucking on the cocaine water all day and night. After a while, the rats were put together and objects that they could play with and clamber over were added to the communal living area. They were, in short order, all drinking plain water only.

The detoxes I had via the NHS were all administered professionally and kindly. I came out the other side healthy and full of optimism. The difference that last time was that I emerged feeling loved. I had something at stake. I'd seen it on those cardboard badges.

GRIT IN THE SPONGE

You can drive round and round the multistorey at University Hospital Llandough looking for a parking space until you've either recovered or died. Drivers exchange predatory glances as people return to their cars, carrying news that's written on their faces. I've got a blue disabled badge, though, so I can manoeuvre past the queue and into a prime spot near the exit. I feel eyes on me as I hop out of the car and saunter easily towards the concrete steps, briefly tempted to affect a limp. I've got the badge because I'm a support worker and I'm required to pick up people who would qualify for one if they were driving themselves. On this occasion, though, my client will be going nowhere.

Andy brings out a parental streak in all the professionals who work with him. Shy, polite and well meaning, he has slight learning disabilities and a permanent nervousness that contradicts his masculine bulk. He's called three times in the last ten minutes to check I'm still coming. I have the impression that he's been let down a lot. His eyes are always scanning me for a sign that I might do the same.

Opposite to the orthopaedic unit, you can see straight down to the sea at Penarth, where Grandad's second cousin became the first one-legged man to swim the Bristol Channel. I wonder if he had a parking badge.

Reception in the Hafan y Coed unit is staffed by conspicuously cheerful people, and an enormous television screen is showing *This Morning*. The walls of the corridor to the wards display artwork and poems from patients. Snatches of them lodge in you as you approach the double doors. *We grow better tomorrow when we plant seeds today.*

To the right is Alder Ward. Here, people who arrive in crisis are assessed and either decanted back into the community or distributed amongst the longer-stay wards. I'm most familiar with Pine Ward. That's the addiction unit, where people come to be detoxed and set back on their feet.

Today, I'm headed for Willow Ward, which is through another set of double doors and down two flights of stairs. As you descend there is a palpable dimming of the light. You are pushing further into the place, away from brightness and towards something quiet and insulated.

I head through the final double doors and I'm on the bottom corridor. At the door for Willow Ward, I ring the bell and read the list of items it is forbidden to bring on to the ward: lighters, bank cards, alcohol, energy drinks, pornography… I ring the bell again. The glass in the door is frosted, and you can't hear if the bell is ringing or not. Laptops, cutlery, cash…

A nurse comes to the door.

'Hi, I'm looking for Andy. I'm his support worker.'

'Which Andy?'

'Oh sorry. Andy Davies.'

'He's been moved, love.'

'Ah, right. Do you know where to?'

'Sorry, no idea. You'll have to ask at reception.'

I trudge back up to the light and glance at the television as I wait for the receptionist to finish a phone call. Holly Willoughby's militant commitment to conformity has me tucking in my shirt; if there's one place you want to pass as normal, it's here.

'How can I help you?'

'Hi, I'm looking for one of your patients. He was on Willow, but they've moved him, and I don't know where.'

'What's his name?'

'Andy... Andy Davies. I'm his support worker.'

The receptionist looks at me, suspiciously I think, and starts searching on his computer.

'Andy Davies, you say?'

'That's right.'

'Do you have a date of birth?'

A *proper* support worker would know Andy's date of birth, probably by heart, or have it written in a hardback work diary that they carry around for moments like these. I search through the emails on my phone and find one about Andy's birthday.

'Sixth of the seventh, nineteen eighty-nine.'

'Well, I'm afraid I can't find him on the system. Are you sure he hasn't been discharged?'

'He can't have been. He's on a section thr—'

My phone rings. It's Andy.

'Where you to?' he asks urgently.

'I'm in reception. Which ward are you on now?'

I hear Andy asking a member of staff.

'Maple Ward, mate.'

'No worries. I'm on my way.'

I nod to the receptionist and head back down the corridor.

Hope. Hold on. Pain ends.

Descending the stairs again, I'm chilled by the implications of them not knowing where Andy was.

Willow is to the right on the bottom corridor, Maple is left, then an immediate right into an alcove with no natural light feeding through from above. I press the doorbell. I read the sign.

Knives, matches, medication or drugs of any description...

The door opens and a burly nurse looks at me inquisitively.

'I'm here to see Andy Davies. I'm his support worker.'
'Oh, ok. Come in.'

He lets me past him and gestures to a door on the right. 'You'll have to wait in there.'

The front door is on a weighted hinge and seems to take an age to clunk shut. When it does, the LED light on the waiting room door changes to green so the nurse can open it with his pass card.

'Wait in there. I'll go and get him.'

I sit down on a sturdy, wooden chair. Its plastic cushioning exhales as if it's relieved to have me. It's darker still in here. The door I came through has a red LED on it now, as does the one that leads to the ward at the other end of the room. I look at my phone, but there's no signal. The neutral colours of the room put you on notice that you're to be calm. I'm not calm. I'm thinking about calm things, though: lapping waves and waving palms. Lapping palms and waving laps.

Time passes.

I examine my hands under the artificial light. There are less of those little skin tags on the backs of them nowadays. Someone told me they were caused by stress, so you've got to call that a win. I *am* doing better. The chances of ending up back where I started must have retreated. I mean I've still got to keep trying hard – keep working and not take a backward step – but I'm definitely further along now. Not out of the woods, but certainly heading towards their outer edge. Definitely.

Where are they?

I get up to look out of the window into the corridor. It's thick glass, but I can make out muffled shouting from somewhere. Nowadays, admittance to these places is reserved for those who are in such difficulty that they can't be reached by community nurses or the sort of medication available from GPs. The bar is set so high that nobody could possibly fake the symptoms of the illnesses that are treated here.

Andy's journey to Maple Ward started on Tuesday afternoon three weeks ago, when he called me just as I was leaving for home.

'Alright Andy, what's up? We still on for coffee in the morning?'

'Yes mate. Can we go to Cathays?'

We always go to the coffee shop in Cathays. It's next door to the Lidl, so we do Andy's shopping then head there. Flat white for me, Diet Coke for Andy. Twice a week, every week.

'Course we can, Andy. Could we chat then? It's just I'm nearly in the car.'

'Er, yes mate, it's just…'

'What's up? You ok, Andy?'

'Yeah, mate.'

Paid empathy is always a trade-off. You're working for money but also because you care, and those two impulses don't sit too well together. Tomorrow, when we go shopping, I'll be all ears for Andy. His conversation is slow and repetitive but often contains insight and wit if you have the patience to persevere with him. Now, though, nine hours and fifty-five minutes into a ten-hour shift, I'm not really present for him. I'm going through the motions before I can turn my phone off and go home. Something nags, though; he usually calls me at 8.01 a.m., just after I switch my phone on. Other clients are fond of a last-minute request for assistance before we go home, but I've never known Andy to call at this time of day.

'You sure, Andy? You sound like something's bothering you.'

There's a long pause so I sit on a wall in the car park and let him assemble his thoughts.

'What I was gonna say is…'

Another long pause ensues, so I light a cigarette. It's a conflicting situation. The reality that our relationship is governed by the clock is accepted by both of us without discussion. I try never to seem reluctant to be there for Andy or to make him feel less than welcome company and usually that's authentic. Right now, though, I want my mind back: to be able to think about whatever I please, to drive home in this bright sunshine and smile at my wife. This makes me feel like a bastard and a fraud as well as frustrated and trapped. Best chivvy him along a bit. He probably just wants some fags dropping in. I can do that on my way home, no worries.

'Come on, Andy. What's the matter, bro?'

'I wants to murder my dad. I've bought a knife.'

You might think that sort of revelation would trigger an urgent response from emergency services, but over the next week, I had to plead to get Andy seen by a psychiatrist, who deemed him 'non-urgent'. I then had to call the police again twice because he'd called to tell me he was stabbing pieces of cardboard to 'practice'. The first time the police attended, they told him to 'chill out and watch a film'. They finally sectioned him on the second visit.

Now, as I'm peering through the glass, he's been here two weeks and the meds have started to kick in. The nurse walks past, so I knock on the window and look questioningly when he turns round.

'Sorry, it's been kicking off. I forgot all about you. I'll go and get Andy now.'

I admit to having a rather dramatic cast of mind, but being locked in an underground room in a psychiatric hospital and forgotten about is surely a legitimate anxiety, isn't it? It's not about me, though, I remind myself. *Poor Andy is locked down here for real and his only respite is coffee out with me, so pull yourself together and enough with the* One Flies Over the Cuckoo's Nest *fantasies.* Here he is.

'Hello, mate. How are you?' he offers with a nervous smile. He looks awful, unshaven with sleep in his eyes and food down his sweatshirt.

'Ah, you know.' We exchange another smile; he's used to my miserabilist tendencies.

The first of three doors is unlocked and we sign the book releasing Andy for an hour.

'Rhys Webb has retired,' he tells me. Rugby is what we have in common. A while ago I'd encouraged him to join a local team, and it had been the sun and moon to him while it lasted. His week had a focus: training on Wednesday and a game on Saturday. He had news to tell me when I saw him. He loved it. Eventually, I got a call from the Welsh Rugby Union safeguarding department. The club had raised concerns about Andy. Perhaps a mainstream club wasn't the right environment for him. Maybe he'd like to try his hand at 'all abilities' rugby – they have some great schemes in Cardiff that Andy could join in with. When I put it to him, I was seared by the pain and humiliation on his face. No, he wouldn't.

'We'll have no players left at this rate, mate.'

We're making our way up the stairs, and natural light emphasises the sense of escape as we make it to the ground floor.

'Reckon we'll be thrashed at the World Cup.'

I nod at the receptionist as we pass, all normal like.

I can sense Andy's anxiety rising as we approach the exit. It's not because he's about to go outside, where it's bright and loud and people are rushing about. He's fine with that. He needs a lighter. On the ward, he's allowed one cigarette per hour and the lighter is signed in and out when he goes out to the garden to smoke. He loves a cigarette, does Andy, and he's got his tobacco in his hand ready. He doesn't like asking for things, though. Tiny kindnesses carry weight for Andy. It's if he's been allocated a smaller share of goodwill than the rest of us and, if he uses it up, he'll be cast out. Before he's forced to say anything, I hand him a lighter.

'Thanks, mate,' he beams.

Andy's not allowed outside the hospital grounds, but opposite the psychiatric unit there's a coffee shop with seats outside.

'What do you fancy?'

Andy's frantically trying to light his roll-up.

'Diet Coke, mate. I'll wait here if that's ok, Ben.'

He looks at me hopefully.

There's a problem here. I've signed to take responsibility for Andy whilst he's off the ward, so if he decides to disappear whilst I'm getting the drinks…

'Er, ok. But you'll stay here, right?'

'Yes, mate,' he assures me.

I go in to join the queue and immediately regret my decision. I want to trust him. I *do* trust him, but you wouldn't blame anyone for wanting out of the situation he's in right now. If it were me, I'd be off without a doubt, and that's exactly why people like me shouldn't be put in positions of responsibility like this. These people need dependable support from professionals whose own lives don't threaten to shatter every time some pressure comes on.

I crane my neck to try and see Andy out of the window as the queue moves forwards.

'What can I get you, love?'

'Er… a flat white and a Diet Coke.' Hard-pressed medical staff are rushing through their lunches at the tables around me. They look so solid – so *on* it.

I rush outside with the drinks and Andy is smiling at me, puffing away.

'Thought I'd run off, mate?'

At least one of us has a grip of the situation. We sit down at a sunlit table and watch taxis dropping off patients and picking them up.

When someone's been as unwell as Andy has, the rules of conversation change. Where once you could assume common ground for the discussion, now you are alert to hazards that could open up and swallow you both if you stray from narrowly marked-out pathways.

'Don't reckon Gatland can weave his magic this time, Andy.'

'No, mate.'

There's discomfort around his eyes – an uncertainty, as if he's weighing his responses to check they are appropriate. I'm doing the same.

'Are they looking after you in there?' I ask.

'It's alright. I had jacket potato for my tea yesterday.'

'Nice one. Got to keep your strength up.' Listening to that platitude fall out of my mouth persuades me to try to sit with silence for a bit. Andy stares into the distance and a tall, dissolute looking guy comes over to fill the vacuum.

'Got a cigarette I could have, buddy? I wouldn't ask but I'm stuck in here and they don't sell them.' I hand over a fag.

'Should have told him to fuck off,' Andy tells me after he leaves. 'He's probably out here asking for them all day.'

'I'm a pushover,' I admit. Andy laughs so I probe a bit.

'How's the medication they've got you on?'

'It's alright, mate.'

'Does it make you drowsy?'

'Yes, mate, but I don't mind.'

'You seem a bit calmer than you were.'

'Yes, mate.'

'Have you been having any more upsetting thoughts?'

'About what?'

'Well, in general. About your dad maybe?'

'No.'

I brighten at this. Andy does seem calmer and, when he was admitted, they seemed confident the meds would work after a while.

'Ah, that's great, mate. I could ring him if you like.'

'Why?'

'Just to let him know that you're feeling better and there's no need to worry anymore.'

Andy smiles at me and asks, 'Worry about what?'

I pause a moment to weigh this up. He seems happy enough and I don't want to push him. On the other hand, the last his dad heard about his son was when the police turned up and told him to keep his doors locked. If there's better news, then he needs to know.

'That he's in danger.'

Andy finishes his roll-up and smiles at me again. 'But he is.'

'I thought you were feeling calmer now.'

'I am, but I still wants to murder him… because of what he done.'

Dropping Andy back at the ward, I tell him I'm off tomorrow and will see him in a couple days.

He shakes my hand, beaming. 'Thanks for that, mate.'

He disappears through the double-locked doors, and I climb back up the dim stairwell into the yellow afternoon. As I reach my car, I realise that I forgot to look at the sea.

I don't want to do anything. It's my day off and I want to spend it doomscrolling through Twitter, occasionally insulting politicians and liking memes. I want to close the curtains and let the screen flicker me into a dissociative state. I want to be a spectator, not a participant; to sit still and let the world flow around me until I'm drowned by it. So, I go out. That train of thought never leads anywhere good, and besides, it's going to rain tomorrow. For some reason – any reason – I go out.

Since moving to the Rhondda, I've been rationing out local sightseeing trips so that I don't become over-familiar with the area too quickly. I'm trying to outwit my psychology and postpone the point when I can drive from Brynmawr to

Porthcawl without noticing anything or feeling the peril of possibly getting lost. Over three years, Cardiff was stripped of all mystique on account of my job. Once it had been a mythical place of pilgrimage that I dreamed of and spied through the empassioning prism of Six Nations rugby on the telly. Driving around its homeless shelters, mental health units, drug treatment centres and crack houses for ten hours a day, four days a week, turned it into a Christmas bicycle left out in the February rain. This isn't to say I don't still love it. Cardiff inhabits me like a flawed relative whose every misdeed is forgiven, but from whom you'd rather not hear on your birthday.

Fuck off, Cardiff – you're drunk and I'm at the opera.

Sometimes, whilst living in Cardiff, I'd drive up to the Rhondda on my own to absorb its otherness. Navigating around the narrow streets of stone terraces and up the steep banks to viewing points, I'd gather fibres from my imagined roots, overlay the stories I'd been told onto the landscape. Wistfully, I'd replace the missing Dai caps and boots on passers-by and hear the hooter, the silver band and the call for solidarity.

Leaving my Rhondda Fach terrace to visit Penallta, I'm struggling to detach from this absurd fantasy of this place that I carry around as a crutch. Down the street is the convenience store where I buy my fags or vape liquid depending on where in the cycle of that particular addiction I am. To the right is entrance to the bypass, which replaced the railway line as a final admission that no more empire-building steam coal would be leaving from here. It's my day-to-day: a place where I get angry if I can't find a parking space and where council tax bills arrive. I still thrill to the views from Penrhys, where Grandad's parents are buried, but that road is also a shortcut to Asda at Tonypandy, where Churchill stained history in 1910 and avocados are often on a three for two deal. So, today, I'm off to find a bit of reverie before my brain turns the whole country commonplace.

To love the Valleys is to love a mottled sky. The muted greens and blurred purple of the mountains are at their best beneath a canopy that promises deliverance and threatens consequence simultaneously. Clouds rush around this country in pursuit of the fugitive sun. While jackdaws circle a sainted patch of blue in Trealaw, the sinners in Ferndale must sit through a thrumming sermon that washes their afternoon away. Nothing is settled; anything is possible.

Heading east across the A470, through Nelson and Ystrad Mynach, angry outbursts of rain spatter the car, triggering the automatic wipers into brief action. Sometimes, they'll only wipe two or three times before the sun pokes through and I have to put the visor down to see properly. I slow down, respecting the elements. To the north lies Aberfan.

My shift pattern means I have three days off, and this is the first. My inclination is always to spend it wound-licking. There's a reassuring mountain of pop-psychological advice that endorses doing the thick end of fuck all whenever you feel like it. If I'm 'decompressing', 'letting the world take a turn' or 'taking time to be', I could assemble a mighty defence of it from the pronouncements of the wellbeing industry. In my case, though, it would be dishonest. One day of doing nothing can easily turn into a decade if I'm not careful. With the curtains closed, the phone off and an intoxicant to hand, I'm safely strapped into a spacecraft, sailing further and further away from anxiety until I crash. So, day one of 'me time' has to feature purpose or, at best, I'll pitch up back at work on Monday with nothing to show for it. On to Penallta.

The car park sits high in a wide, open space that wouldn't be out of place in the American Midwest. The sky here is white and still: a neutral canopy that contrasts with the animated drama that overlooked the narrow streets I've left behind in the Rhondda.

Whose Song to Sing?

I consult the board which offers a choice of walking trails around Parc Penallta. It's not been long since I was too overweight to attempt anything like this, so I pick the easiest one and tell myself I'll be back to do the others.

Setting off down the path, I make some mental preparations. Firstly, of course, it feels easy doing this bit; it's downhill and I'm only a few steps in. *On the way back, you'll have to climb up here again and you won't be so jaunty then, will you?* Every step down means one back up later. That's physics, or geography, or both.

Actually, the real problem here is biology. Decades of cramming fags, lager, cheese and drugs into my mouth whenever it wasn't singing or otherwise drowning out dreaded silences have washed up on the beach of my half century like an oil slick. I'm sick of the sound of my rasping breath every time I expend a calorie. *Keep walking, and try not to throw a seven.*

People often view addictions as a good time gone wrong – as if the addict doesn't know when the party is over and leaves with their pockets bulging with goodies from the buffet. They just need to sort themselves out; to grow up; to get a grip. But taking responsibility is a leap of faith that requires confidence in your environment. If you have that, then the thrill of a challenge is all the buzz you need. If you start from fear, then you meet life like a skittish horse at a fence.

I'm round the corner and the car is out of sight. The first part of the trail leads into a wooded area that is coming alive at the end of winter. Insects and budding twigs are here to tell me I've made it through another one and, though the ground is sodden, I'm upright on it.

So here we are, *in nature*, just like every sorted-out human tells us to be. Away from the city grind and work, I allow my senses to fill with wonders and am restored to oneness… Am I bollocks. I look at the black suit jacket I'm wearing, the one I always wear, and the unsuitable loafers that threaten to send me slithering down a bank and wonder whose idea this was. *Where's your Gore-Tex clothing, eh? You haven't even got proper walking shoes that support your ankles or something, let alone a pair of those sticks with spikes on the end. You're a shambles.*

Dithering along the track, I'm acutely self-conscious – I'm as out of place as if I'd stumbled into a mosque or a strip club. Occasionally, someone suitably attired passes me, and I'm struck by how purposeful they look. They move quickly, presumably on a pre-planned route. Some nod hello; some don't. I prefer it when they don't.

The woodland here is described as 'developing' on the park's website. Like my self-awareness, it's only sprung forth thanks to the intervention of well-meaning people after many barren years. In Parc Penallta's case, those barren years were due to the landscape being captured by the Industrial Revolution: a couple of centuries during which much of western humanity was sucked into a machine before being spat out into the Information Age with nothing to do. All over South Wales, there are tracts of land like this that have been repurposed for 'leisure'. Neat and tidy grasslands are crossed with well-signed paths and little bins for dog turds. Occasionally, trickles of coal dust emerge above the turf, refusing to be buried by a greenwashed facsimile of nature or defined by historical information boards. You do well to tread lightly in this country. As you dash around the aisles in Asda, you're likely to be walking over the bones of lost colliers whose lives have been condensed into a tarnished plaque by the trolleys out front. You might be offered a 'pitman's platter' in the cafe along a nature trail or in a heritage-themed pub. At the industrial park, where you turn up every day to input data and die inside, there might be a preserved pithead winding gear watching over you. Your fool boss might exhort greater efforts 'at the coalface' before replacing you with AI. You might book a weekend visit to the Rhondda Heritage Park for the 'Welsh Coal Mining Experience' and stand in the cage as it clanks and rattles down to the face without moving an inch. If you do, you'll be accompanied by a guide who once did it for real: he has dust on his lungs and a self-assurance you will never enjoy.

As everything real floats off into digital spaces to be archived, monetised and fenced off from grimy fingers, the remaining tools and machines from our recent past have become fetishised totems of longed-for solidity. We cling on to any lump of iron we find, hoping it will weigh us down to a place where specific words, foods and dances belong. It wasn't like this for our parents. They wanted out of it as fast as they could go. And who could blame them? If you'd grown up with the filth and ill-health that industry brought, you'd want a nice office job, wouldn't you? You definitely wouldn't dream of running an artisan smithery from a museum that sells your ironic horseshoes in the gift shop next to the commemorative fudge.

When I was little, David seemed to be able to fix anything. There was an endless stream of classic cars on the drive, often in pieces so small that they were unrecognisable. Each one, though, would come together into gleaming wholeness as my old man's weekends were spent doing what his old man did for a living. He'd carried an understanding of physics into a career as a highways engineer. Before I went to bed, I'd wish him goodnight as he pored over giant technical drawings at the kitchen table. Sometimes, he'd take me to a site he was working on, and I'd hold the staff whilst he peered through the level and wrote down calculations.

I enjoyed holding the staff. Little boys want, above all else, to do serious things with their dads. They don't want toys, not really. They want tools and responsibility, whatever they tell you. I wasn't cut out for that life, though. Even at the time, I understood that it would never be me looking through the level. Where David saw the angles and forces at play in the world around him, I saw the looks on people's faces and

Grit in the sponge

picked up their whistled tunes. Holding the staff was the best I had to offer and, every now and then, it granted me admission into his life. It was something.

I wasn't allowed near the cars, though. He'd seen enough of me dropping anything I ever held to know I'd cause problems.

'You'll get grit in the sponge and scratch the paintwork.'

With car maintenance out of the picture, my life took a course away from David's. As he clanked away in the garage, I'd be in a book or learning to gossip with my mum. I picked up the complex rhythms of female conversation that turned on a sixpence from engaged compassion to withering contempt and back again over a single coffee in Beatties lounge. I learned to talk as a pastime without purpose and to enjoy company and then bitch about it when I got home. In the library, I'd pick out books *because* I didn't understand them. All the empty space where spanners and chrome polish might have been were instead filled with words, words, words.

By the time David left, we were different species in the same enclosure, skirting each other in silence save for the occasional outburst of territorial screeching. After he left, I missed him. He might have only said twenty words a day, but ten of them would have been funny, even if I was their target. The 'verbal diarrhoea' he diagnosed in me was and still is a tic. It's one thing cramming as many ideas into your head as possible, but what do you do with them once they are there? Slowly rebuilding a 1959 AC Aceca, though? That tells its own story.

You'll appreciate, then, that when I eventually faced expulsion at school, and David was summoned from work to learn of my wrongdoing from the chief master himself, it didn't augur well.

David left when I was fourteen and, for a while, Mum and I coexisted pretty happily. We were in the same big, detached house in Solihull but with next to no money. On a Friday, we'd watch *Cheers* together, she'd have a miniature bottle of wine and I'd have a cream soda. It was our treat for the week out of the £30 David gave us to live on. I didn't see him for a month or so after he left but, eventually, he and I fell into a routine of going out once a week on Thursdays. It'd be to a balti house in Sparkhill usually, and I'd be allowed two beers from the off-licence next door: Raven's Superbrew was my favourite.

'Tell him we need more money,' Mum would urge me. 'He owes us.' So I did, and it went up to £60 a week. Four miniature bottles of wine on a Friday – one of them for me.

When Mum's whirlwind romance with our family doctor took her off on a series of exotic holidays, it was really something to see her happy again. She stopped wearing beige and got her hair done. After one of these jaunts, she settled into life at her lover's flat overlooking a lake. My food would be delivered twice a week and stacked in the freezer. Most weeks Mum and her boyfriend would invite me out for dinner. I had a new love too: there were bottles of it left carelessly behind in the dining room cabinet. It helped me sleep in an empty house with the lights on.

The day the school called David, I'd been sent home. He phoned me to say he was on his way to the meeting. I was to catch a train into Birmingham and meet him in the car park at the back of New Street Station. Nothing good ever happened to anyone in the car park at the back of New Street station, and I paced around it in dread of what was to come.

I'd been rumbled, exposed as the off-the-rails nascent alcoholic I'd become at sixteen. David had always been clear that I wasn't bound for success, and now the school was going to confirm it for him. My ocean of prattle was about to break over the rocks of adult judgement and leave me with silence: no lessons, no school choir and no Dad. *What the fuck am I going to do?*

His company Sierra pulled slowly into view, and the rush of passengers swarming in and out of the station blurred

Monet-style into my anxiety. As ever, David's face gave nothing away. 95 per cent of his emotions were conveyed via a slight narrowing of the eyes or a lifting of the brows. The rest exploded in laughter or anger without warning; you cherished the former and feared the latter.

I climbed into the passenger seat and the ordered, pristine habitat of a man who was too smart to cause the sort of trouble I was in. There were no empty crisp bags, no cassettes and no discarded receipts. If you opened the glove box you'd find this year's Birmingham A to Z; if you popped the boot there would be a briefcase, and inside that would be pens, documents and a thousand pounds in immaculate £20 notes. You never knew when you might need it.

Silence reigned for a while as David assembled his thoughts. Unless he was raging, every word he ever said could have been etched onto stone, such was their permanence. Whatever was coming would not be up for discussion.

'Well, Benjamin, you've done it now, haven't you?'

This might not sound encouraging, but my heart lightened at these words. In the grammar of our relationship, 'Benjamin' suggested things might not be as bad as I feared. My mum used the longer version of my name when she was cross with me, and David found nothing – absolutely *nothing* – as funny as seeing my mum lose her temper. He'd dedicated a quarter of a century to honing his technique at enraging her so that when she reached the apex of her fury, he could laugh and say, 'Nasty…' I suspect on some level they both enjoyed it. It was a cruel game, but at least it was a game.

He rarely addressed me by name at all, but if he did, 'Benjamin' indicated he was taking the piss by mimicking my mum at her most serious. The atmosphere in the car loosened.

'I'll tell you now that the chief master – or whatever he calls himself – is an absolute prick.'

'Er, what did he say?'

'Well, first off, he said it was good to see me. He has the cheek to summon me from work and then says that. I told him it was good to see *him* after you'd been at the school for five years. Anyway, the upshot is they haven't got any proof you did anything, so don't admit a thing and you'll be fine. Remember, admit nothing. I'm going back to work. Don't let this happen again.'

My God, he's actually on my side. He loves me.

And that was it: no explosion of anger, no recriminations, no concern at all for anything except getting away with it. I've got away with a lot since.

Purposeless walking disquiets me. If you're just at large, bimbling about, things can only happen *to* you. If you have a destination in mind, you can persuade yourself that you have a hand in your own destiny.

At Penallta, it's all about Sultan the pit pony. At the end of my brave trek across municipally managed outdoorsia is a public artwork of heart-stirring ambition. High on the edge of a ridge, the ground becomes scalloped with sweeping terraces of grassed-over coal spoil that you can clamber up to observe the surrounding patchwork of green and grey. From the air, the sculpture reveals itself as a galloping horse, its hooves, tail, mane and eyes black where the spoil has been exposed.

I walk along Sultan's spine towards his great eye, the white sky thinning out my internal chatter until it's just a feeling. *Poor ponies down the mine, blind from the dark. Poor, blind ponies, in the dark mine.*

Andy looks sharper: his clothes are clean, and he's had a shave.

'I'm allowed out, mate, as long as it's with you,' he smiles.

I look up at the nurse for confirmation.

'Don't be running off, Andy,' she says. 'Be back in two hours.'

We find the car and high tail it out of there. Leaving a place like Hafan y Coed is what cars were invented for. Each press on the accelerator takes Andy and me further away from confusion and confinement.

'Caerphilly mountain?' I suggest.

'Yes, mate!'

Once we're up there, sat outside the shack with a Mountain Burger each, we munch silently for a while. The late afternoon sun hazes over Coed y Werin, gentle and optimistic.

'So, how's it been whilst I've been away?'

'Good, mate.'

'Are you feeling any happier?'

'Yes, mate. I'm getting better now.' Andy smiles easily, without the 'please-don't-notice-I'm-not-okay' rictus he's been relying on recently.

'Ah, that's good, mate. They said the meds would take a while to kick in.'

Andy nods.

We talk over the upcoming Rugby World Cup – being normal, both of us, in the Spring warmth until time runs out.

'Back to the nutty place,' Andy sighs as we get back in the car.

'Not for long, mate. You'll be home soon. So, Andy,' I probe, before we descend into the shadows on the valley floor and join the A48 traffic. 'How are you feeling about your dad now?'

Andy stares straight ahead. 'It's alright, mate. That was… a misunderstanding.'

MONKEY PAWS

At fifty-two, I have cause to thank myself. Blinking out of my hotel window into the pre-dawn, I can see the tailfins of planes lined up over the road at Sydney's Kingsford Smith airport. I've splashed out on a room at Rydge's, so I just need to wheel my case a few yards and I'm there. If I'd followed my usual penny-pinching instincts, I'd be looking for a bus now.

I like being on my own in airports. The peculiar otherness of them, odd-shaped vehicles, poker-faced passport rituals and off-schedule drinking is best appreciated if you have nobody else to talk to. You feel intrepid as a solo traveller. In charge of your own destiny, you stride around the concourse beholden to nobody: a citizen of the world.

The few quid I have to splash out with have come from writing. I rode my luck after being asked to cover Wales in the rugby and have ended up with a twice-weekly politics column. Alongside my real job supporting homeless people in Cardiff, I fire off spiteful, sarcastic pieces about our largely useless politicians. I've saved a year's worth of fees from this column and cashed them in on this trip. It feels like robbery.

After checking in at the Thai Airways desk, I breeze through security and head off to find the gate. When I finally reach it, my health app tells me I've done 8,000 steps. And it isn't even 7 a.m. yet. Anything I do today, however unhealthy, is now justified. I check out the bar options and find them lacking. A pay-to-use airport lounge is an extravagance, but nobody can see me. Nobody even needs to know.

My eventual destination is Phuket where my wife, Susie, has been visiting her friends for a week. We've been married for five years, during which I've done a master's degree, held down a proper job, published two books, and bought a house in the Rhondda. Initially, our marriage resembled one of those television programmes where someone buys a dilapidated property, having seen its potential. But it was me who was Susie's do'er upper, and she had me knocked into shape lickety-split. Sort of.

This trip has flowed from several long-running narrative strands. Fifteen years ago, I went to Hull for drastic treatment for the alcoholism that was dragging me under at an alarming pace. That moment of need was met by a new force in my life, Eric – Daddio, my natural father.

After receiving the details of my adoption from Social Services in Dudley, I had found my birth mother easily. I looked up private investigators in the Yellow Pages and gave a guy called Mac – a pleasingly gumshoe name – the details I had learned about my mother. They were twenty-five years out of date, but he called the next day and told me he'd found her. Mac's fee was £50, and I had it ready in my hand when I knocked on his door.

'Sit down, young Ben,' Mac instructed. He was in his fifties, friendly and charismatic. His office was a blizzard of paper, the sort of stash as you'd imagine a PI would accumulate.

I handed over the payment and he passed me an envelope.

'Right, in there is her address, phone number and the names of your brothers and stepfather.'

Stepfather... Brothers!

'This must be a big thing for you,' Mac smiled. 'Are you coping alright?'

Whose Song to Sing?

I was... I think. I mean, it *was* a big thing but, at this stage — the Schrödinger's birth family moment — it was also deliciously exciting, like being at the top of a log flume. I nodded, lost for words.

'It's been a nice job for me,' Mac continued. 'Most of the time, I'm following around after bastards who are cheating on their wives. It's lovely to do something like this. I really do wish you all the best with it.'

He rose and opened the door for me.

'Thank you so much,' I managed as we shook hands.

'Truly, it's my pleasure.' Reaching into his pocket, Mac retrieved one of the twenty-pound notes I'd given him. 'Go and get yourself a drink, Ben,' he said, pressing it into my hand. 'Hope it all goes well for you.'

A month later, I was dithering around the corner from the Grand Hotel in central Birmingham. Writing the letter had been tortuous. Draft after draft had been completed and binned:

Dear Mary...

Dear Mrs Kearney...

Hi!...

It felt as if I were sending a letter bomb, something that could upend a household and cause untold and lasting damage. Every statement had to be meticulously qualified to remove all traces of entitlement.

If you prefer not to reply, I quite understand...

Eventually, Dawn snatched a completed draft from me, stuffed it in an envelope and posted it. Never without a stamp, Dawn.

Dawdling down the narrow street at the side of the Grand, I was in distress. The sensory onslaught of a city centre was swirling around me at a moment when I seemed weightless. I'd brought myself out here, away from the questionable solidity of my relationship with Mum and David. As precarious and fractured as that could seem, it was, at least, identifiable as a base point. Now, I was spacewalking. Mum was devastated I was doing this. I should never have told her. I was risking the little security I had for an unknown quantity.

I leaned against a wall, hyperventilating. *Why am I doing this?* It's a question that still troubles me. I can present a convincing case: I deserve to understand my origins and find out about the genetics that went into making me and what those might mean for my health in the future. Who could argue that I'm not owed an explanation for my adoption? I could look at you with fierce, hurt eyes and demand all that so persuasively that you'd be ashamed to challenge it. It's not the whole story, though. Idle curiosity played a role in the enterprise that, at least, equals all those noble motivations. *Am I breaking my Mum's heart just to scratch an itch?* As horns honked and shoppers bustled past me at midday on a Saturday in Brum, I was frozen in a psychological bear trap. *I'm searching for authenticity here, but my search is selfish and shallow. My need for authenticity betrays how fundamentally fake and diminished I am. I should be still and quiet. Three-dimensional people are being hurt by my cartoonish indelicacy. Go home!*

Still, the undeniable rectitude of my endeavour – or the urgency of my curiosity – set me straight. *Deep breath. Go to the hotel.*

Mary was a lovely person. We chatted for several hours. She'd been young, she explained; she'd had no choice, really. She'd always thought of me and was glad I'd got in touch. I came away with two new half-brothers yet to meet and a feeling of overwhelming gratitude that no grisly details had been uncovered – that my origin story wasn't a violent one. I was relieved, also, that she was ok. Her life hadn't been easy, but things had worked out. We stayed in touch, and her husband became a treasured friend. That day, Mary wondered if she could write to Mum.

'Under no circumstances is that woman to write to me. You do what you need to, but leave me out of it.'

That was, very clearly, a final decision. I knew Mum would react this way before I brought it up. I'd decided, though, that I ought to live in the light. All this taboo-breaking action had convinced me that the truth was nothing to be afraid of. If I could cope with it, why couldn't everyone else? I had become tyrannical in my imagined innocence. *None of this was my doing*, I told myself. I had been an object in this story, debated in court with a changeable name and no say in my destiny. Surely now, when all I wanted was for everyone to get on, they owed me that. Didn't they? The truth, of course, was that the door I'd pushed open led down to some unbearably sad memories for people who were only young themselves when all that had occurred.

When I pressed on to find my biological father, I felt carried by momentum. Having crossed the Rubicon in meeting my mother, this seemed inevitable. Complete the set, why not? I told David that I was doing this in advance. Over the phone I delivered a much-considered speech explaining my decision and emphasising that it changed nothing between him and me. For some reason, I considered that dynamic to be under my sole direction. He couldn't have been more reasonable.

'I'd want to know if it was me,' he reassured me. I was impressed. See, it didn't *have* to be the histrionics and recriminations that Mum had served up. There was an adult way to approach these things, and David was taking the high road. Good on him. Women, eh?

I tracked my father down using Friends Reunited. Again, my initial message took dozens of drafts to perfect. The format is similar to a spec letter offering your services to a potential employer: 'I am a conscientious offspring with a great deal to offer...' You mustn't sound too desperate, though. Whilst employers are charmed by enthusiastic applicants, putative family members might find puppyish advances to be alarming. *So, tone it down, Ben, be cool.* 'So, I, like, exist and shit…' It's a demanding exercise in creative writing and a strange use for language skills. It did the trick though. Intriguingly based in Australia, this guy – my father – was conveniently visiting the UK in a few weeks.

We met in Horts Wine Bar in Five Ways, Birmingham. It was a chintzy place and popular with office workers, so lunchtime just before Christmas was busy. A bit overwhelmed by the noise, I scrutinised every male in there who was older than me as I sat and waited. I hadn't seen a photograph of Eric; he could be any one of them. *I hope it's not him… Or him for that matter…*

After a while, a large group in front of me broke up, and stood behind them was a bloke who looked so much like me as to be impertinent. Generously proportioned, with thinning hair, a goatee, black shirt, black trousers, black shoes and, well, *my* face if it had been marinated for a while. This was my father, alright.

Hug or handshake, what's the protocol here? Haven't thought this through, have you? Oh, hug then, cool.

'Look Ben, a table has opened up – go and grab it,' Eric said. 'What do you want?'

'Guinness, please.'

I bag the table and watch this new creature as he negotiates the bar using a fair imitation of my own mannerisms and facial expressions. *This is so strange…*

'Two pints of Guinness please, love.'

He turned towards me; nodded; smiled.

'That'll be £6.20.'

He pulled out his wallet then started going through his pockets, frantically patting himself down. Turning back to me, he goes, 'Haven't got a fiver, have you?'

My face dropped at speed.

'Only joking,' he laughed.

The precise wrongness of this thrilled me. Moments like that, when we are balanced between two futures, are usually fraught with solemnity. I didn't want to be solemn! Neither did I want to be nervously polite, nor wracked with worry about misstepping a tiny bit. I wanted to have a laugh with someone who looks like me and feels that same way.

The conversation that followed has continued ever since. Some people you can just talk to, easy and free. The next night Eric came to see me play music in a pub. Brian was there, wet-eyed with emotion for me.

'How does it feel to find your long-lost son?' he asked Eric after we'd all had a couple.

'Well, it's a big thing, Brian. I mean, you never know when you're going to need a new kidney, for starters…'

I needed a way to address this man. Our resemblance and easy companionship felt like more than acquaintanceship from the off. He'd called me 'son' reflexively, then apologised and took it back, saying he hadn't been thinking. I smiled, unsure what to say – it seemed wrong but felt right.

I tried out 'Daddio' in a text message. He took to signing cards that way. It was dumb and might even seem creepy to you – I dunno – but it filled an oddly shaped linguistic void. What are you *supposed* to call someone who looks and talks like you, someone who walks around with half your genetic information, if you can't call them 'Dad'? 'Mate' doesn't really cut it. The addition of a jaunty 'o' at the end took the weight out of it and distracted from the shifting loyalties that were, like it or not, at play. You can't feel guilty about a name with 'o' at the end of it; that would be silly, wouldn't it?

When we met, I was nearing the depths of my drinking problem. Daddio would come over from Australia a couple of times a year for business or to see family, and it would be party time. We'd meet at rock shows or restaurants with plenty of family and friends in tow and drinks flowing. I'd been immediately welcomed by this new group of people. The echoing quiet of only-child life in Solihull had been my experience of family. This was noisy, warm, instinctive and fun. At the apex of the family, Joan, my grandmother, reigned over her four surviving children and countless grandchildren, dispensing endless love and twinkling wit to all. Nearly ninety when I met her, she was still out dancing several nights a week and her have-a-good-time-all-the-time ethos defined the family. Everyone was in business; everyone was travelling; everyone was laughing. Whatever tomorrow brought would be made fun one way or another. I found immediate shelter under her wing, no questions asked.

So, initially, I could hide the trouble I was in because we always met at social occasions. After a while, though, my physical decline became visibly obvious. Daddio started to venture little pleas, artfully masked with humour, to look after myself better. I was past that, though. When addiction becomes a full-time deal, it accelerates beyond the pace at which you can adapt to the change. I was running down a hill and momentum prevented me from stopping. It was a case of seeing where I'd land.

After my friends, Paul and Brian, vetoed my final descent and detoxed me back to sanity, I was at a crossroads. The process had been harrowing: the full premium experience, complete with convulsions, continual retching and ataxia so severe that I couldn't walk at all for a couple of days. When I could walk again, it was initially around in circles as my brain and limbs were not communicating with each other. I emerged very subdued and unsure what to do with myself.

When Daddio came to visit next, he was clearly shocked at my appearance. As I sipped a lemonade outside a pub, he pressed me about what was wrong. The problem here was that I didn't know. There was an unendurable ache in my guts that had been dulled by alcohol, but what put it there wasn't clear to me. All I was sure about was that it was nobody's fault but my own. Lots of kids are adopted, and lots of them subsequently emerge from family breakups without becoming the embarrassing mess I was. Daddio looked stricken at the state of me and offered practical help.

'What would change things for you, Ben?'

Legally murky psychedelic treatments for addiction don't come cheap but neither, I suppose, do chances to redress the past. As much as I told him he owed me nothing, this kindly man quietly repaid something on his own account. He paid for the iboga treatment. And what do you know, the treatment worked! I'm all better. Thank you for listening. The End.

Well, not quite. In time, though, the benefits began to emerge. Whilst I was, and still am, prone to sliding down the snakes, I found that I didn't slide as far. I had a new ability to put a stop to things before it became impossible to find a ladder. How much of that was due to the iboga treatment and how much was thanks to the proof that people cared about me, I couldn't say. Incrementally, though, I began to benefit from better decisions. Instead of comfortingly impossible dreams of musical stardom, I started to wonder if I could manage small achievements in the world that existed around me. Perhaps I did have something to offer?

I'd always told Daddio that I had no interest in visiting Australia. The truth was that I couldn't afford the air fare and was embarrassed about it. Five years married, at fifty-two, with a mortgage and a spare pair of shoes, things had changed. His recent health scares had prompted him to suggest a visit rather more firmly.

'Come over and spend some time. We never know how long we've got.'

I've never quite got used to being anything other than utterly skint as an adult. Susie rolls her eyes when I come home with out-of-date bread. I *could* afford the trip, though, just. So, we agreed on an adventure. I'd meet Daddio in Cairns, and we'd drive through the outback down to the Gold Coast, visiting family there before finishing at his place in Sydney. I booked a flight via Bali on the way out and Thailand on the return. That meant Susie could visit her friend in Phuket and I could meet her there. It was all a long way from throwing up bile in frozen bedsits – very swank.

I hadn't heard from David in quite a while. Occasionally, I'd ring, but he and Jakki, who was now his wife, screened calls. She usually claimed he was in the bath when she called me back. I sent presents for their birthdays and Christmas. I invited them to our new home. They didn't come.

In summer 2024, whilst Daddio was visiting and we were discussing the trip, my phone rang showing David's number. This had become so unusual that I was scared. It had clear potential to be bad news about David's precarious health. He was eighty and had a number of threatening conditions. I excused myself and took it in the bedroom.

'Hello Benjamin!' he began. His tone was affectionate and cheerful, as if we spoke every week. He wanted to know if I remembered the details of a bass player whom Jakki had brought to a rehearsal when she and I had abortively tried to start a band thirty-five years ago. It seemed oddly random.

The conversation petered out after about ten minutes, but I encouraged him to call more often.

'Really. It would be lovely to hear from you.'

I didn't hear from him more often though. I hadn't really expected to. But maybe he'd like to hear more from *me*? A friend of mine told me he'd been to look at a Vernon-Derby racing car. David had restored one of these back in the 1970s, and they were very scarce: a perfect excuse to call him up. I tried three times over a couple of weeks in September but there was no reply. He wasn't even in the bath, as far as I knew.

Then, at the end of November, Jakki called. David was in Heartlands Hospital, and she said that I should get there immediately. Susie and I battled through Storm Bert up the M5 to Birmingham and arrived at the hospital mid-afternoon. In the waiting room outside David's ward, the BBC news was showing footage of flooding from the bottom of our road in the Rhondda.

Inside, David was hooked up to machines, his hair thick and brown as always. He had the same thoughtful look that he always wore when sleeping, as if figuring out some tough maths in a dream. I stood quietly and stared at him for a moment before Jakki came rushing in, accompanied by a neighbour who had driven her to the hospital.

'I had just stepped out for some air. You should have called me before coming in.'

Here we go.

A discussion with the consultant revealed that the game was up. He wouldn't be leaving this place. I thought back forty years, almost to the week, when I'd heard the same news, in the same hospital, about Grandad. Then, I'd run full pelt down the corridors, flinging open the door to a cold night and screaming into it. Now, I just nodded and listened to Jakki blame the doctors.

I sent the neighbour home after it got dark and drove Jakki back to Solihull. My childhood home, now David and Jakki's home, was, in many ways, a museum. The carpets, kitchen units and curtains were all the ones my mum had picked out in 1974. The National Trust couldn't have preserved it better. Missing, though, was any trace that I'd ever existed here. Not only were all photographs of me gone, but the painting of a steam train I'd bought David for his retirement was no longer on the wall. None of the carefully chosen gifts I'd sent them both over the years were in evidence. When I got up to fetch a glass of water, Jakki sneered to my wife, 'He likes to wander round to see everything is in order.'

To escape the atmosphere as much as anything, I offered to fetch a takeaway. Sat in the Indian restaurant waiting for the food, I ordered a pint and tried to process what was happening. Even the beginnings of grief were forestalled by the overwhelming aversion I felt to going back into that house. That expensive, rectangular space – where my mum had been bounced around the kitchen, where I'd been left alone long enough to drink bleach at fifteen and where, right now, my wife was being lectured on how Britain should expel its immigrants – was supposed to be my home. I ordered another beer and asked them to keep the food warm. It felt safer and more welcoming on the bench of the takeaway than in that empty, loveless box.

When I returned the television was blaring racist comedy songs from YouTube and Jakki was demanding that we agree that Tommy Robinson is a national hero. Susie, soldier that she is, shot me looks of solidarity, mouthed 'love' and feigned exhaustion so we could go to bed.

After visiting the hospital the next day, I said I had to go home. I'd agreed to appear in court for one of the homeless people we worked with, and that was a solemn promise but also a blessed relief. When Jakki went to complain to a nurse about something, I made myself mindful with David. In contravention of his 'don't-monkey-paw-me' horror at my childhood attempts to hold his hand, I stroked his palm . We'd had good moments, lots of them.

I hurriedly whispered to him, 'I love you.'

The next evening, when I got home from court, Jakki called me. It was best, apparently, if I didn't come again. The doctors would need space around the bed. Also, the nurses had been instructed not to update me on David's condition if I called. If I wanted to know, I could ring her. She was sure I'd understand.

'Just tell me when it's over.'

Later, Susie held my hand in the funeral car, crammed in with Jakki, her nephew and his wife. I'd never met them before. Susie carried on holding it in the crematorium as I stared at my shoes whilst a thoughtful, religious cousin eulogised David as best he could, having seen so little of him in recent years. David's sister wasn't there; they had become estranged. Nobody except the neighbours, Jakki, and Jakki's nephew had seen David in a long time. A photo montage played on the wall of the hotel where the wake was held. His life from a wartime child to aged husband flashed by. There he was on a bicycle in black and white and there again with his AC Aceca. There was even one with Mum, now long gone but survived by her choices in interior decor. Susie squeezed my hand as I watched, wondering if maybe... Nevermind. To be fair, I don't take a very good picture, so no harm I suppose.

Driving home, I wished I'd been able to show him my car. It's pretty poky and he'd have appreciated the roar when my right foot pressed viciously down on the accelerator and took Susie and I away from all that for good. She stroked my hand as it purpled on the gear stick, and I bit on my lower lip. *Croeso i Gymru* never hit so hard.

Cape Tribulation in northern Queensland is named for the perilous time that Captain Cook spent there repairing the hull of his ship after damaging it on the coral offshore. If he'd failed, then the dense rainforest behind the bay likely held dangers that would have ended his story.

Daddio is taking a business call in the shaded car park, so I've set off to look around. There's nobody here. The mid-afternoon sun refracts off the water – a million diamonds lapping gently onto the curved bay. I'm overdressed in the jacket I wore on the plane from Bali. I'd arrived at 6 a.m, and Daddio took us straight to a crocodile park where, bog-eyed and discombobulated, I peered out of the boat and watched our prehistoric pals jump up for chickens that the guide dangled off a fishing rod.

'You can throw that float in for me if one pulls me off the boat,' she instructed. 'It won't help, but you'll feel like you tried to do something.'

After lunch, we'd set off north to explore and by the side of the road I spotted a tall, black, ostrich-type bird with a turquoise head clambering up a verge into the forest.

'A cassowary,' Daddio informed me as I gaped in wonder. Who knew such things existed? I was a long way from Kansas.

I take the jacket off and set off to walk around the bay, feeling the heat on my arms and sweat trickle down from my hat. It's silent save for the crickets behind me in the greenery. Powdery white sand gives way beneath my feet and the light is unsettlingly sharp, like being inside an overexposed photograph. The sea is gentle and inviting and, as I potter round taking in the otherness of it all, I consider stripping off and running into it. *Who would know?*

'Bloody hell, you gave me a fright!'

Wandering back towards the path from the beach to the carpark, I encounter Daddio looking breathless and fraught. I've been gone longer than I realised.

He points to a sign: 'Strictly No Swimming. Saltwater Crocodiles. Extreme Danger!'

'Oh, I'd seen that,' I lie. 'I just went for a wander.'

The beginning of a road trip, especially a long one, is a heady delight. This drive will take ten days, down from Cairns to northern New South Wales, before we head back north again to the Gold Coast. If you consult a guidebook, it will tell you to take the coastal road, along which there are sea views, beaches and inviting, touristy towns. We're not doing that. The alternative route winds inland through the virtually empty grasslands, where cattle are herded by helicopter.

From Port Douglas we climb up a long, gradual hillside. As a first glimpse of Australia, this landscape challenges preconceptions. Instead of the dusty, orange desert of Castlemaine XXXX adverts, or the beachy attractions of *Home & Away*,* this area offers lush, tropical farmlands and winding mountain roads. The ascent up through Mount Molloy builds expectation yet further. It's as if we are chugging up a rollercoaster with who-knows-what awaiting over the crest. Daddio and I have never spent this length of time together before and the road will be long and empty. That's the point.

As we descend into Mareeba, the landscape begins to sparsen. Behind us, the sense of abundance is almost comical. People were seemingly able to grow anything and make a living from it. 'The Home of Mango Wine,' proclaims one roadside sign.

We need a map. There's only going to be a couple of forks in the road along the whole trip, but they are important ones that we cannot miss. One misstep in the sort of terrain we are heading for could have life-changing consequences. We try stopping at a few places to purchase a map, but nobody seems to have one. It's a concern; a little cloud in our big, blue sky. Daddio is more decorous in his breakfasting habits than I, so I wolf down my bacon sarnie and leave him to politely nibble his whilst I head for a bookshop I'd seen when we pulled into town. Praise be – the bookshop has a road map of Queensland. Heading back to the café with it, I feel childishly proud. *Look. I did it!*

I silently interrogate that feeling as we clamber into the big Toyota Land Cruiser that Daddio has hired for the trip. *I'm,*

---

* Yes, I arrived in Australia with formidable cultural understanding of the country to inform my visit.

Monkey paws

like, *fifty-two. Should I really be* this *in need of validation?* Well, seems I am – for the time being, at least. What of it?

We've got to put some miles on to make this trip viable. The first stretch is nearly five hours, during which we see no other cars. Occasionally, an articulated road train will come roaring past. These things couldn't stop if they wanted to, so the somnolence of a long, straight road must be prickled with alertness, no matter how deserted it seems. As the route opens out into scrubland, there is plenty to look out for, though. For the first time, I see an emu that doesn't have a light entertainer's arm up its arse – then another, and another. There are galah parrots wandering around in a layby where we stop so I can photograph the five-feet-tall termite nests that line the highway on both sides. Within the nests are complex cities. I speculate on the family dramas, politics and crime contained within them. Does the character of one differ from that of another? What unseen forces and instincts are at work in there? Or in us, come to that?

In the early afternoon, we pull into the Greenvale Roadhouse. It's a rickety old structure with petrol pumps and a cafe just off the highway where a country road spikes off towards the back end of nowhere. The heat is so fierce as to be comical.

Thanks to satellites, there is Wi-Fi available* so, after ordering a sandwich, I start looking for a hotel in Charters Towers, where it seems we'll be by this evening.

'Where are youse from then, fellas?' The owner grins at us, joining his wife, Mandy, who's been bantering with my dad for ten minutes. I'm all UK stutter and murmur, completely missing the pitch of the place.

---

* Simultaneously wondrous and terrifying. No corner of the planet goes unscrutinised; we are never alone.

'He's from Wales and I'm from Sydney, mate – you know – civilisation,' Daddio grins back.

'Fuckin' 'ell,' the owner replies, as he slumps down on a couch. 'I could tell you were fuckin' trouble the moment you pulled up in that.' Pointing to our enormous, gleaming white hire car, he stretches out his long, sunburned legs and takes a load off from whatever has left his singlet, shorts and boots caked in red dust.

'I went to Sydney once…' he begins. A car pulls out onto the highway at speed and his wife is suddenly action stations.

'That was Chip. Wonder what he's after in a hurry! I'm fuckin' callin' him, eh?' Mandy disappears with her mobile.

'Chip's the local cop,' the elderly Aboriginal cook explains. 'He isn't allowed to do anything exciting without his deputy there finding out about it.'

'She's as nosey as I am!' Mandy calls from the back room.

'Yeah, I was eighteen,' the husband continues. 'We couldn't get a drink anywhere. Ended up in a Kings Cross strip joint just because we were thirsty!'

'A likely story,' Daddio snorts.

'Straight up! Mind you, there were fifteen of us from Weipa. We've grown up all our lives around Black fellas and our manners didn't translate to the big city, apparently. We were ordering a bottle of rum per round, and they said that wasn't on. We were like, "We're not even pissed, mate!" Anyway, they didn't seem to mind our money in the strip joints. You live and learn!'

Before we leave, they've rung ahead to Charters Towers and sorted us a motel room.

On the road down, there are a couple of clouds in the sky. We scrutinise these for meaning, because the news is warning of cataclysmic weather ahead. Cyclone Alfred is building out in the ocean off the Gold Coast and predictions about if and where it will make landfall are indicating that our intended route – that takes in visiting my brother in Mullumbimby and my uncle's family at the Gold Coast itself – might be impossible. The longer the cyclone builds out at sea, the greater its force, so phone calls are going back and forth with expressions of concern all round. So far, though, all we've seen are these two clouds.

Charters Towers is an old gold-mining town. Its architecture tells a story of rise and decline. There are a dozen or so ornate old banks and even a stock exchange to pay testament to the town's historical wealth. The paint on these buildings is peeling, though, and the bunce was spirited away from here long ago, leaving a discernible resentment in those left behind. They remind me of the crumbling old buildings back home in the Rhondda that were similarly built on extraction and then left to the birds when the mines closed down.

That sort of story makes for a particular sense of humour. After we've dumped our bags in the motel, we find a skilled exponent of it behind the bar at the White Horse Tavern. It's a big old boozer with a bar on one side and a pokie room at the back. The bar's empty except for us, but Sharon, who is working behind the bar on her own, has to stand in a particular spot where she can keep an eye on both rooms.

'If it isn't nailed down, they'll have it!' she explains.

'Is there a lot of crime round here?' I ask.

'It's getting worse. The little bastards think they're above the law.'

'The police are a waste of breath where I am too,' I offer in sympathy.

'Same all over, I reckon.'

'Fancy a drink, Sharon?' Daddio chimes in. She's around my age with dyed black hair, wearing denim and a storied complexion. Like all proper Queenslanders, she enjoys a Bundaberg Rum.

'Fuckin' government's only put the tax up on my rum,' she complains, 'as if there isn't little enough enjoyment left in life.

Fuck 'em!' She downs her glass, pours another one and gets us beers, waving away our money.

'I got robbed last week. Little kid, only thirteen, snatched $50 out of my car when I was at the lights.' In the way of storytellers, Sharon warms up to her theme. 'So, I call the cops and tell them. I've even got the little bastard's name. Two hours later, and they still haven't done anything. So, I call them again and ask what they're doing. It's *sensitive*, they tell me. I'm, like, stop right there! *Sensitive?* I don't care if you're Black, white or brindle, you're not fuckin' robbing from me. If youse won't do anything, I'll deal with it myself.'

She takes a breath, so I get another round in.

'Right enough, I hear nothing. So I goes out looking, find him in about fifteen minutes. He's already spent $15 and says he's given the rest to his sister. So, I sling him in the back of the car and take him home. I'm back onto the cops, "You'd better come and pick up your boy, before I kick the shit out of him!" They're all "You can't do that anymore, Sharon." I go, "Oh can't I? Well why don't you come round here and fuckin' watch me?" Right enough, they turn up then! I still had to go get the money off his sister though. Useless fuckers!'

Before we go, Daddio asks about the Chinese place over the road.

'Yeah, it's ok. Order from the menu, though, don't go near that chew-'n'-spew buffet or you'll be in Charters Towers longer than you planned...'

The road ahead seems endless. Hours pass with nothing but asphalt curving into the horizon and open country either side. A kangaroo, alive or dead, is news. But we do have music. I've compiled hundreds of tracks on a playlist to see us through the journey: Waylon Jennings, Miles Davis, The Incredible String Band, Chuck Berry, John Prine, Sierra Ferrell, Minnie Riperton, The Everly Brothers, Ry Cooder, Muddy Waters,

Emmylou Harris, Julian Cope, The Cure, Pentangle, Slade, Townes Van Zandt, Calexico, Frank Zappa, Lord Buckley, and the Pendyrus choir. It's a map of my own taste; something to show off to a man I desperately hope is impressed.* I took weeks to create it back at home, imagining how the songs would sound on the other side of the world. The hypnotic chug of J.J. Cale's stoner boogie floats over this landscape like it was written for it. Davy Graham's metallic, Moroccan-infused English folk cuts across it like a reminder that nothing is comfortable for long – not if you want to get somewhere.

The vastness of the landscape and the time we have forces our life stories out of us, as we knew it would. There are sharp differences between his hardscrabble beginnings in a large, boisterous family and my cossetted only-childhood. We compare relationship histories, test each other's worldviews and see how honest we can get before it all becomes too much. Strange, significant similarities surface: pubs we've both drunk in, places we've been, ways we cope. Anxiety emerges as a theme and as something that has followed us both marring experiences that should have been enjoyable, and hobbling our ease in the world. Our humour has no taboos on the journey. Birmingham piss-taking is a peculiarly jagged cultural jewel and we both possess it. It's our love language. Spending each night in a new town – Emerald, Roma and Toowoomba – gives the trip an epic quality. It's a serious thing we're doing here: finding each other and repairing holes we'd left through our absence. The grandeur of our journey seems fitting, as if our story deserved world-class locations against which to unfold.

As we leave the unpretentious fun of Roma's moustache-'n'-mullet pub scene with a racing tip from a horse trainer

---

* He was. Who wouldn't be? Contact me for a private consultation to address the shortcomings in your own music collection.

and bellies full of steak, the air is becoming heavier. So far, Cyclone Alfred has been something we've been seeing on the television in pubs. Sparkly-toothed news anchors are predicting devastation not seen since the 1970s. Now, Alfred's approach seems to be for real. They still don't know where it's going to land, and both of our upcoming destinations are right in its way. After weighing the risks, we drive towards it.

This might sound as if it's setting up an exciting action scene later in the story, but I'll have to disappoint there*. The climactic point in this narrative is our decision to go. According to the news, it's a foolhardy and dangerous decision, but we take it anyway, and the reason is that relatives are expecting me. Daddio says they will be disappointed if I don't show up. This hasn't been my experience of family life since Grandad died forty years ago. I've been an embarrassment, a nuisance, a drunk – it's better all round if I *don't* show up, even to death beds. So, the notion of people being *upset* if I don't make it, and of someone being willing to take physical risks to ensure that I do, is both bemusing and thrilling.

There is a bit of weather, for sure. When we reach Toowoomba, the rain is falling and the town is in crisis mode. Nearly all the shops and restaurants have signs explaining that they are closed due to the imminent apocalypse. The pub is open, though, and running a blues jam. There's camaraderie in there as we all wonder what's heading towards us. The musicians are superb, causing me to wonder at the odds of making it in music at any level. If you can be this good and end up playing an afternoon shift for free in Toowoomba…

---

* Strictly speaking, I don't have to. I could fabricate a scenario in which we're cut off by raging torrents and have to shelter in a cave having relationship-defining conversations. Bit of a prompt there for anyone thinking of picking up the film rights.

Monkey paws

Heading east towards Mullumbimby the next morning, we start to experience the full drama of the situation. The highway down to the Gold Coast is closed, so we use the back roads around Tambourine Mountain. Flooded fields have merged with rivers so as to be indistinguishable, and are running alongside the road and threatening to overwhelm it. In Canungra, where we stop for coffee, people are huddling in the cafes because their houses outside of town are without power. There's plenty of 'she'll-be-right' Aussie stoicism in the air, challenging the sheeting rain to do its worst.

Back on the road, we're racing, acting on rumours that the roads we're driving will be closed soon. Visibility is poor as the deluge overwhelms our wipers and blots out the sunlight. Any notions I'd brought with me of the parched desert in *Walkabout* are long gone now as we negotiate fallen trees and abandoned vehicles.

As we pull into Mullumbimby, it begins to clear. We park outside a spiritual bookstore and watch a white-bearded starchild make his way past the organic produce shops, blowing bubbles through a plastic hoop to express his joy at existence. Grinning with relief at making it in one piece, we head inside The Middle Pub for a schooner. Make that two schooners.

'You should chew that steak slower,' Daddio instructs. I look up, bemused and mid-chomp.

'Eh?'

'You're wolfing it down. Be careful.'

My brother Jack, is barely suppressing a laugh. Ten years my junior, properly Aussie and a GP here in Mullumbimby, we've met a couple of times in the UK. We exchange glances, amused by Daddio's tendency to overthink things when it comes to the people he loves.

'He's made it this far – he'll be alright, I reckon,' my brother offers.

'Do I have medical clearance to continue?' I enquire.

We're having a laugh, the three of us. It's a dynamic I never expected to be part of, and I'm so caught up in the novel experience of family life being so easy and warm that I have to tell myself just to be and not to squeeze the moment so tightly that it bursts.

In bed, back at Jack's, I listen to Alfred's final assault batter down on the flat roof above my room. *I'm not just observing this*, I tell myself, *I'm a part of it. I am.*

The next night, we're at the Gold Coast where the cyclone has hit hardest. There is a fifteen-foot drop in places where the beach has been carried away, and electricity is patchy across the resort town. My uncle, who is nearly eighty, lives with his son on the fifth floor of a tower block where the lift is out of order because of flooding in the basement. He's ok but can't get down the stairs, so I head up them to see him. Daddio doesn't fancy the climb, so it's a solo trip.

Despite multiple heart-related health scares over the years, he remains handsome and possessed of an effortless cool that sees him able to carry off Ray-Bans in any situation. Like many in this family, he's been around and ran businesses in the UK and America. I've seen him often back home, but he's recently retired to Australia.

We stand on the balcony, take some selfies and catch up. He's all stories, a walking screenplay of a man who has seen life go from poverty to riches and repeated the process as providence demanded: a twentieth-century life that would be impossible in the risk-assessed, corporately policed world we're in now. As long as there are dice, he's rolling them. I soak it up, loving the largeness of his presence, Again, it's easy. He's not wondering why I'm there, just clinking a glass because I am. Family.

It's family, too, when we finally reach Daddio's home on the northern beaches of Sydney. It's family when his wife,

Monkey paws

Alison, ushers me, smiling, towards my room and offers to do my washing. It's family at my younger brother Fred's birthday party, which is celebrated in the same Chinese restaurant every year and has an extra guest without comment or drama. It's family when my sister, Liz, and her husband, Chris, take me out to see the underground history of the area* and then share a beer on the way back. It's family when their little boy sits and chats for twenty minutes, wondering which countries I've visited. I'm unsure because I am still becoming accustomed to leaning on something that doesn't give way. None of these people owe me a damn thing. And I must have been the cause of some turmoil, crashing into their lives full-grown and unfamiliar. I'm not sure how I'd have taken it, in their shoes.

On my last day, Daddio and I take an Uber to Manley and then the ferry into Sydney. Sailing, as the convicts used to, into Circular Quay is an affecting experience. The visuals of the Harbour Bridge and the Sydney Opera House are so familiar as to seem slightly unreal when encountered *for real*. Their shapes and colours are already imprinted on me and the reality of them is familiar yet at odds with the imagined version. How much of life, I wonder, is like this? Our imaginings lead the way, only to be superseded by experience.

I'm sailing into Sydney with a man who has existed for me, in abstract form, since I was six years old. Initially, there were no parameters on how I imagined him. With no information at all, he could have been anyone and anything. Occasionally, as a kid, I'd daydream about who he was. *Could be him*, I'd think as a random bloke passed me by while I was out and

---

* As well as important Aboriginal sites, the area around Narrabeen hosts the overgrown and deliberately forgotten headquarters of Sydney's NAZI party. On its stone walls, dates from the 1930s are carved alongside swastikas and double-headed eagles.

about. Or if I saw someone on the news who was convicted of a terrible crime. After meeting my birth mother, I had the beginnings of a pencil sketch of him. He was darker than I am, from a large family, and he was driven to succeed. That's what I had to go on when I was looking around Horts Wine Bar for him at our first meeting. I have him in three dimensions now, though. As we disembark next to the opera house, I look at him with his back to it and feel the dissonance fizzing within me as make-believe is confronted by reality. I've got to know him over the last couple of years, but far more so over the last couple of weeks.

It's St Patrick's Day and the city is in an excitable mood. Along the quayside, the pubs have all set up outdoor marquees with bands playing and bars serving drinks. You can just wander down it picking up a pint in each and listening to the music. I don't want to leave Australia, but this does feel like a great send-off.

We're feeling sociable. A group of retired cops from Queensland are down for a piss-up, and one of them has been to the Rhondda! By the time we've finished celebrating that synergy, we're pretty sure he's walked past my house – 85 per cent sure, at least. *Have another one.*

At the end of the night, we go to the left luggage store to collect my bags. My flight for Bangkok leaves in the morning so I need to take the train out to the airport and my hotel. We are beerily emotional – it'll be months before we see each other again and we've become accustomed to each other being around over the last couple of weeks. There are hugs and a tear or two. I jump on the train before it all gets too much. As it speeds through the darkness, I reflect on my astonishing good luck. Setting out to find my birth family, I'd had to discipline myself to be ready for the absolute worst. I'd steeled myself to the possibility that I was the product of rape, that my birth parents may no longer be alive, that I might be rejected by them or find I was nothing like them and didn't share any values. I'd shed layers of armour as things worked out at every turn. Warm breezes of acceptance had pushed me through all of that and then across the world to Sydney Harbour.

So, in the airport lounge the next morning, with time and a hangover to kill, I feel grateful. I send a text message to Daddio thanking him for the extraordinary time I've had. When I think of him, I smile. Charismatic, popular and successful, he remains plagued by self-doubt. He's at once the brightest light in the room and its most uncertain occupant. His family know he loves them – that they are the world to him. They know through his actions and because he tells us, sometimes in the middle of the night, if he feels so moved. He worries so that we don't. It defines him.

My head is *banging*. I still like a drink now and then, but extravaganzas like Paddy's Day in Sydney are rare events nowadays. I shouldn't, but I'm having a beer to wash down the ibuprofen and take the edge off. I was never bound to be a poster boy for sobriety, but it isn't actively killing me anymore. This isn't the UK, where pre-flight drinks are traditional whatever the time. There's a discernible sniffiness when I ask for a beer and a negative atmosphere when I return for another one.

'I'll sleep on this flight if it kills me!' I offer brightly. *Tough crowd.*

There's still a couple of hours until my flight boards, so I fetch some noodles from the buffet and push them round a bowl. *Noodles for breakfast, but if you ask for a beer, they can't handle it. Weird.*

I plug my phone in to charge and open my email account. Amongst the credit card offers and guitar adverts, there's one from the government. Since David's funeral, Jakki seemed always to be mentioning his will when I called to see how she was. It was very simple, she'd said, the solicitor had never seen probate issued so swiftly. She never mentioned what was in it, though, so I'd ordered a copy from the Probate Office and here it was. The very first line revealed David's priority in the document.

'I hereby confirm that I make no provision in my will for my adopted son…'

Jakki's nephew and each of his children are all mentioned on the next line; their unfamiliar names listed in full, for accuracy. I had been prepared not to receive anything of substance, or even be mentioned at all. To find that he had gone into a solicitor's office thirteen years ago bound and determined to repudiate me was something else.

'Give me another beer… please.'

I make my way to the gate feeling that I've been impaled on something. There's a dull ache at the centre of me. Initially, I'm paralysed with it, as if any movement or thought would fatally disturb the stake sticking out of me. I pop a sleeping pill on the plane and drift off, having strange dreams before awakening into renewed pain and drifting off again. The stake starts to work loose as I get to grips with it, splintering inside me with each insight. I remember how impressed I'd been at David's calm reaction to the news I was looking for my birth family. I'd contrasted his cool, seemingly adult approach with Mum's howling objections and judged *her* for making it difficult. A shard of overwhelming guilt twists off the stake and is left inside me as I try to wrench the thing out, half-pissed, drugged and at 30,000 feet above the ocean a world away from home. *Sorry, Mum. I'm so very sorry.*

Ten hours of woozy flying allows some time for the news to settle a little. For all that my relationship with David had been complex, difficult and nuanced, I had always found a way to rationalise that it was, ultimately, built on mutual affection. He'd had a loveless childhood himself so found it difficult to express his feelings. We were very different in character, so naturally we'd clash here and there. I was pretty wild as a teenager and young adult; that must have been hard for him to experience. I've got dozens of these excuses I could produce for every hurtful situation he threw my way. *Deep down, he loves me – he must do.*

Well, no, apparently, he didn't. Here, in black and white, are his last words on the matter. Now that nothing more can be said, or pleaded, I must reimagine my entire life with that fictional affection subtracted. I stare at the blank screen in the seat in front of me as we hurtle through the sky and project onto it memories that will need to be refiled under new categories. A little, blonde boy on holiday walks down the seafront, trying to hold his father's hand.

'Don't monkey-paw me.'

EPILOGUE

I'm in a wooden cabin in Lo Ba Khao village on Koh Phi Phi, Thailand. We've come back from a memorable lunch in a cafe by the dry riverbed. Just as I was about to crunch into a spring roll, I had seen something move in the corner of my eye.

"Kin' hell!' I splutter. 'Look at that!'

Susie turns to look at the riverbed and sees an eight-foot water monitor moving across it. It stops for a moment, flicking out its tongue before ambling mechanically under the bridge with its peculiar turned-in feet and magnificent tail behind it. Then come its pals, six that I count, one of whom scampers through a patch of water at top speed, showing us how he could take a monkey or small child.

I've been away from Susie for over a month, travelling through Australia, and her tenderness outweighs David's posthumous scorn quickly and utterly. Spite is such a small creature when you stand it next to love.

I've been providing hilarity and consternation in equal measure. We're not in the bit of Koh Phi Phi that everyone stays in. Oh no. On my insistence, we are on the other side of the island in search of an 'authentic' experience.* This required us to take a longtail boat from the port, where there are nightclubs and a Burger King, for heaven's sake, around

---

* I know, I hate me too.

Epilogue

the coast to this quiet village. Unfortunately, when the boat arrived at Lo Ba Khao bay, the tide required us to walk the last hundred metres through the sea. The two young Chao Ley* who were operating the boat cheerfully hoisted our suitcases on their shoulders and skipped off towards the shore. Susie was pretty nimble too, whilst my progress was rather more stately.

The first bit was fine. Lowering myself gingerly off the boat, holding my suede loafers,† I allow my 5X linen beach pants to soak up to my thighs and find a footing on the seabed. No worries. It's soft sand and easy enough to walk on. *Stroll ashore!*

The problems started when I encountered some rocks on the seabed. I am an indoor person whose extremities are unused to rough surfaces. My baby-soft tootsies, the cause of some envy in other circumstances, recoiled from the stony surface, so I set off on a circuitous route looking for a sandy path to the shore.

The Chao Ley were, by now, nearly on land. Susie, who grew up on the Cornish coast without shoes, was not far behind them. I seemed to have found a navigable way forward when I encountered another carpet of rocks in my way. *This can't go on. Come on, you've got this.* So, without a thought for my sole,‡ I tried to go over them. Almost immediately, I found myself recoiling from a sharp bit of rock and thrusting my leg out sideways to find something better to stand on. Unfortunately, my foot landed on a large, rounded rock and slipped off it straight away.

Sploosh!

---

* Sea gypsies. You learn this sort of thing when you venture beyond Burger King.
† Get in there, Marco Polo.
‡ Oh yes, we're punning now. It's the epilogue, and I'm giddy at the thought of freedom.

Mayday!
Lord, help me!
I listed back in the water, which came up to my neck, as my arse rested on the rock and my knees poked out at chin-level.

'Are you ok?' called my wife – Marina, girl of the sea – barely suppressing her laughter.

'Fine!' I spluttered, spitting seawater, 'Never better.'

'Need any help?' she offered with wifely concern.

'No!' I snapped, in husbandly humiliation.

As I floundered about, trying to get a footing so I could stand up, I remembered my bag. Man-bags attract a degree of ridicule from people who aren't as secure in their masculinity as perhaps they should be, but I find them to be a practical way of keeping credit cards, paper money, vital electronics and passport in one, easily accessible place around my neck. Unfortunately, as we know, I was now *submerged* up to my neck and, whilst I'd demonstrated rare practicality by using the man-bag in the first place, this hadn't extended to buying one that was waterproof. I unzipped it as soon as I was upright and found it to be wetter than an otter's pocket.

So, my stay in Lo Ba Khao has included an unscheduled digital detox. The Kindle, praise be, has survived, but my phone won't charge and the screen doesn't work. There are bank notes drying under the air conditioning unit, along with my passport, which has the pages propped apart with coins.

My phone lights up. It's ringing, but I can't see who it is or answer the call. Then Susie's phone rings.

'For you,' she smiles.

It's my son. He's twenty-seven and training to be a ship's captain in Norway. He's lived there since he was six years old and, thankfully, wasn't around for much of the dysfunction described in this book. He's bright, beautiful, and calm: a credit to his mother and her husband. I'm proud to bursting of him but have no right to be, not really. We are close in our own way, though, sharing a sense of humour and an easy, affectionate relationship. We've always hugged. That he doesn't seem to resent me for my absence during much of his life feels like a gift I barely deserve. My heart soars whenever I see his name light up my phone.

He's concerned. An earthquake in Laos has reverberated through Thailand, bringing down buildings in Bangkok. I explain about the phone and why I haven't seen any news. We chuckle at the irony of him knowing about the quake in Kristiansund whilst I'm oblivious in Thailand. He's relieved I'm ok. We'll meet up in the summer when I'm back in Europe and he finishes his exams.

'Love you.'

'Love you.'

'Love you,' I tell Susie as I hand back her phone. Now everyone's had some love.

It's a happy, teary feeling I'm experiencing. I love travelling above all other pursuits, and one reason is that you can recontextualise yourself away from familiar scenes. Here, in a wooden hut, with the burning afternoon sun outside and the joyous shouts of little Thai kids flying kites from the house next door, I can see myself without the confusion of connections, obligations and assumptions that come with life at home. I'm not Ben the support worker, or Ben the writer, or Ben the guitar player, or Ben the adoptee, or Ben the alcoholic, or Ben the Brummie, or Ben the please-let-me-be-a-Welshman. I'm just here, in my boxer shorts, feeling the enormity of what my son's concern for me means, the luxurious sweetness of my wife's affection and the sure knowledge that what I've left behind in Australia will be there when I return some day.

I love and I am loved.

Tomorrow, we'll set off for home, via Singapore. I moved to Wales ten years ago and, almost from the moment I arrived, my life began to change in a dramatic fashion. Opportunities for my writing and music seemed to open up without my even seeking them. I found friends everywhere, from drug treatment centres to the Senedd via Hay Festival and Tylorstown RFC. It was as if Cymru knew that I'd treasured her since I was a child and been her fiercest defender and most ardent admirer. Her heart seemed open to me.

When my *tadcu* offered me the stability and affection I was lacking from other quarters, it came wrapped up in his Welshness. The few words of *Cymraeg* and the songs that he taught me were how family love was codified for me. Today, if I hear a rare hateful word out and about in the Rhondda, it sounds like a bum note in a song. Something that doesn't belong there.

Those songs aren't my songs, though, not really. My accent doesn't fit around their musicality as it would if I'd grown up wearing daps instead of pumps. Still, I've loved them all my life, paid them attention and championed them. Welsh culture has a welcoming vastness that allows for generosity. Those songs stiffen hamstrings and moisten eyes all around the world.

Are they mine to sing? I hope so; they are the reason I can sing at all.

ACKNOWLEDGEMENTS

It didn't so much take a village to raise me as a demographically significant subset of the West Midlands conurbation. Recalling all the kindness that has come my way over the years is warming and humbling but, in this instance, it also makes me fraught with worry. I know that if I tried to list all the people who have saved me from circumstance and righted my missteps, I would be bound to leave out people who deserve a place. And so I've lost more sleep over this part than the rest of this book put together.

I've also enjoyed extraordinary support for my writing. The Welsh literary community fosters a nurturing environment, and I've benefited immeasurably from the wise counsel and warm encouragement that it offers. In particular, the Hay Festival Writers at Work programme, organised by Literature Wales, is where I came to believe I could produce something worthwhile. The friendships I made there changed my life.

So, to minimise the risk of spending the rest of my life haunted by omissions to either list, I'll restrict this to people who helped directly with this book. Thank you to so many for much else besides.

clare e. potter has read this book in its entirety, starting from the first essay. She's advised, encouraged and occasionally cajoled me through this process with characteristic sensitivity, acumen and passion. *Diolch, butty.*

Lea Millership, Dan Hartland, Sam Annetts and Stan

Mir looked at bits and bobs too. Sending the manuscript out seemed emotionally reckless at the time, so I must trust them.

At Cardiff University I was lucky to experience Richard Gwyn's course on the creative process where I learned to calm down and transgress cheerfully. It was also here that I received sensitive insights from Ailbhe Darcy that caused me to expand my ambitions for my work into something that was book length. Tristan Hughes stylishly navigated my petulance in response to wise criticism.

I next carted this project to Swansea University where David J. Britton and Jon Gower both offered inspirational mentorship at a time when I was unable to make the most of it. My failure to keep up with the programme there is a real source of regret, and I hope that sticking with the book itself redeems me a little in that regard. Jon's wider advocacy for me and his friendship have meant the world.

At Calon, I am indebted to Amy Feldman for taking a chance on me in the first instance, and to Abbie Headon and Katherine Venn, whose expertise has made bringing the book to fruition possible. Caroline Goldsmith's exceptional feel for sentences and tone has improved the book immeasurably. Thank you to Hannah Dafforn for impeccable proofreading. Thanks to Siôn Tomos Owen for helping with the Welsh in the book.

Some truly exceptional writers have read advance copies of the book and been kind enough to provide words of endorsement. The generosity of spirit offered by Rhian Elizabeth, Niall Griffiths, Peter Finch, Leanne Wood, Ailbhe Darcy, Catrin Kean, Abeer Ameer and Horatio Clare has sent me reeling, to be honest. I admire them all without reservation and am so proud of their support.

Eric Hodges, Stephen and Sue Clarke, Paul Calver, Louise Walsh and Sarah Dolman have all, at different times, stepped

Acknowledgements

in to save me from imminent peril in my life. Without them, I don't think I would be here at all.

To everyone *in* the book, I mean no harm. Put me in yours, if your recollections differ.

Susie is at the beginning of this book and the end as my wife, pal, editor, inspiration and all sorts of other good stuff. She knows I luvs her coz I buys her chips.